P.G.H. Fender

To Sir Derek March.
9th December 1989.
Hoping that you find it an interesting
"Sutcliffe" to Arlott's Hobbs.

Ethel & Chris Martin

"THE TWELFTH MAN."
Cartoon by A. A. Mailey.

[*Frontispiece.*]

Arthur Mailey's sketch of a dejected Fender outside the England dressing-room, having been told that he had been omitted from England's team for the first Test match at Sydney in 1920–21

P.G.H. FENDER

A BIOGRAPHY

RICHARD STREETON

Foreword by John Arlott

THE PAVILION LIBRARY

First published in Great Britain 1981

First published in the Pavilion Library in 1987 by
Pavilion Books Limited
196 Shaftesbury Avenue, London WC2H 8JL
in association with Michael Joseph Limited
27 Wrights Lane, Kensington, London W8 5TZ

Consulting Editor: Steve Dobell

British Library Cataloguing in Publication Data
Streeton, Richard
P.G.H. Fender
1. Fender, P.G.H.   2. Cricket players—England—Biography
I. Title
796.35′8′0924   GV915.F/

ISBN 1-85145-143-9
ISBN 1-85145-117-X Pbk

Printed and bound in Great Britain by
Billing & Sons Limited, Worcester

Cover photograph reproduced by courtesy of the Press Association

INTRODUCTION

Percy Fender died on 15 June 1985, peacefully in his sleep, shortly after supper, in an Exeter nursing home. He was aged 92, the world's oldest Test cricketer and, as his obituary in *Wisden* later stressed, he was the last survivor of those who played county cricket regularly before the 1914–18 war. During the final fortnight of Fender's life, his name and lifestyle, unknown to him, were once more being discussed in print.

Newspapers were full of the way Fender, and others, were portrayed in an Australian television series called 'Bodyline'. For five days the series had occupied British screens each evening. It infuriated those involved in 1932–33 who were still alive, and earned ridicule from anyone knowledgeable about cricket. To be fair, the series also brought immense pleasure to millions of viewers outside these categories and it has since been repeated.

Fender was depicted as a Bertie Wooster type character, wearing a monocle and playing a ukelele. To his family's knowledge Fender did neither. Even the actor concerned admitted later that he knew the interpretation of the role was wrong. He had performed to order, though, as the script and production demanded.

In a letter to me, Fender's daughter, Patricia Bensted-Smith, said: 'My father never knew about the "Bodyline" programme – we all felt it might have finished him off. While we acknowledged that it was a programme made *by* Australians, *for* Australians, and was intended as entertainment for the general public, and not specifically cricket lovers, we felt that "Pop's" character was a diabolical distortion.'

On a happier note, the family confirmed that the work involved in Fender's biography, and the aftermath to its first publication, in February 1981, brought him much pleasure in his last years. He bore up well as he fulfilled several requests for interviews – not least when he continued to defend Jardine stringently, as the fiftieth anniversary of 1932–33 approached.

Fender's ninetieth birthday also rekindled the media's interest in him. Among old friends to get in touch was a fellow Old Pauline, the artist Harry Jonas, also aged 90. Jones delivered a portrait, commissioned sixty years earlier and until then never finished!

Fender was also in the headlines when his world record 35-minute hundred was equalled, after 63 years, on the final day of the 1983 season. Steve O'Shaughnessy, playing for Lancashire against Leicestershire at Old Trafford, plundered his runs against deliberate long hops and full tosses, in what *Wisden* termed 'farcical circumstances'. These were not the fault of O'Shaughnessy, who was the first to deprecate his own feat.

Fender sent a congratulatory telegram to O'Shaughnessy, who was taken to meet Fender at Horsham by Brian Bearshaw, the cricket correspondent of the *Manchester Evening News*. O'Shaughnessy, aged 22, showed Fender the bat he had used and his face dropped a mile, momentarily, when Fender pretended he had been presented with the bat as a gift. 'Ye Gods, it was heavy. I could still hit a six playing back with that one,' the 91-year-old Fender told the author later.

By January 1985, Fender's health began to fail, with loss of appetite a major worry. Constant medical supervision was advised and he was reluctantly persuaded to move into a nursing home at Exeter, near where his son, Peter Fender, lived. He died on a Saturday evening, and Sunday's radio and television news bulletins – dominated by a Middle East airport hi-jacking – still found room to mention his death.

The author was at Northampton, where a packed house groaned sympathetically when Fender's death was announced on the loudspeaker. Not many present could have actually seen him play. Monday morning's newspapers all carried remarkably full reports. *The Times* and *Guardian* both had long, front page stories, as well as two columns inside on the obituary pages.

Fender's funeral, on a windy, rainswept afternoon, brought representatives and wreaths from many cricket and other organisations, to the hilltop cemetery on Exeter's outskirts. At a family lunch beforehand, by specific request in Fender's will, close mourners drank his health in Krug Non-Vintage, 'to cheer him on his way'.

When Peter Fender decided to have the headstone on his father's grave inscribed 'A Record Innings', it was a felicitous choice in several ways. No-one who met P.G.H. Fender, or saw him play, will ever forget it.

Harpenden, 1987   Richard Streeton

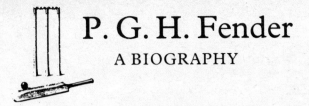

P. G. H. Fender
A BIOGRAPHY

by Richard Streeton

Contents

Foreword

The most remarkable aspect of Richard Streeton's biography of P. G. H. Fender (for he comes from the age of full initials for amateurs) is that it has not been done before. Certainly books have been written—or autobiographies published—about far less interesting cricketers. 'Bill' or 'Percy George' as he was called, was consistently one of the liveliest thinkers and most exciting players in the cricket of this century.

As a batsman he was extremely capable, basically orthodox but skilful in improvization or calculating risks in the attacking role he enjoyed, and which he strategically set himself in the Surrey team he captained. As a bowler he practised primarily the leg-break which he pushed through and spun so hard as to leave, after more than fifty years, a clear memory of the ball's sharp spin-swerve in towards the batsman's legs before it bit and turned away. He bowled the googly, too; a really sharp quicker ball, and juggled with scores of experiments and tactical variations on the theme of temptation. In the field he was generally at slip, where he took some prodigiously distant catches. These three departments afforded ample opportunity for the spectacular, of which he frequently availed himself. As a captain he was thoughtful, original and positive; constantly scheming to overcome the shortcomings of Surrey's limited bowling.

Unmistakable on the field, lanky, bespectacled, curly-haired, slouching along, hands deep in pockets and wearing a grotesquely long sweater, he was immortalized by Tom Webster. The caricaturist, for his part, had a stained-glass window of his victim made for his Highgate house. To a schoolboy spectator who found some efficient cricketers dull to watch, Fender was infallibly entertaining. He thought much about the politics of cricket; he did not suffer fools gladly; he spoke his clear mind; he had the knack of being right in his judgements and he resented the feudal attitudes within the game. All this combined to make him less than popular with the Establishment.

Gifted individualist as he was, he had immense respect for

other players, including those under him; especially Jack Hobbs, whom he held in deep personal affection. The feeling was reciprocated. Sir Jack referred to him more than once as 'the best captain I ever played under,' explaining: 'He was quick and clever and he thought out more batsmen than any other captain I ever knew—he had to with us in the twenties.'

One of the few to play top-class amateur football and county cricket, Fender's speed of reaction made him a talented if unorthodox goalkeeper. Despite a shattered leg, he was far more athletic than he looked. He still is highly respected in the wine trade, and the fact that he continues so capably as a vintner after the loss of his sight is a tribute to his acumen, memory, stamina and determination.

It is surprising that he never wrote an autobiography, for he was—and, no doubt, still is—much more literate than most cricketers. As this book shows, he has a retentive and orderly memory, a balanced mind, and a pretty wit. Of his five books, *An ABC of Cricket* is perceptive and lucid; while the accounts of the England–Australia series of 1920–21 (in which he appeared valuably in three Tests), 1928–29, 1930 and 1934 were as precise in their reporting and as keenly and objectively analytical as any ever written.

His readers must congratulate Richard Streeton on recognizing such a worthwhile theme, and be grateful that the absence of *The Times* for so many months allowed him time to work on the project he first communicated over oysters and Chablis at Brighton in 1978. Happily, too, he proved not only an accurate reporter, but a sympathetic listener, encouraging a good talker to search his memory and talk. Only thus have we documented evidence of that comic morning at Leyton in 1925 which, recounted in an after-dinner speech, once drew down on this writer's head an attack on grounds of falsehood by a statistics-blinkered fool who could find no mention of it in *Wisden*. This is an authentic view of a phase of cricket: for many, too, it is a nostalgic backward look to the 1920s world of Jack Hobbs, Patsy Hendren, Tom Webster, Herbert Sutcliffe, Frank Woolley—and Percy Fender.

JOHN ARLOTT

Preface

There were worse ways for a cricket reporter to fill the unforgiving minute during the eleven months when *The Times* did not appear than to sit at P. G. H. Fender's feet and listen. Fender, blind and in his eighty-eighth year, was a generous host over countless hours in his study. As the wine flowed, so too did his conversation and it provides the basis of this biography. Sometimes a ten-hour visit would not yield a paragraph until that day's farewells were being made, but the wait was usually worth while.

Old men's stories, like many an angler's yarn, have to be treated with caution. In these pages, the irrelevant, the uncheckable and, it is to be hoped, the libellous—and this last was seldom far away—have all been rejected. Fender's memory was remarkably good and my basic intention to produce a factual, sourced book was made easy. Occasionally the confirmatory researches in books, newspapers or with those of Fender's contemporaries still alive made it necessary to make minor amendments to the story being told, but not often.

Fender was always more aware of his shortcomings than anyone and in old age was willing to acknowledge the mistakes he had made more readily than he ever did at the time. It would have been out of place, therefore, to allow the writer's opinions to intrude when dealing with contentious matters. Judgement has not so much been shirked as passed to the reader to form his own from the evidence provided.

Apart from Fender himself, it would not have been possible to write this book without the co-operation of his daughter, Patricia Bensted-Smith, with whose family he now lives at Horsham. Her patience and tolerance were endless during my numerous visits and overnight stays. Not every woman turns a stranger loose in her home to scour the family belongings from attic to basement for relevant material; nor in her own absence confers the freedom of her kitchen. Mrs Bensted-Smith did both.

I owe an enormous debt as well to the Newspaper Library staff of the British Library at Colindale. It remained a constant source

of amazement, during long days of research, that I could request
newspapers from all over England, Australia and South Africa,
from sixty years ago and longer, and have them placed in front of
me within a few minutes. Similarly, nothing was too much trouble
for the staff at the Surrey Records Office, Kingston-upon-Thames,
the BBC's Written Archives Centre, Caversham Park, Reading,
and Mr Stephen Green, the MCC curator at Lord's.

Several members of the Association of Cricket Statisticians
were generous to me with the fruits of their own researches, culled
often from old scorebooks, notably George Russ (Surrey), L. T.
Newell (Northamptonshire), Leslie Newnham (Essex), E. K.
Gross (minor cricket), Roy Wilkinson (Yorkshire), Peter Wynne-
Thomas (Nottinghamshire), Robert Brooke (Warwickshire) and
Radcliffe Grace (Australia). Mr H. A. Osborne, the Sussex CCC
librarian, and the secretariats of all the county cricket clubs, in
particular Lancashire, also helped me considerably.

For details of Fender's schooldays, I must thank Mr M. C. R.
Roe, the archivist at St Paul's School, and Mr Brian O'Gorman,
the cricket master at St George's College, Weybridge. Help with
Fender's football activities came from Mr N. F. Epps, hon. secretary of the Corinthian-Casuals FC and Mr Jack Rollin of the
Sunday Telegraph. Valuable aid about Fender's service in both
world wars was provided by staff at the RAF Museum, Hendon.

Above all, though, many cricketers and cricket writers, some,
alas, now dead, were unstinting in the time and help they provided
in letters and conversations. Among those who played with
Fender, I would acknowledge, in particular, the co-operation of
Andy Sandham, Alf Gover, Bill Bowes, 'Monty' Garland-Wells,
Ben Bellamy and E. M. Wellings. Among journalistic colleagues
and friends, I owe much for guidance and support to Brian Chapman, John Arlott, Irving Rosenwater, Norman Preston, John
Kay, David Frith, Reg Hayter, Gordon Ross, R. L. Hollands,
J. D. Coldham, Fred Speakman, Edward Grayson, Terry Cooper
and E. K. Brown. My thanks must also go to Michael Fordham
for his statistical appendix and to Miss Wendy Wimbush for
typing the manuscript. There were many others who contributed
to the entire project, not least my own family, who assisted with
proofs and indexing. I remain grateful to them all.

RICHARD STREETON

Harpenden, 1980

1. The captain England rejected

Almost alone in cricket folklore the place held by Percy George Herbert Fender has depended on something he failed to do rather than what he did. 'The best captain never chosen to lead England,' has been the verdict passed down to later generations. As an all-rounder his greatest deeds were with Surrey and included the fastest hundred made in a first-class match. That innings remains Fender's main legacy to the record books but hardly explains the multitude of stories and legends that continually surrounded his name. He was what was known in his own day as a card; now it would be said he did not conform, or that he was a rebel. He was descended on his father's side from Scottish border outlaws and a number of Fenders ended their days being hanged for stealing English sheep. His mother's forebears were Huguenot refugees from France, who settled and prospered in Gloucestershire. Hereditary instincts were always apparent in Fender's cricket: he batted and bowled more like a buccaneer than a conscript and his captaincy had an astuteness then rare in the county game.

Fender's contemporaries were unanimous in the 1920s that he manipulated the thin Surrey bowling resources with an almost miraculous flair. There were differences in cricket leadership in that era, of course, even if the emphasis was seldom as fixedly on attack as some writers have claimed. Wickets were more palpably sought, with containment and run-saving fields spurned as routine tactics. A greater use of spin bowling brought the chance to vary the tactical thinking and, most significantly of all, to maintain a respectable over rate. Fender's gifts as a captain, though, would have marked him out in any period of the game, irrespective of tactical trends or bowling cults. He had a deep knowledge of cricket, its history, laws and technique, and the judgement to interpret pitches and match situations. He kept dossiers on players and had a knack for recalling a batsman's weaknesses in matters of bowling and strokes and, equally important, his preferences. Fender had the insight to utilize these things at the right moment, and harnessed to this were the craft and knowing instincts of a

successful gambler. His ability was all slightly tinged, too, with
gamesmanship, though always within the laws.

As a player Fender had the ability to scale peaks reached by
few, though, like Constantine's, his talent was erratic. The full
potential was only fulfilled intermittently and not often reflected
in the scorebook. A rapid-fire fifty, three or four opportune
wickets, or a couple of brilliant catches: Fender's cricket tended
to be explosive and relevant. It brought disquiet to opponents
and excitement to spectators. 'The type who would win a match
but would rarely be at the top of the averages,' was how the
Australian critic A. G. Moyes summed up Fender in *A Century
of Cricketers* (Harrap, 1950). It seems incredible that Fender
failed to win more than thirteen caps even in a period when
numerous all-rounders flourished and fewer Test matches were
played. Above all there has remained the long unfathomed mystery of why Fender—accepted as the supreme tactician of his age—
was not chosen as England captain. 'I wish he could have captained
England; for surely he earned it,' was R. C. Robertson-Glasgow's
view in *More Cricket Prints* (T. Werner Laurie, 1948). Throughout the twenties the leading cricket writers were astonished by
England's rejection of Fender: it was a door that stayed permanently closed, locked and heavily bolted in his face.

Fender has disposed of several myths about the subject that
were first suggested at the time or have become accepted since.
One was that he failed to get the captaincy because it was thought
he was Jewish; second because he was not a university man; and
third because his business as a wine merchant came close to being
considered 'trade' in the class-riddled society of those times. To
modern readers these may seem distasteful and unnecessary
things to raise, but sixty years ago, sadly, they were meaningful.
Fender denied he was Jewish and in any event he did not believe it
would have told against him if he had been. In the second case he
pointed out, correctly, that England had already chosen several
captains who were not Oxford or Cambridge men and that they
were to do so again. Finally, to sell wine for a living was a perfectly
acceptable occupation by the 1920s.

To find the real reasons why Fender was never England captain
it is necessary to enter a delicate labyrinth of personalities and
prejudices. Time eased the hurt a little and Fender in old age
agreed there had been occasions when he was too sharp, or too
outspoken, for his own good. The English have always had

reservations—a positive distrust, in fact—about clever people, as numerous politicians who failed to disguise their cleverness have found to their cost. The cricket Establishment in Fender's day was no more hidebound than that found elsewhere in public life. They would have been suspicious of Fender's shrewdness in cricket and would have resented the instances when he acted contrary to normal practice. Not to do the 'done' thing was the biggest sin of all in those days in every sphere and Fender always had an approach and a mind of his own. Like many such men, too, he could be brash and tactless, however justified were his motives. To use a homespun phrase, Fender's face often failed to fit in the circles that mattered.

Fender was already aware by 1923 that senior officialdom regarded him with only qualified approval. He had been vice-captain of the MCC team to South Africa in 1922–23 but was not asked to lead either team in the two Test trials held in 1923. His own form and his leadership of Surrey had been outstanding and not for the first time, nor the last, Fender's case was lobbied in print at great length. The newspapers continued to ignore the pointers and they made Fender and Arthur Gilligan the front runners for the England captaincy in 1924. F. T. Mann and G. E. C. Wood were lesser candidates mentioned by the press for the job of leading England against South Africa, in what was the first home Test series for three years, and then to Australia the following winter. (Mann was to emerge as MCC's first choice all along, but he was unavailable to tour. This will be discussed in a later chapter.) The cricket writers were extremely critical by the standards of those times when Gilligan was chosen to lead the England XI in the Test trial and was then confirmed in office for the first Test match.

Cardus in the *Manchester Guardian* spoke of Lord's having reasons 'not apparent to the man in the street'. H. J. Henley in the *Daily Mail* said 'the best captain in England has again been passed over', and G. A. Faulkner in the *Westminster Gazette* described it as 'one of those incidents that cause a jar the more one thinks about it'. The *Daily Express* noted: 'Happily there is still time for reflection and reconsideration. The selection committee have not finally committed themselves. Let them beware lest a blunder be committed which will put into the shade all the blunders—and they have been many—which have distracted our post-war cricket.' Fender was naturally disappointed but, deep down, Gilligan's appointment did not surprise him. The two men were close friends and the day before Gilligan left for Australia in September he was a guest at Fender's wedding. By then Fender was out of the England side and an episode had occurred which effectively finished his Test-match career for good. Certainly Fender remained convinced that it cost him any lingering hopes he still held of captaining England.

The incident which finally made Fender *persona non grata* came in 1924 when he was rash enough to cross swords, woundingly, with Lord Harris, arguably the most influential figure English cricket has ever had. Lord Harris, President of MCC in 1895, was in his seventies and still held the powerful office of MCC treasurer. He was an autocratic figure at Lord's, serving cricket and cricketers faithfully by the dictums of his time, and a man of rigid principles throughout his long life. Fender remembered him as 'a fair but formidable man'. The first link in the chain of circumstances that led to Fender's incurring the baronial wrath was the dreadfully wet start to the 1924 season. The South Africans, needing more practice than most visiting sides as they adjusted to turf wickets, were badly hampered in their opening matches against Leicestershire and Derbyshire. At both games the captains agreed to cover the wickets and 'Plum' Warner in the *Morning Post* on 6 May, like other journalists present, wrote that this covering was contrary to the regulations. Warner added that the MCC committee might have something to say, 'though the practice has before now obtained at cricket festivals such as Scarborough without any notice being taken of it by MCC . . .'

MCC's response came in a statement which was carried by the newspapers without comment on 22 May. They reminded everyone that covering was in contravention of the appropriate law and went on to claim no knowledge of what had happened in the past at Scarborough in the following terms: 'They now, *for the first time* [author's italics] are informed that it has been for a long time a regular practice to cover the whole of the pitch at Scarborough and possibly at other matches. . . .' This seems to have been extraordinarily naïve of MCC in view of the stature of the Scarborough Festival, with which most of the leading players and officials were usually involved. They escaped any adverse criticism in the national press on this aspect, however, but it was touched upon by Fender in a letter on the whole subject of covering which was published soon afterwards.

Fender was ill-advised enough to recall an occasion at Scarborough a year or two earlier when Lord Harris himself had sought Fender's advice on how covering facilities there could be improved. They had walked across the Scarborough ground together during a stoppage for rain, and when Lord Harris raised the matter Fender had recommended more tarpaulins rather than the type of covering in use. Lord Harris had agreed and said that he would have inquiries made. In other words, Lord Harris, of all people, must have been fully aware of Scarborough's use of covering in the past. Few things could have been more calculated to embarrass Lord Harris and MCC than Fender's disclosure, though in itself it made no impact on either the media or the public. A reader's letter in the *Cricketer* in October 1924 was the only other instance where MCC's two-faced approach to the matter was mentioned in print. A Mr W. F. Curtis of Leicester noted that the pitch had once again been covered for the Yorkshire v. MCC match the previous month at Scarborough—in the presence of the festival's patron, Lord Hawke. Mr Curtis recalled MCC's strictures on the subject the previous May and, with tongue in cheek presumably, he wondered if MCC had now changed its mind. This letter provoked no further correspondence or, if it did, the letters were not published.

Whatever the rights and wrongs, Fender had obviously behaved extremely tactlessly and it need hardly be stressed that he never regretted anything as much in his life. The next time Fender was at Lord's, one of the pavilion attendants told him: 'His Lordship would like to see you, sir, in the committee-room.' Fender had already had one 'wigging', as he put it, from Lord Harris, who had remonstrated with him about his habit of leading amateurs and professionals on to the field through the same gate. 'We do not want that sort of thing at Lord's, Fender,' was a summary of that first occasion—guidance given kindly but firmly, and above all explicitly, as Fender recalled. This time Fender's memory was of Lord Harris's extreme anger. He was told something along the lines: 'Don't you ever write anything about me, my views or MCC in print again, young man.' Fender was left in no doubt that he had blotted his copybook badly and that the affair would not be forgotten.

Lord Harris died in 1932 and it has proved impossible to trace any reference by him to what went on that day in the committee-room between himself and Fender. MCC confirmed for the author that Fender's name did not appear in any minutes that dealt with wicket covering in 1924 and the present Lord Harris was unable to help either. He knew his father had several disagreements with Fender, but the family had no record of them. Even when Lord Harris's initial anger passed, the matter must have rankled at Lord's for a long time. It probably brought the breaking-point in what had seldom been an uncensorious view of Fender, who was adamant it was not entirely coincidental that his Test career virtually ended at this time. Nor was he ever asked to tour abroad with MCC again. Fender had been involved in every Test rubber played by England since the First World War. He won his first three caps in the final games of the 1920–21 series in Australia and he played in the last two Tests of 1921 in England. On tour in South Africa Fender played all five Tests of the 1922–23 series and he was picked for the first two Tests in June 1924. After that he was dropped—the man hailed in the press as the best all-round cricketer in England.

It was an unhappy time for Fender in other ways as well. During the second Test at Lord's he had to contend with unsought publicity when his engagement was leaked to some newspapers. The resultant fuss in the middle of a Lord's Test was a further contributory cause of disfavour with the Establishment. Nor had there been any let up at that time to the unsavoury campaign in some newspapers about the captaincy. They continued to dwell on possible reasons for Gilligan's selection ahead of Fender and this speculation was embarrassing to everyone. An outburst in a Sunday newspaper by Parkin, the Lancashire bowler, who criticized Gilligan's handling of England's attack helped to close the official ranks even more firmly behind Gilligan. In addition, Fender lost all bowling form for several weeks and there were also unfounded rumours that he was not available for Australia.

Fender finally knew for certain that he was out of the selectors' reckoning when Gilligan was injured in the Gentlemen v. Players match at The Oval in July. Gilligan was hit over the heart by a ball from Howell and, though he hit a hundred the next day, it was an injury which affected Gilligan's own fast bowling for the rest of his career. Gilligan stood down from the fourth Test at Manchester and J. W. H. T. Douglas, approaching forty-two, was hastily recalled as England's captain and added as vice-captain to the early list of tour choices. There were many unexpected selectorial decisions by England in the twenties, not least for the

1924–25 tour, but to many people this was turning back the clock with a vengeance. Fender did actually play in one more Test match. He began the 1929 season in remarkable form and was picked for the first Test against South Africa at Birmingham under J. C. White. Fender in old age did not even remember this late recall by England. In his own mind his Test career ended in 1924. The newspapers, incidentally, never did face the facts and continued their advocacy of Fender for several more years.

In the closing years of his life Fender confessed he had tilted unwisely with authority for as long as he could remember, though he also believed his unconventionality was frequently only ahead of its time. The first brush with those in high places that he could recall came when he was about eleven and at St George's College, Weybridge. Fender headed the winning goal from a corner in a house match and was later reprimanded by his housemaster, whom he had expected to be pleased. 'That sort of goal is a professional's trick, Fender; no proper footballer scores a goal with his head.' Later, a century he made for St Paul's School against Bedford was not mentioned when he irritated his cricket master by bowling lobs in the same match. A draw had looked certain and the fact that Fender snatched several wickets with his lobs and took St Paul's close to victory was considered unimportant. In county cricket the Lord's officials were not the only ground authority he upset by leading all his team through the same gate. Fender actually went further at The Oval and tried to get the Surrey amateurs and professionals to use the same dressing-room. He was dissuaded after talking with Hobbs and Strudwick. 'With respect, Mr Fender, we like to talk about you and laugh at what you might do next,' was the gist of what Hobbs told him, and Fender had the perception to let the matter drop.

Fender was the first man in English press boxes to use a typewriter, thus disturbing with metallic clatter traditional havens of quiet in which everyone wrote copy by hand. Fender had to ride out several storms of protest from colleagues and once at Leeds from a persistent woman spectator sitting nearby. Fender in his most charming manner offered to type the threatened letter of complaint to the club secretary for her.

He enlisted the aid of clothing manufacturers to provide lighter cotton vests and underpants for cricketers; he helped design a different-shaped Surrey cap with a larger peak that shielded the eyes more effectively. One spring, a leading baseball coach on a visit to London was invited to The Oval to help improve throwing techniques at fielding practice. All things, possibly, of small import, but they confirmed Fender as an innovator.

Like many quick-witted men Fender could be impatient with those lacking his ability to see ahead and he could be downright prickly with those he felt to be wrong or out of place. He was definitely intolerant of authority or tradition if he felt it to be out of step with the prevailing circumstances. In his thinking he was thrustful and never hesitated to cut corners, attributes he brought not only to cricket but also to his business life and to the bridge he played at the highest level. At the same time Fender was a stickler for things to be done properly and never allowed himself or others to desert the high standards of behaviour and commitment he set. If he was a man who tended to be respected rather than revered, his own professionals admired him enormously as a person and player. He was looked upon with the utmost suspicion, undoubtedly, by those who knew him least.

Andy Sandham played throughout the time Fender led Surrey and summarized a theme consistently reiterated among his age group: 'Mr Fender always knew too much for the others—committee men, groundsmen, the other team or their captain. It did not make him popular, but he was too clever for them.' Fender's ceaseless plotting was stressed with admiration by all his generation in their books: famous professionals like Hobbs and Strudwick, as well as Sandham, together with those like Hammond and Sutcliffe from other counties. Then there were the fellow amateurs like Arthur Carr, who believed Fender rather than Chapman should have succeeded him in 1926; and deep thinkers on the game like Jardine and Wyatt, who were unreservedly generous in print. Fender's discernment and the wide range of his scheming were the chief feature of the books he wrote on Test matches, which according to secondhand dealers remain in demand. These are *Defending the Ashes* (Chapman & Hall, 1921), which dealt with the 1920–21 series in which Fender played; *The Turn of the Wheel* (Faber & Faber, 1929) which described the 1928–29 rubber and was, perhaps, the best of them all; *The Tests of 1930* (Faber & Faber, 1930); and *Kissing the Rod* (Chapman & Hall, 1934). The penetrating insight into cricket strategy on every page make the mind boggle at Fender, day in, day out, practising for Surrey what he preached.

Captaincy was the part of cricket Fender came to enjoy most.

It added mental spice to what was otherwise only a physical activity. He believed there were two fundamentals to cricket leadership. First to keep the opposition unsettled by doing the unexpected, or at least to make them wonder. 'Post an extra slip whether the ball was turning or not; it might make them think it was turning.' Second to keep his own side informed of his plans in order to enlist the maximum co-operation. He was especially strict about the need for bowlers to bowl to their field; everyone had to work together. This trait for ensuring that everyone was briefed fully on the tactics to be used was a feature of Field Marshal Montgomery's leadership in more exalted spheres. Fender arrived at St Paul's as Lord Montgomery's schooldays there were ending. It might not be too far-fetched to wonder if there was a master or cricket coach at St Paul's who instilled this precept of full briefing into all his pupils.

Inevitably some of the unexpected wins Fender contrived for his side became exaggerated in the telling. The point was reached when he would be credited with ruses and captaincy coups not intentionally planned. There were also the legends, one of the best being of how Fender allegedly 'conned' Leicestershire at the old Aylestone Road ground. On the third afternoon, as the match drifted towards a draw, it was suggested to the Leicestershire captain that he should declare at tea-time. Surrey had an awkward journey to Bradford that evening, several players had minor strains, and a break from fielding would be a considerate gesture. With what seemed a safe lead the Leicestershire captain complied. Fender led the assault on the 150 required and won the game with a six into the pavilion. He was later presented with the ball used—inscribed with his 91 not out in fifty minutes. There were Cardusian echoes about this story. Sir Neville, who admired Fender's captaincy, would say that if it were not a true story it deserved to be. The 1923 *Wisden* referred to Leicestershire's declaring 'very rashly', as Surrey won by 6 wickets with time to spare. Fender did not think he would have been as blatant as the story depicted. 'I think Surrey were underestimated, even if the odd seed might have been sown in the chap's mind.'

Fender in the same conversation remembered a club match when he himself was duped by Beverley Lyon, whose captaincy of Gloucestershire between 1929 and 1934 showed much of the same boldness and imagination that characterized Fender's handling of Surrey. 'I always had a fellow feeling for Bev Lyon,'

Fender said. 'I felt he was the only other county captain juggling like myself with a restricted attack to try and make things happen.' The time when Lyon outwitted Fender came early in the season on an appallingly cold day with traces of snow on the outfield. Fender had spent a long time struggling to avert defeat and his side still had 3 wickets to fall as the final half-hour began. After a further fifteen minutes of purgatory in a biting wind, Lyon said: 'I've had enough. What about going off?' Fender was only too thankful his concentrated effort for survival had finished and agreed straight away. Only in the dressing-room did some of his team express surprise that Fender had accepted the chance of a draw. Fender had taken his side to within 15 runs or so of victory. 'Bev thought it very funny; he decided to try it on but never dreamt I would fall for it.'

As Fender's first-class career ended in 1936, an attempt must be made to convey something of his mode and style for those who never saw him play. Tall (6ft 2in), lean, almost gawky, and with a forward stoop when walking, he had a reach which gave an impression that he had been born with longer arms than other batsmen. There was a flurried, whiplash character to his strokes with an obvious contribution from strong, supple wrists: what appeared to be the same shot would send similar balls flying in a variety of improbable directions. He played mostly on the front foot and, basically, had two favourite strokes: these were variations of the pull, and a shot that propelled the ball between extra cover and third man, something of a cross between a sliced drive and a square cut, and there were recorded instances of its bringing 6 runs. A minor idiosyncrasy to record was that Fender did not regularly wear a left-hand batting glove.

Gerald Brodribb worked out that Fender's biggest scores averaged 62 runs an hour over his entire career. Jessop with 80 runs an hour headed the list, followed by Constantine (79), but Fender was among the leading ten. Cardus in the *Manchester Guardian* once described Fender as 'nature's second edition of Jessop'. Fender's approach to batting was helped by the fact that he played for a high-scoring team but even his rearguard actions, like those of Marshal Ney in the retreat from Moscow, tended to be spirited affairs. Fender had a favourite stratagem whereby Nos. 6, 7 and 8 in the order, were expected to slog. Fender usually filled one of these places and at least one of the three would succeed. If the earlier batsmen had done their job, Surrey's position was further cemented; if there had been a breakdown, the initiative was wrested back. Always, let it be noted, the belligerent approach.

In no part of cricket was Fender more of an experimentalist than when he was bowling. It led Ronald Mason, his memory jogged by Fender's appearance, to compare him, in *Sing All A Green Willow* (Epworth Press, 1967), with Groucho Marx. Mason wrote that Fender had clearly decided the only way to compensate Surrey for a lack of differing styles in attack was to provide them all himself: 'As if Groucho were suddenly to impersonate all his brothers in turn. . . .' As a young man Fender bowled medium-fast and Surrey's necessity would often make him revert to this later. In his heyday, though, he became a dangerous legspinner, with more googlies employed than usual. There was also a brisk top-spinner that brought many caught and bowleds; a quickish off-break, and the intentional full toss or long hop also earned wickets. Fender used a short run, but his arms and wrists flailed like the proverbial windmill and he aroused the curiosity of coaches by using the thumb and the first two fingers only for everything he attempted. Several of his contemporaries remembered the snap of Fender's long fingers as he tried to impart the maximum turn and he was among those who could, literally, make a ball 'hum' through the air, though the scientific explanation for this has never been found.

Fender believed that few bowlers used the width of the crease enough. He claimed he tried never to bowl two consecutive balls from the same place, nor to release them with his arm the same height. All this variety made him unpredictable and, at times, a costly bowler, but he was seldom easy to play. Dick Williamson, who reported Yorkshire cricket for sixty years, once watched Fender take a crop of wickets and remembered: 'I have never seen better "bad" bowling if you can understand that. Every ball was different. There was some rubbish sent down but you were aware all the time of his mind ticking over and the ball might have been deliberate.' As a slip fieldsman Fender was one of the best in England, with a talent for anticipation and mobility. He preferred to be the outside slip, second, third or fourth, and was particularly adept at those awkward catches that looked like falling short. He believed he was helped with these by standing in a 'starting blocks' position, one foot in front of the other, rather than with his legs straddled. This stance might have originated from the pain that developed in his left leg when it was jarred by a lengthy spell in the field.

Fender fractured this leg in five places playing football late in 1918 and the extent he suffered in later years was not widely appreciated. Fender's healed leg emerged from its plaster cast slightly shorter than his right leg. A built-up heel of spongy rubber helped disguise a minor limp and eased the pain from jarring. When batting, Fender inserted an iron bar inside his left pad to give additional protection to the mended bones. There were also little-known stories behind the famous Fender elongated sweaters and his glasses which, with several physical characteristics, made him such rich material for the cartoonists, whose influence and popularity were so great before live photography in newspapers became commonplace.

Fender, like many entertainers in sport with a mercurial talent, possessed his full share of showmanship. In the case of the sweaters the cartoons came before the actuality. He admitted that once Tom Webster began to draw him with those long sweaters down to his knees, he made a point of buying excessively large ones and stretched them downward whenever he could. Something similar applied to the round glasses that became so familiar to cricket enthusiasts. Early in 1922 Fender found he was getting headaches. A family friend, one of the royal family's ophthalmic specialists, tested Fender's eyes and had the glasses made up for him. Soon Fender discovered there was nothing wrong with his eyes and the original lenses prescribed were so weak as to be virtually plain glass. He had, however, escaped any more headaches: a triumph for psychosomatic healing. Fender being Fender, he continued to wear them and the cartoonists continued to caricature them. Some years later Fender did need glasses, but it helped explain why when he first wore them he was more than once described as having removed his glasses in mid-over and continuing to bat just as well. It was a habit that caused E. H. D. Sewell to omit Fender when Sewell once chose a 'Giglamps XI' for an imaginary match. It was ironical, therefore, to find Cardus in the *Manchester Guardian* writing about Fender in the 1924 Test trial as follows: 'He often drives a straight ball to the on with a cross bat and, at such moments, one has reason for imagining that Fender's spectacles are like Sam Weller's doubly magnifying glasses of "hextra" power.'

2. A cricketer is moulded

Fender and Surrey have always been so synonymous that it tends to be forgotten that his initial four years in first-class cricket were spent with Sussex. Lengthy school holidays with his maternal grandparents at Brighton brought a residential qualification in their wake for a promising young amateur in those more lax times. Fender's performances in local club cricket earned him the chance to develop his game at the well-conducted Sussex nursery and at seventeen he made his county debut for Sussex in 1910, within a few weeks of a premature departure from St Paul's School, West London, during his final term. Later Fender utilized his Balham birth to join Surrey in time for the 1914 season, a move made to facilitate work with his father's London firm of wholesale stationers. Early ambitions to become a barrister were scotched because the family could not afford to help him financially. Few lists of players capped by two counties include Fender, but Arthur Gilligan did give Fender a Sussex cap, retrospectively, in the late 1920s. It was an agreeable gesture and typical of Gilligan, who wished to remedy what he felt had been an oversight by Sussex.

Early cricketing days for Fender followed a pattern common to most boys with enthusiasm for the game and were traced by him in a most readable book he published in 1937 called *An ABC of Cricket* (Arthur Barker). This also contained some excellent instructional tips written as his county career closed, all still relevant, of course, to this day. His mother's maiden name was Herbert and it was from this side of the family, and especially from his mother, that Fender derived the active encouragement for his passion for cricket. His father was less involved with the game. He always grumbled, good-naturedly, that it cost him an extra sixpence on Saturdays to woo his future wife, when he came down from London at week-ends, as she would be ensconced all day in a deck-chair at the Hove ground. Without quite having to telegraph the details to her after a day's play, as did W.G. and E.M. to Mrs Grace (still the only woman to appear in *Wisden*'s births and deaths), Fender always found his mother the most dedicated and best informed of his critics. She seldom missed a game at The Oval in later years and failures and shortcomings had to be explained at the maternal post-mortems.

Grandfather Herbert played with Brighton's well-known Brunswick Club and so, too, did other members of his family. He was always credited with helping 'Punter' Humphreys, one of the last lob bowlers, to perfect his technique. Fender lacked the expertise to bowl underarm himself in county cricket, though instances are on record that he would do so to point the message if he felt a declaration was overdue! He was aware, however, of the potential in a slow, dropping full toss, and these often yielded a catch or would be missed altogether and would go on to hit the stumps. Oval *habitués* in the Fender period will confirm the success these balls brought him more than once against known big hitters like F. T. Mann, the Middlesex captain, and others. 'They would be slower to what I had been bowling, thrown up high and would drop just short of the block hole,' Fender said. 'They might cost a few runs but they got their share of wickets.' In view of what has been recounted about the relationship between Fender and Lord Harris, it is worth noting that they shared a respect for the possibilities of lob bowling. In his book *A Few Short Runs* (John Murray, 1921), Lord Harris wrote: 'But before I leave the [bowling] department, I should like to add this: it seems to me a great pity that lob bowling is not more cultivated.'

Alf Gover, whose formative years as a Surrey player were spent under Fender's captaincy, has never forgotten how a tempting leg-side ball brought Fender the wicket of Arthur Carr, one Whitsuntide at Trent Bridge. Gover was at forward short leg and Fender warned him to fling himself flat when he tugged at his shirt collar before bowling. 'After an over or two Percy George tugged at his collar; I ducked as Carr swung wildly at the full toss that came along. It was still high in the air as Fender called out "Carr, caught Gregory, bowled Fender", and so it was. Fender and Carr stood together in the middle of the pitch and watched Gregory take the catch on the midwicket boundary. "You so and so," Carr said. It amused us because we knew Fender was staying at Carr's house for the game. Mind you, with Carr, it only worked once.'

Fender's grandfather and his two uncles devoted many hours on a narrow back lawn to the family version of cricket that the space permitted. A soft rubber ball was used and the youthful

P.G.H. batted with a tennis racket. (The first proper bat he owned came as a bribe to stop him from biting his nails.) All the time-honoured rules of such family occasions applied: you could be caught full pitch off a fence; it was six and out if the ball went over the wall; and there was an abrupt cessation of play, and pocket money, if a window was broken. Footwork and the improvisation and skill needed to place the ball wide of the fieldsmen in the limited area were the lessons Fender remembered longest from these early days. Fender at this period was, by his preference, a left-handed batsman before the uncles persuaded him otherwise. He was virtually ambidextrous at cricket until he was about twelve and certainly the first hundred he ever made came as a left-hander in a local boys' club match. 'One of my schoolboy idols was E. H. Killick, a tiny left-hander whose late cutting always sticks in my mind. I remember going through a phase of trying to cut everything and this, perhaps, made me bat left-handed whenever possible.'

Fender could not remember why his uncles were against him batting left-handed. 'But in those days you did what you were told.' The uncles were adhering, probably, to the nursery dictums of the time as laid down by every governess. These good ladies, practically without exception, used to go to great lengths to rid their charges of any leaning towards left-handedness. If modern psychiatric thinking is correct, they did a great deal of harm, too, by so doing. Another possibility was that the uncles were following the precepts of Sir Arthur Conan Doyle, a favourite author in the Fender and Herbert households, who around this period was urging that all left-handers should be outlawed from cricket. The truth will never be known about the avuncular insistence that Fender bat right-handed. It remains a tantalizing thought that, had he been left alone, his unorthodox hitting might have been enhanced further by the advantages that seem to accrue to left-handers. As a bowler Fender was always out of step (yes, again!) with the majority, in that he did not mind bowling to left-handed batsmen. 'In some ways I even preferred them and fancied my chances. They did not always seem to me to play as straight and a good number of them could not "pick" my googly very well.'

One of the Fender uncles, Percy Herbert, who was a good club cricketer, was later given the chance by his famous nephew to make his only first-class appearance, or rather not to make it, in what are believed to be unique circumstances. In 1920 a fixture was arranged at The Oval between the Gentlemen of the South and the Players of the South as a benefit for J. J. Reid, the pavilion attendant. On Saturday, 3 July, the Players scored 551 for 9 against an incomplete Gentlemen's side, who fielded a substitute all day. On the Sunday Fender asked his uncle to make up the Gentlemen's XI and on the Monday Percy Herbert travelled to The Oval to play. It rained, however, all day and again on the Tuesday. There have been instances of cricketers neither batting nor bowling in their solitary first-class match; but to be credited in *Wisden* with playing but never actually seeing a ball bowled, or even treading on the field, must be unique.

Fender had a special bond of affection with his grandfather and as soon as he was allowed out on his own, he was a regular spectator from the pavilion at Hove with the older man. Grandfather Herbert would leave the house first but Fender became adept at sneaking his way into the ground without paying, and joining him. Not a word would be spoken between them but they became a familiar sight to other members and the players, it seems, both sitting bolt upright at the back and highest seat level, the top-hatted bearded old man and the young boy in knickerbockers, unmoving and watching every ball with rapt attention. This was from about 1900 onward. C. B. Fry and Ranjitsinhji were the first batsmen to enchant Fender and for an impressionable boy there were, presumably, worse pairs to seal a lifetime's dedication to cricket. Ranjitsinhji was past his best by the time Fender played with him in the Sussex side, but Fender has retained a special memory of one occasion when he and Ranjitsinhji batted together.

The match was Sussex v. the Australians at Hove in late July 1912. It was the first time Fender played against an Australian team and Ranjitsinhji, despite a heavily bandaged, strained wrist, made a brilliant 125 before he ran himself out. As C. G. Macartney scored 142 and 121 in this game, batting in each innings for less than two and a half hours, the spectators over the three days might be said to have had value for their money. Ranjitsinhji, in the sense that he needed incentives, could be a lazy cricketer, according to Fender. His mastery was such that he might not always apply his gifts fully without an additional spur. There have been great players in our own time to whom the same stricture could be applied. Ranjitsinhji's team-mates, knowing this quirk, would stimulate his interest in the form of small bets. On this occasion

Ranjitsinhji had accepted wagers that Sussex would get first innings lead. Sussex were struggling on the second day against an Australian total of 398 when Fender, with only a handful of county games behind him, walked out after tea at No. 8 with Sussex 268 for 6.

Ranjitsinhji, who had reached his century just before the interval, assured Fender there was nothing in the Australian bowling to worry about and told him to play his natural game. This was what Fender seemed to have done because, according to the *Sussex Daily News*, they added 51 together in twenty minutes with Fender, 'hitting in powerful and resolute style', driving three fours against Matthews and hitting Whitty over mid-on for six. What the newspaper could not be expected to disclose, however, was the remarkable private challenge that Ranjitsinhji set himself during this stand. He casually suggested to Fender between overs that it might be 'interesting' to nominate in advance the strokes he intended to play. 'I'll send the first ball down to Kelleway's left hand at long leg and the third ball to his right—he's always slow to get back; we'll run 2 each time.' Sure enough the famous leg glance brought this about with Ranjitsinhji reminding Fender, as they crossed, to run 2. In another over it was late cuts to Bardsley at deep third man which first brought 2 runs to the fieldsman's left and then 2 more to his right. There were some drives through the covers, too, and it did not matter what sort of ball was bowled, Ranjitsinhji never failed to achieve what he warned Fender to expect.

Fender went on: 'It did not last long; he soon tired of his "fun and games" but it was incredible to me at the time and still is. I had always been told he could do anything with a bat if you got him interested. This was an example of something that he set his mind to himself.' Ranjitsinhji was eventually run out when he called for a run as he played a ball straight to mid-on. Fender believed it was Matthews who threw down the stumps direct as Fender sent him back. He did not see Ranjitsinhji to speak to again that day and next morning found him in the amateurs' dressing-room surrounded by the morning newspapers. 'You must have a lot of friends in the papers, young man; they all say it was my fault—and it was,' he added with a smile. Fender scored 69, with one six and twelve fours, in sixty-five minutes, before he was bowled by McLaren, the Australian fast bowler. Sussex finished 9 runs short of the Australian total and the match was drawn.

Reverting to Fender's schooldays, he had three years in the St
Paul's XI, starting in 1908 when he was awarded his colours a
few weeks before his sixteenth birthday. (Fender was born on
22 August 1892, though *Wisden* for some reason gave his birthday
as 10 August until the matter was put right from the 1923 edition
onwards.) He seems to have been a normal boy academically,
doing better in English than in mathematics or the classics. His
reports are preserved at St Paul's and the over-all summary of his
work in his last year comments that 'His character has become
steadier.' In addition to cricket Fender played fives for the school;
he had some success at boxing, the school coach at this time,
incidentally, being 'Peerless' Jim Driscoll; and at track and field
he was a shot putter. There are few mentions of him as a rugby
player, though he seems to have been a reliable place kicker in
house matches. Fender's own memories one particular winter, are
of dislocating a shoulder playing full back in his first match of the
Christmas term, and then doing the same thing to the other
shoulder in the first match of the Easter term.

Fender did excel at fencing at St Paul's, where his long reach
was an advantage, and he must be one of the few county cricketers
to have fought a duel. It happened when he was working in Belgium a year or two before the First World War. A lifetime later
Fender was still reluctant to go into details, but apparently he had
been paying too much attention to a girl who was unofficially
engaged to an officer in the Belgian army. Fender was challenged
to a duel by his rival and a type of foil was the agreed weapon. 'We
were both very young and hot-headed. Almost as soon as we
started I nicked his arm and that was that, our seconds being as
anxious to finish as we both were.' Fender remembered enough of
his fencing to realize that his opponent knew little of the sport.
'Fencing, I always found, was the only sport where, deep down,
you know within seconds of starting, who is going to win.'

In England about a year later Fender received as a gift a magnificent swordstick direct from the Wilkinson sword firm. He made
inquiries, but all they would tell him was that the order had been
placed anonymously from Belgium. If Fender asked about the
order, he was to be told it was a gift 'for an Englishman who fenced
better than any Englishman has a right to do'. Fender still has the
swordstick, which he only used once in anger, as it were, when he
defended himself from being 'mugged' one night outside an
Estoril casino, while holidaying in Portugal. One of his assailants

ran on to the sword in the dark, but was able to run away and was never caught.

The first mention of Fender as a cricketer in the *Pauline* has him playing for the under-16 Colts on 29 June 1907, against the Charterhouse Maniacs. Fender opened both batting and bowling, making a chanceless 94 before he was stumped off a lob, and taking 3 wickets with the ball. His 1st XI debut was against the Incogniti on 23 May 1908, when he helped redeem a poor start with an innings at No. 3 and he kept his place in the side thereafter. The match mentioned in the first chapter, when Fender was reprimanded for bowling lobs, came in 1909. On a wet, deteriorating pitch he hit 145 out of 218 as St Paul's reached 249. Bedford Grammar School on their own ground were 104 for 9 when the game was left drawn. Fender took 3 late wickets and tried 'at least four varieties of bowling', according to the *Pauline*. His promise that year was rewarded by selection for the Public Schools against MCC, his first appearance at Lord's.

Most of the Public Schools side in that game on 2 and 3 August 1909 went on to play for their counties. Other than Fender, those to make the biggest mark on cricket history were M. J. Susskind, a South African Test player, and R. St L. Fowler, who stamped his name in such emphatic manner on the Eton v. Harrow series twelve months later. Fender contributed little to the match, making 28 and 0 and bowling 3 overs without taking a wicket. Among the schoolboys *The Times* saw, 'no-one of exceptional merit but there were several most useful cricketers likely to do well in future'. Early in 1910 Fender made 146 against Mill Hill in an away match, one of six sixes he hit breaking a window of an adjoining house, but soon afterwards his school life ended. His father and the High Master of St Paul's had an altercation about cricket taking precedence over other school activities. Fender was immediately withdrawn from the school by his father, though there were several weeks to go before the term ended.

The High Master at St Paul's at this time was Dr A. E. Hillard, a distinguished classicist. (The name may invoke mixed emotions to anyone who ever used the famous Hillard and Botting Greek textbook at his own school.) The details about the row remain obscure to Fender, who listened anxiously outside the High Master's study to the raised voices during a Monday lunch-time. It was connected with Fender's playing in a club cricket match the previous Friday and Saturday, which had been 'whole day holidays'. A necessary letter of clearance from the Fender parents never reached the school. When the High Master that Monday morning got to hear that he had played in the match, Fender was sent with a letter to the West End club where his father always lunched.

Mr Fender left his meal unfinished and summoned a horse-drawn cab, which was kept waiting as the quarrel with the High Master ensued. Fender never did learn what was in the High Master's original letter, but he remembered returning to his father's club and helping to finish an extremely good lunch. *Wisden* gives the matter an oblique reference in its comments on St Paul's season that year: 'Two players, Buckley and Pender [*sic*], stand out from the rest, and it was unfortunate that the latter's services were not available all the term.' Thus can all human drama be buried between the good book's thin lines of small print.

The 1910 school averages show that Fender played seven innings that term against most other people's sixteen innings. His early departure did not preclude him from figuring in the *Pauline*'s critiques, with the same themes recurring that had been in the magazine a year earlier. In 1909 Fender had been told that he was careless and was a rash hitter and that in bowling he 'would do well to stick to one style and avoid mannerisms'. Fender topped the batting averages all three years he was in the 1st XI but again in 1910 he was mentioned as 'still inclined to take liberties before he is really set', while the writer goes on: 'A good bowler when he chose but too fond of affected peculiarities of action.' These remarks show that in approach and style, perhaps, the child's cricket was father to the pattern that the man's would take. It could also be deduced that Fender's experiments were frowned upon from his earliest days but that already there was never any shortage of ideas in his cricket thinking.

Fender had been chosen to play again in 1910 for the Public Schools at Lord's when his school life ended so suddenly. Having to stand down from this match rankled as much as anything connected with his departure from St Paul's. The MCC Secretary, Mr. F. E. Lacey, as he then was, even had to give a ruling about Fender's position, as Captain E. G. Wynyard, who was responsible for getting the Schools' team together, was not clear where Fender stood. MCC took the line that Fender could no longer be considered a schoolboy, which was perfectly fair but naturally was a bitter disappointment to the player. As he did every summer Fender went to his grandparents at Brighton and quickly became involved with local cricket. His potential was already known and on 13 July some newspapers listed him in the Sussex team to play Leicestershire the next day at Hove, but R. B. Heygate, who had been indisposed, made a quicker recovery than expected and was able to turn out. Fender went off to Leyton instead for a 2nd XI match where he hit 82 (thirteen fours) and the *Sussex Daily News* referred to 'the St Paul's school star', as follows: 'He is a fine punishing bat with a good reach and plenty of scoring strokes and he gets great power into his shots.'

A few days later Fender was included in the Sussex team to play Nottinghamshire at Trent Bridge, starting on Thursday, 21 July. Sussex were playing at The Oval when the names were announced and Fender earned his selection by some fierce hitting on the Hove ground for Old Eastbournians against the Sussex Martlets. Fender had no membership qualifications to play for the Old Boys' side but, batting No. 5, scored 147 not out (one six and nineteen fours) in a total of 294 for 7. The next highest score in the innings was 36. Sussex Martlets made 123 for 3 and the mixed feelings they probably had about their opponents' 'guest' player were not recorded.

Fender's own summary of his first-class debut was: 'I scored one run, took one wicket and held one catch in the first innings—and did not do so well in the second.' Sussex batted first on a wet wicket and were already struggling when Fender arrived at No. 6—'A well built young fellow standing well over six feet high,' said the *Nottingham Evening News* and the newspaper continued: 'There was not, however, much opportunity of estimating Fender's powers today as, having scored a single off the first ball he received, he was out, caught at the wicket to the third. . . .' (c Oates, b Iremonger, to be precise). When Nottinghamshire batted, Fender took a good catch 'high up at short leg' to dismiss Hardstaff, and later he had George Gunn leg before. Fender does himself a minor injustice in his summing up of his performances in this game as he actually made 2 runs in the second innings before being caught by Wass, again off Iremonger's medium-paced off-breaks.

'The shortest county career of all time, I reckon, sir,' was Albert Relf's greeting in the dressing-room. This bit of leg-pulling, it transpired, was a comment on anyone having the ill luck to be caught by Wass. For all his gifts as a bowler, Wass was regarded as one of the poorest fieldsmen in the game. (Wass, according to legend, indulged in poaching during the winter months, but was always careful to trespass only on land belonging to Nottinghamshire CCC members as they were less likely to prosecute him.) Fender, in fact, remembered this catch to Wass as being one of those instinctive self-protective ones that stuck. A vigorous pull stroke towards mid-on sent the ball skimming straight to what are politely known as Wass's nether regions. Sussex played seven more championship games that year before Fender was next chosen for the county, this time against Worcestershire.

There is no intention to take the reader through Fender's career, match by match, but this second game for Sussex caused him several embarrassments he has never forgotten. Fender was playing in one of those lavish country-house weeks that the Kaiser, Adolf Hitler and social change have all had a hand in removing from the English scene. This particular game was at Warnham Lodge, near Horsham, on the private ground owned by Sir Henry Harben, corner-stone of the Prudential Assurance Company in its early days, and a dedicated cricket enthusiast. Sir Henry was eighty-seven when Fender knew him and in the tradition of all such cricket hosts, mentors and patrons, he exercised his rights to the full. By 1910 Sir Henry often used a wicker Bath chair and he would insist on being wheeled into position at the bowler's end, over by over. There, next to the umpire, he supervised his guests' playing of their cricket. Fender, with several hard, low and straight hits, had already broken some spokes and done other damage to Sir Henry's Bath chair, when the uniformed telegraph boy of that era came out to the wicket and delivered the summons for Worcester.

Sir Henry's good humour and enthusiasm were seldom known to desert him, but they had been thoroughly tested under fire from the crease this day. Permission for Fender to break off his innings and depart was readily granted. Trains on the Sussex branch lines were none too plentiful even in those times and it was early evening when Fender reached his grandfather's house in Brighton. He found that the laundry had failed to return his only other pair of flannels. After a frantic hunt he managed to get a cheap pair in a back-street shop he persuaded to open, and finally set off for London. By the time he crossed to Paddington he found there were no trains to Worcester until sixish the next morning. A porter, with tongue in cheek, or possibly on commission, directed Fender to a hotel, one of those tall dwellings that still stand not too far from the station. It proved to be a hotel of sorts but one with other good reasons for making male arrivals especially welcome late at night.

Fender was puzzled by the amusement he seemed to cause in the foyer when he asked for a quiet room where he could get a good night's sleep. He was even more bewildered later by the succession of female callers at his door asking if he had everything he needed. Fender was still a few days short of his eighteenth birthday and from a sheltered background, but finally the penny dropped. He fled back to the station long before dawn, without, he thinks, paying any bill, and spent what was left of the night on the platform. The train was late arriving at Worcester and he almost missed the start of the match. He duly received a thorough dressing-down from H. P. 'Bertie' Chaplin, the Sussex captain, whose military background had greatly extended his vocabulary. Fender's unhappy experiences were not finished yet. He had an undistinguished game and during the match was sent off the field by Chaplin to borrow some other flannels. The cheap pair he had bought were so transparent against the sun that they induced ribald remarks from the crowd.

Fender scored only 12 and 4 in his two innings and did not bowl, but he has a feeling that he stayed at the wicket longer than these scores might imply. Long enough to admit, candidly, that for one of the few times in his life he took steps to avoid facing particular bowlers. In the first innings it was the fast bowling of R. D. Burrows that scared Fender; in the second innings he changed his approach and tried to stay with Burrows when he found W. B. Burns even faster. Fender's reactions did not go unnoticed by his fellow players. Such things never do, in fact, even to this day and Fender has always remembered the kindness and tact with which H. K. Foster, the Worcestershire captain, dealt with the situation.

Foster sought out Fender after the game and said something to the effect: 'I don't blame you for preferring Burrows to Burns, who is as fast as anybody for a few overs. By the way, I like that square cut of yours. If you find you can go on making that stroke without getting out, you keep on playing it and you should get plenty of runs.' The only other matter worth mentioning from this game is that Worcestershire in more than one press account are referred to as 'the Sauce county', an expression that none of us in modern press boxes has dared to inflict upon our readers.

In the years that followed, Fender came to prefer batting against fast bowling rather than spin, and this is borne out by the details of some of his most successful innings. He blandly explained: 'You can only score really quickly for any length of time against the faster bowlers; the slower ones can stop you with defensive fields if they are good enough to bowl to them. [!] Against fast bowlers it goes farther and faster, and you can have more chance off the edge if you don't hit it properly. Hit it hard and try and hit a four from the first ball of the over. It seems to annoy them more than it does a spinner; and remember, they still have five balls of the over to bowl, and they have lost their head already.[!!]'

When Fender was the Surrey captain he had a reputation for being intolerant of anyone who flinched against fast bowling. He believed it was a fair contest if the batsman had a bat in his hand. For this reason he would never have worn a helmet, he said, preferring to protect himself by his own efforts. Alf Gover remembered Fender's unselfishness in connection with fast bowling. 'I joined him once against Larwood and Voce and was a bit apprehensive. He told me to stay with Larwood. "He'll bowl straight at your stumps but I don't trust Voce; I'll look after him and I'm going to hit him over extra to show him what I think of him." And he did, too, and Voce was furious,' Gover said.

Fender's first job that autumn took him to some mills at Horwich to learn about paper manufacturing. Twelve-hour days in a north country factory for meagre wages, with a full share of the dirtiest and most menial tasks, were a harsh introduction to the outside world for Fender. It was an experience he has never forgotten and it did him, he said, a lot of good. He had excellent digs with a family called Polkinghorne. Fender in later life was a renowned gourmet and the terror of numerous head waiters. It was instructive, therefore, to hear him enthusing seventy years later about Mrs Polkinghorne's cooking, especially her stews and rice puddings. He also recommended as a 6 a.m. delicacy on a winter's morning, egg and bacon placed to cook on an unlagged pipe in the mill's boiler room. On bath nights in the digs it would take longer to clean the bath afterwards than it had done to wash. The highlight each week was Saturdays in Bolton. If he had been on night shift, he would sleep for a few hours and then travel into Bolton (8d return); a steak lunch (1s 10d) at his favourite local, the Black Dog; on to Burnden Park to watch Bolton Wanderers (6d or 1s); back to the pub for another steak followed by the local music hall

(2s) before getting the last tram back to Horwich. 'A marvellous day for around ten shillings,' he recollected.

Fender had one frightening accident at the mill, which could have ended his cricket life there and then. While he was threading paper through some big compressed cotton rollers, his left hand was trapped. The job was done standing on a plank above a pit. As Fender felt the rollers tighten on his hand, he had the presence of mind to jump off the plank and the weight of his body literally wrenched his hand out of the rollers. He was fortunate that only the tops of three fingers were crushed. Two years earlier, another man's arm had been drawn in up to the elbow and the arm had to be amputated. In due course Fender's fingers healed but they were left about a quarter of an inch shorter and were always to remain stiff, with little feeling in them. Certainly he does not think he could have grasped the ball firmly enough to bowl if it had been his right hand. Later we shall see that these 'dead' fingers may have cost England a Test match. Not for the squeamish to dwell on, but Fender in later years, as a party trick, used to stick pins in his damaged finger ends, without, of course, feeling anything. Meanwhile, even Fender lost no time in disposing of the customary souvenir presented by his workmates: his own finger nails recovered from the rollers and mounted on a piece of cardboard!

Fender's cricket early in the 1911 season, while he was still at Horwich, was played with the Manchester Club, whose home matches took place at Old Trafford. Ernest Tyldesley and Harry Makepeace were among others in the same Manchester side. Fender was included in a Lancashire trial once and the county hoped for a time that he might play for them in 1912. By then, however, Fender had completed his time at Horwich and returned to Brighton. At this time his father always allowed him lengthy summer holidays to play cricket, but in 1911 he was again chosen for only two first-team games for Sussex and did little against Warwickshire at Chichester or Lancashire at Old Trafford. Though he played almost every day, Fender's cricket was inconsistent and a lack of stamina may have been responsible. He had been a delicate child and physically his frame had still not hardened. Vallance Jupp was a professional on the Sussex staff at this period and he was considered the far sounder prospect. Jupp, later to do so much for Northamptonshire, was a year older than Fender and several times was chosen ahead of him.

It was half-way through the 1912 season that Fender finally secured a regular place in the Sussex team. He came into the side on 20 June against Cambridge University at Hove and proved his usefulness at Horsham in the next two games with a maiden hundred against Oxford University and some wickets against Surrey. This was the first time that the delightful Horsham ground had been allocated two fixtures. It was a compensatory gesture to local supporters, who had gone without a visit by the county the year before when an agricultural show took precedence for the use of the field. A Horsham and West Sussex Week, as it was designated, was an experiment, therefore, and watched closely by the Sussex authorities. Fender could not have chosen a better opportunity to create a good impression.

The excitement and sense of special occasion engendered by a county match at somewhere like Horsham in those unsophisticated times cannot be appreciated today. The stranger can arrive now for an equivalent occasion and he is fortunate if there are even AA route signs to indicate the match is taking place. Horsham in 1912 was a mass of bunting, flags and streamers and at night there were fireworks and 'electrical illuminations'. The band from Christ's Hospital attended, 'cheered on by their fellow pupils', and so, too, did Mr William Law, the local town crier and champion of England, 'clad in all his glory of habit'. Mr Law, one reporter noted, was more willing to sign autographs than some of the cricketers. Newspaper accounts say that 'the gentry were there in large numbers, both to justify the fixtures being given to the town and to organize their country house parties.' In the evening there were special concerts and drama presentations, including entertainment by the HAMS (Horsham Amateur Minstrel Society). Needless to say, the law of general cussedness saw to it that the weather spoiled things with untimely rain during the six days of festivities but, it seems, 'Nothing could dampen the enthusiasm aroused by the return of county cricket to the town.'

When the game with Oxford began on the Monday, the attendance was about 2,000, which was felt to be disappointing. Sussex batted all day for 414 for 8 before rain brought an end at six o'clock. Fender (133 not out) and the wicket-keeper, George Street (26 not out), had added 94 in forty minutes for the ninth wicket. Oxford's bowling was not especially strong, but Sussex had lost 6 wickets for 187 before Fender and Chaplin put on 99 together in fifty minutes. Fender, coming in at No. 6, was 66 not out at tea

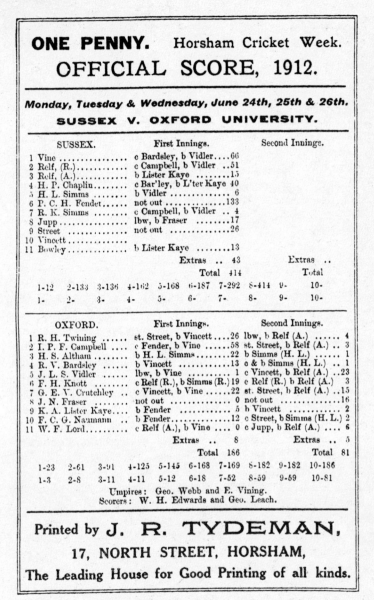

ONE PENNY. Horsham Cricket Week.

OFFICIAL SCORE, 1912.

Monday, Tuesday & Wednesday, June 24th, 25th & 26th.

SUSSEX V. OXFORD UNIVERSITY.

SUSSEX.	First Innings.		Second Innings.
1 Vine	c Bardsley, b Vidler	66	
2 Relf, (R.)	c Campbell, b Vidler	51	
3 Relf, (A.)	b Lister Kaye	15	
4 H. P. Chaplin	c Bar'ley, b L'ter Kaye	40	
5 H. L. Simms	b Vidler	6	
6 P. C. H. Fender	not out	133	
7 R. K. Simms	c Campbell, b Vidler	4	
8 Jupp	lbw, b Fraser	17	
9 Street	not out	26	
10 Vincett			
11 Bowley	b Lister Kaye	13	
	Extras .. 43		Extras ..
	Total 414		Total

1-12   2-133   3-136   4-162   5-168   6-187   7-292   8-414   9-   10-
1-   2-   3-   4-   5-   6-   7-   8-   9-   10-

OXFORD.	First Innings.		Second Innings.	
1 R. H. Twining	st. Street, b Vincett	26	lbw, b Relf (A.)	4
2 I. P. F. Campbell	c Fender, b Vine	58	st. Street, b Relf (A.)	3
3 H. S. Altham	b H. L. Simms	22	b Simms (H. L.)	1
4 R. V. Bardsley	b Vincett	13	c & b Simms (H. L.)	1
5 J. L. S. Vidler	lbw, b Vine	1	c Vincett, b Relf (A.)	23
6 F. H. Knott	c Relf (R.), b Simms (R.)	19	c Relf (R.) b Relf (A.)	3
7 G. E. V. Crutchley	c Vincett, b Vine	22	st. Street, b Relf (A.)	15
8 J. N. Fraser	not out	0	not out	16
9 K. A. Lister Kaye	b Fender	5	b Vincett	2
10 F. C. G. Naumann	b Fender	12	c Street, b Simms (H. L.)	2
11 W. F. Lord	c Relf (A.), b Vine	0	c Jupp, b Relf (A.)	6
	Extras .. 8		Extras ..	5
	Total 186		Total	81

1-23   2-61   3-91   4-125   5-145   6-168   7-169   8-182   9-182   10-186
1-3   2-8   3-11   4-11   5-12   6-18   7-52   8-59   9-59   10-81

Umpires : Geo. Webb and E. Vining.
Scorers : W. H. Edwards and Geo. Leach.

Printed by **J. R. TYDEMAN,**

17, NORTH STREET, HORSHAM,

The Leading House for Good Printing of all kinds.

1. The score-card printed after Fender made his first hundred in a three-day match for Sussex at Horsham in 1912 and, all told, batted two hours thirty-five minutes and hit eighteen fours, mostly by brilliant driving. 'He forced the pace and hit out in dashing style,' according to the *Sussex Daily News*. Rain disrupted the rest of the match, but Sussex completed an innings win on the Wednesday.

Fender's first game against his future county brought him two failures with the bat but an analysis of 5 for 42 in Surrey's second innings, including the much-prized wicket of Jack Hobbs. Four of the wickets were bowled and in three instances the batsmen's middle stumps were 'lowered', as contemporary accounts put it. Hobbs, who had made 65 and was, presumably, well set, was one of these. Sussex lost the game by 78 runs on the third afternoon, when they collapsed on a wet pitch against Tom Rushby and W. C. 'Razor' Smith. Later in the summer, against Hampshire at Eastbourne, Fender had a spell of 4 for 9 in 4 overs, hitting the stumps each time and bowling 'quite fast'. He usually bowled slightly above medium pace at this time, but it was about now that he first became fascinated by the possibilities of spin bowling. The seed was sown, apparently, by watching the turn that Vine could get in the nets with leg-breaks, even if the professional did not always risk them in matches.

Another aspect of Fender's cricket in which he had not yet found his true *métier* was fielding: he was seldom put in the slips but was known as a whole-hearted chaser in the deep. At least two of his catches that season earned him a lot of kudos. After hitting 83 against Gloucestershire, and sharing a ninth wicket stand of 131 in seventy-five minutes with Street, Fender caught A. H. G. White with what seems to have been a brilliant effort. Fender, the *Sussex Daily News* reported, 'while running at full speed took the ball with the right hand close to the ground, not far from the pavilion rails. A finer piece of work has not been seen upon the ground for many a long day. . . .' His other widely reported catch was taken one-handed above his head at long-on to dismiss Rolland Beaumont, when Sussex played the South Africans.

Fender had twinges of conscience about this catch for years and wondered if it should have been allowed to stand. He had to back-pedal to the boundary rope and finally leaned backwards to take it, with a spectator's hand propping him up. The Laws in 1912 were not too explicit on whether Fender had infringed the rules, though it was possible that he might have done. An MCC ruling, applicable to 1912, allowed fieldsmen to lean against a boundary wall or fence to catch a ball outside it—but this was different. (It is interesting to remember, by the way, that it had been only two years earlier that batsmen had first earned six runs for hits over the boundary; before that, a six had to be hit out of the ground.) Talking about this catch, Fender noted he had broken one of his own precepts by having to move backwards. 'I always insisted my deep fieldsmen stood deep, right on the edge of the field. It is much easier to run in than to run backwards. You've got to bear in mind the difficulties of taking a deep field catch if you put somebody two-thirds of the way back, trying to do two jobs.'

Fender played for Sussex from the start of the 1913 season, passing 1,000 runs for the first time, and he was chosen for the Gentlemen against the Players at The Oval and Lord's. His form, though, was curiously uneven that summer. In May and June he left an imprint on almost every match, with either bat or ball, and scored six fifties and one century in his first twenty-one innings. After that he fell away dreadfully and his remaining thirty innings brought only one further fifty and hardly any wickets. It was easy to understand why *Wisden* commented that there were times when he 'was scarcely worth his place in the eleven'. There does not seem to have been any suggestion, however, that he should have been dropped. A part explanation, too, for his deteriorating form could have been the discomfort he had had from early July onwards from a carbuncle in his groin. This had to be lanced more than once and was of the sort that lingered longer in the days before antibiotics.

A strained leg muscle was the published explanation for Fender's standing down from the Sussex team against Leicestershire immediately prior to his appearances for the Gentlemen, but the carbuncle was the true reason. Like many cricketers of his time, Fender was absent from few matches for strains and other injuries. He would often miss Surrey's games against the Universities in later years, in order to rest or for business reasons, but seldom failed to turn out otherwise. Fender believes players were hardier in his era than their modern counterparts. He deliberately did not say 'fitter', as he appreciated the difference and did not think it would have been true anyway. Life in all spheres, though, was harsher in many ways sixty and more years ago, and Fender is not alone in thinking this had a beneficial effect on character and resilience.

Many cricket professionals were not paid in Fender's early days, of course, if they were unable to play. In addition, injuries like chipped bones were not spotted instantly by X-ray examinations. Neither was rest always considered to be the solution for muscle tears. Fender and his contemporaries never trained with the same physical intensity before a season, or on tour, that has now become the norm. They prepared for cricket by playing cricket, with long periods in the nets and in local matches, before the first-class season began. In Fender's case the most frequent injuries he suffered were dislocated fingers while fielding. Andy Ducat, in the Surrey days, became most proficient at putting them back there and then: one more attribute of a man whose gifts at different times brought him England cricket and football caps, the managership of Fulham FC and the cricket coach's job at Eton.

Fender probably should not have played for the Gentlemen as he felt far from fit, but he was reluctant to miss his first representative games. His role was insignificant in both matches, which were played successively, with only Sunday intervening. Jessop in the first, and Sydney Barnes in the second, were the outstanding performers and exemplify the standards beside which Fender's own cricket was slowly being developed. Fender was caught first ball at The Oval off his Sussex team-mate, Albert Relf, one of 7 wickets to fall for 38 in the first hour..Conditions were wretched, but what *Wisden* termed 'utter fiasco' was avoided when Jessop hit 81 out of 111 in seventy minutes. Jessop made 107 in the second innings and Fender was bowled by John Gunn for 10. Needing 433 to win, the Players were 334 for 8 at the end of what had become a fine match. Fender in the second innings had figures of 15—1—68—1, his wicket being W. G. Quaife, who was bowled by one that came back at him. The kindly 'Plum' Warner wrote in his book *Gentlemen v Players 1806–1949* (Harrap, 1950) that Fender's analysis 'gives no idea how well he bowled. Several times he beat the batsmen and only just missed the wicket.' After the week-end a much-strengthened Players' side at Lord's won another good match by 7 wickets. Fender's contributions were 3 and 4 not out and he was given only 1 over.

Earlier in 1913 Fender had first attracted notice outside Sussex when he rescued his team from a poor start against Middlesex at Lord's on 19 May. It was an opportune game in which to do well. Large crowds were present to watch the return of 'Plum' Warner,

who, it was hoped, had finally thrown off the illness which caused
him to miss most of the 1911–12 Australian tour and the following
English summer. Sussex were 15 for 3 on the first morning when
Fender went in and he struck 87 of the next 114 runs in seventy
minutes against Napier, Tarrant and J. W. Hearne. Fender was
missed at slip when 26 but, before he was caught at long-on, he
had hit a six, thirteen fours and six threes. Sussex won by 33 runs,
Warner making an undefeated 88 in the Middlesex second innings.
Fender played several aggressive innings in the next few weeks,
the best coming in a losing cause at Sheffield where Yorkshire
won in two days by 8 wickets. Fender was generously applauded
for 'a dashing and faultless' 76 (three sixes and seven fours) which
ensured that Yorkshire had to bat again.

Excellent form during four successive games at Hove brought
Fender his selection for the Gentlemen, starting with the best
all-round showing he had yet given. Against Cambridge University Fender took 6 for 98 in the second innings, and then made 104
out of the last 148 runs in eighty-five minutes to win the game,
after early wickets had fallen cheaply. Against Oxford University
in the next game Fender took 5 for 21 in the second innings as
Sussex gained an easy victory in a match which has taken its place
in cricket lore because in *Wisden*'s phrase, 'some liberties were
taken with the rules of the game'. Oxford found themselves three
men short in their second innings and Chaplin allowed G. R. R.
Colman, who was not playing in the match, to bat for R. H. Twining. A telegram had recalled Twining to Oxford for an examina-
tion on the second day, while R. V. Bardsley and R. S. M. White,
the other absentees, were injured. Chaplin's decision to allow a
batting substitute was described as 'courteous' by the local
Brighton paper but *Wisden* deemed it 'a very irregular proceeding'.

Scores of 80 and 60 against Hampshire and a rapid 83 against
Nottinghamshire followed and the newspapers began to report
that the refreshment tents emptied whenever Fender went in to
bat. The best of his season, though, was behind him now, but
special mention, perhaps, should be given to the first occasion he
ever played at The Oval. Sussex were thrashed by an innings and
158 runs. They used ten bowlers as Surrey reached 501 for 9
declared. Fairly soon 5 wickets fell, but Andy Sandham (196)
made the first of his 107 hundreds and he and Harry Harrison
(138 not out) took complete control. They added 298 inside four
hours, a sixth-wicket record for Surrey that still stands.

It was an unforgettable introduction for Fender to The Oval's vast playing area at that time. His carbuncle was troubling him and he had to do a great deal of running about in the outfield. In the first over he bowled, he was driven by E. G. Goatly for an all-run six, which he thinks he had to 'fetch'. At least Fender made the top score in the first innings, but it was only 22 as Sussex collapsed for 87. Overall, this was an unhappy game for Sussex, but revenge came in their final match of the season when they won the return with Surrey at Hastings. Fender had no idea as he left the ground on 3 September 1913 that the following year he would be one of the Surrey team who would win the championship.

3. A decisive season overshadowed

Every cricketer has met with one particular season when his life-style in the game suddenly emerged; a time when his career was shaped in its final form, to stay basically unchanged until retirement. It happened to Fender in 1914 and in his case he jumped abruptly into the front rank of English all-rounders and at the same time stamped himself indelibly in the public eye. From the moment Fender began with Surrey, his cricket thrived and became more meaningful. In his second match he performed a hat trick against Somerset and in his fifth he hammered 140 against Warwickshire inside two hours. These feats both took place at The Oval, where Fender and the habitually large and chirpy crowd quickly established a rapport that lasted for the next twenty years and more. Captaincy had yet to come and most of his finest moments as a player also lay ahead. If the legendary ring-master was not yet cracking the whip, the distinctive crowd-appeal and ebullient gifts, however, were in evidence from the start.

Surrey always had great cricketers at the time when Fender played and they included some remarkable characters as well. Other than Hobbs, it was the ungainly, long-legged figure of Percy Fender in the next decades that epitomized Surrey cricket for London crowds and elsewhere. He was, of course, a natural cynosure for Cockney witticisms and manna to cartoonists, who revelled in the black, crinkly hair, expansive brow, beaky nose and later, the round glasses, knotted neckerchief and grossly long sweater. Few players in fact have lingered longer, or more vividly, in the minds of those who watched him in his heyday than Fender as a cricketer and as an individual. Attendances were larger then, interest in cricket more widespread. Remembering this, it can be claimed, possibly, that nobody in terms of personal magnetism has made a similar sort of impact at The Oval since.

There is no need to remind anyone what a momentous year 1914 was in wider contexts, and those who lived through it say that nothing, literally, was to be quite the same again. It is a claim made with more justification, of course, than most of its sort, and cricket, as always, faithfully reflected its era. Surrey's first place in the championship table was virtually unassailable when they cancelled their final two matches, away to Sussex and at home to Leicestershire. By then the First World War had been in progress for nearly a month; the early casualty lists from Belgium and the North Sea were appearing in the newspapers; and both the battle and retreat from Mons had occurred. The fact that cricket should have carried on uninterrupted as long as it did shows what a completely different world it was in every way. Cricket administrators were far from being the only people who failed to grasp that normal life would not continue at home as it had done in every previous campaign fought. England had declared war on 4 August and four championship matches started on 31 August, the day when the Surrey committee finally took heed of growing public disapproval at the continuation of the first-class game.

Surrey themselves that day began a match at The Oval against Gloucestershire, who played with only ten men, Dipper, the absentee, having enlisted. Both a famous letter from W. G. Grace in the *Sportsman* and some acidulous remarks by Lord Roberts in a recruiting speech had a hand in cricket's cessation. Surrey's two fixtures were the only championship games still outstanding. Otherwise the Scarborough Festival and the Champion County versus the Rest of England were all that was left of the programme. Surrey's failure to complete their matches led a number of people to assume that the championship had been left in abeyance. Surrey sought clarification from the MCC committee in the end and with Middlesex, their nearest rivals, raising no objection, they were finally officially declared the championship winners at a meeting on 9 November. It was the only county title Surrey won or shared between 1899 and 1950. By the time the ruling was known, Fender and practically all other cricketers were in uniform or the munition factories.

In all sorts of ways Fender has retained more nostalgic memories about this period of his life than any other and it is not hard to find the reason. His emergence as a cricketer, for instance, was helped by the fact that he had matured in build and strength, though he did not know it was to be the last summer when he was to be free from the physical effects of sundry other set-backs. He found himself invigorated in 1914 by playing with a far more gifted set of professionals than there had been at Hove and he also responded to the stimulus provided by the London environment.

Several years of unrest in the Surrey committee-room and dressing-rooms had been put aside for good and Surrey were a happy as well as successful team.

Fender's own improvement, of course, was overdue for a player with his ability. He was again chosen twice for the Gentlemen and played in twenty-three of Surrey's twenty-six championship matches. All told, he scored 820 runs, took 83 wickets and held 29 catches, a solid and useful season's work. *Wisden* chose him as one of their Five Cricketers of the Year and what was to become a familiar theme was stressed in the pen portrait: 'He is not a cricketer whose value can in any way be gauged from the figures or averages. As a match winning factor he is a far greater force on a side than his records would suggest. Tom Hayward said of him last season that he was the making of the Surrey eleven, and a higher compliment could scarcely have been paid him.'

It was easy to see what Hayward meant. There were not many weak spots in Surrey's resources, but the attributes now sprouted by Fender were precisely those needed to fill the gaps that did exist. Only unselfish hitting was normally required from Fender by the time he batted in a team whose order could start: Hobbs (ten championship hundreds this season), Hayward, Hayes, Ducat and C. T. A. Wilkinson, with one or more from Sandham, Harrison and M. C. Bird also playing, and D. J. Knight available after the Oxford term. It was Fender's bowling and catching ability that Surrey utilized so much more effectively than Sussex had done. His bowling varied between what we now term seam and leg-breaks delivered at a brisker pace than usual. He got through almost 600 overs, twice as much work as he had ever been given before. 'Razor' Smith played infrequently and Fender provided the main support for the faster efforts of Hitch and Rushby. In the field Fender moved permanently into the slips for the first time and his brilliance quickly solved what had been a problem position for Surrey. Fender joined Strudwick, Hobbs at cover point and Hitch anywhere, as the individuals singled out for special mention when Surrey's all-round efficiency in the field was discussed.

Fender's sudden advance as a cricketer was undoubtedly spurred as well by the need to prove to his father that full-time county cricket could be combined successfully with the sales job he now held with Crescens Robinson & Co. Ltd at Newington Causeway. His father was managing director of this firm of wholesale stationers and paper-bag manufacturers. Fender had been allowed to play cricket hitherto through his father's generosity, but there was every intention that his son should have to earn his own living. After his spell at the Horwich paper mills, he had periods during the winters in both Belgium and Paris, partly to learn more about the manufacturing of paper but also to improve his French. He became sufficiently bilingual to find this a great aid in the wine business in later life, and also to be considered during the Second World War for parachuting into France, to co-ordinate work among the resistance movement.

Mr Fender senior believed county cricket consumed too much time to be linked with a worthwhile effort in business, but the son was convinced of the opportunities it offered for meeting people and making sales' contacts. A bargain was struck that Fender should play cricket for a limited period until the matter was proved one way or another. The outbreak of war effectively brought an end to the arrangement, but by then Fender had shown that it was perfectly feasible, in his case, to combine business with pleasure. It brought him enormous pleasure, eventually, to notice that his father was often among the spectators in The Oval pavilion from four o'clock onward. Nothing was said, but paternal pride had become responsible when Mr Fender senior deserted his office early for the first known occasions in his life.

Fender does not remember life ever being as hectic again but, at twenty-one energy and dedication came easily when it was necessary to prove a point to the previous generation. It did seem common-sense to move to London, however, and Surrey during the winter of 1913–14 were delighted that a promising amateur, who had already played for the Gentlemen, should wish to transfer to his native county. The Surrey secretary at this time was Mr 'Billy' Findlay, later to prove himself such an outstanding secretary for MCC, and the registration details were soon accomplished. When Surrey were at home Fender would often be at his desk before 8 a.m. dealing with correspondence and he would return in the evenings, after play, if this had not been finished. Away matches were combined with business trips and Fender, with an eye to the fixture list, would arrange meetings in advance. He found his work contacts enjoyed being privileged guests at county grounds and his whole approach seems to have been a forerunner of the way firms entertain clients when they sponsor matches today. In a short space of time Fender achieved a considerable

success. This is primarily a cricket book, but among his innova-
tions at work were inner and outer cartons for holding salt and
sugar, stronger and waterproof bags for coke, and a new method
for lining women's hat boxes. Fender the bright young salesman
was clearly every bit as resourceful a thinker as the man in later
years who diddled out opposing teams.

Amid his work and his cricket Fender did not neglect the lighter
side of life. Like every other normal young man he thoroughly
enjoyed discovering the varied delights that London society could
offer a bachelor with adequate means, and a man, too, with the
added distinction of being a well-known cricketer. There was
never much time for the Mayfair drawing-rooms, but he was put
up for several distinguished clubs in the area of St James's, and
good food, wine and bridge all became abiding passions. There was
no doubt, either, that Fender was also a familiar figure at more
than one stage door. In short, he lived life to the full like all his
contemporaries, unaware that the entire carefree pattern was
destined soon to be shattered. At this time Fender began a lifelong
friendship with Jack Hulbert, recently down from Cambridge
and embarking on his lengthy career as an actor and musical
comedy star. Fender always had an affinity with the theatrical
world and put money into several musical shows. One winter he
toured America for three months with Hulbert in a production he
had backed.

During this period and later Fender tried his hand at writing
lyrics himself to popular music-hall ditties and more than one of
his efforts were incorporated by Hulbert and others into sketches
over the years. Like many of Fender's diaries, letters and other
mementoes, carefully hoarded throughout his life, examples of
these lyrics were destroyed in the Second World War blitz. He
remembered one lyric he wrote for Hulbert, and P. G. Wodehouse
addicts will surely recognize the flavour of that period:

I'm Reckless Reggie of the Regent Palace,
I'm in love with every girl;
I flirt with Maudie and I flirt with Alice,
I'm a real live Regent Pal;
I'm a nut, I'm a roarer
And I flirt with Flora;
And I dodge her dud of a Dad;
I'm a perfect nob if I spend five bob;
Ha-ha ha-haw, I'm some bad lad!

Another verse began:

> I'm absolutely the absolute it,
> A perfectly priceless old bean.

The verse went on to invoke 'Flappers of sweet sixteen', but the remainder escaped Fender's memory, and we are overdue in reverting to our subject's career in cricket.

The Surrey captain in 1914 was Cyril Theodore Anstruther Wilkinson, whose legal talents were such that he eventually became the Registrar of the Probate and Divorce Registry for twenty-three years. He was a neat, precise batsman, capable of varying his game to the situation's needs, and a firm, tactful leader. Surrey functioned well under his captaincy though Fender did not rate him as highly tactically as he did the forty-three-year-old Hayward, the senior professional, who took over when Wilkinson was unavailable. Both men were unstinting in the encouragement they gave Fender and six years later it was to be Wilkinson who bowed to Fender's flair for captaincy and made way for him. Wilkinson was an England hockey player and a member of the team that won Olympic gold medals at the 1920 Games in Antwerp in circumstances that bear repeating here. Wilkinson and his team-mates clinched the title with a walk-over in the final against France, who were officially described as 'indisposed'. *The Times* referred to 'an epidemic in the French camp', but in hockey circles to this day the legend goes that the French fell victim to the local red wine, freely plied them the night before by their prospective opponents.

Fender's first day as a Surrey player on Saturday, 2 May 1914, against Northamptonshire was mostly spent in The Oval outfield in a biting wind and rain squalls. Surrey had the worst of a drawn game, with little happening to suggest the excellent season that lay ahead. Fender's 26 in the first innings helped save the follow-on. In the closing stages he took a couple of wickets and hit hard for 44 not out in the last forty minutes as the match petered out. Major Philip Trevor, as he then was, had seen enough to comment in the *Daily Telegraph*: 'Fender has already proved his value to the county of his birth.' Fender's hat-trick wickets in the next game against Somerset were all bowled and a news agency report confirmed he was still feeling his way in his method. 'For the most part he bowled at a much slower pace than was his custom for Sussex and it is said he has become a disciple of the "googlie".

One Penny.

Surrey County Cricket Club.

KENNINGTON OVAL.

SURREY v. NORTHAMPTONSHIRE.

SATURDAY, MAY 2, 1914. (Three-Day Match.)

NORTHAMPTONSHIRE.

		First Innings.		Second Innings.	
1	Mr. W. H. Denton	b Hitch	4	c & b Fender	61
2	East	b Hitch	26	c Ducat, b Fender	30
3	Haywood	b Smith	3	c Wilkinson, b Hitch	60
4	Mr. S. G. Smith	c Hayward, b Smith	66	not out	72
5	Thompson	b Smith	56	c Strudwick, b Hitch	15
6	Mr. S. F. Smith	b Hitch	6	b Smith	5
7	Woolley	not out	92	not out	40
8	Walden	b Hitch	3		
9	Wells	b Hitch	25		
10	Buswell	retired hurt	0		
11	Murdin	c Strudwick, b Hitch	0	B , l-b 4, w , n-b , ...	4
		B 9, l-b 3, w 1, n-b 3, ...	16		
		Total	297	declared. Total (5 wkts.)	287

FALL OF THE WICKETS.

1-8	2-11	3-108	4-110	5-134	6-205	7-208	8-293	9-297
1-51	2-134	3-181	4-200	5-209	6-	7-	8-	9-

BOWLING ANALYSIS.

	First Innings.					Second Innings.				
	O.	M.	R.	W.	Wd. N-b	O.	M.	R.	W.	Wd. N-b
Hitch	20.3	4	89	6	1 ...·3	23	1	106	2	...
Smith	30	4	96	3	...	17	3	54	1	...
Rushby	13	4	38	0	...	12	4	27	0	...
Fender	10	2	43	0	...	18	6	57	2	...
Hayes	5	2	15	0	...	8	3	19	0	...
Goatly					...	4	1	20	0	...

SURREY.

		First Innings.		Second Innings.	
1	Hayward	c Denton, b S. G. Smith	43	c Thompson, b S.G.Smith	56
2	Hobbs	c Buswell, b Wells	19	b Thompson	10
3	Hayes	c S.G.Smith, b Thompson	13	c Denton, b Thompson	14
4	Goatly	c Thompson, b S.G. Smith	5	b Thompson	35
5	Ducat	st Buswell, b S. G. Smith	2	not out	36
6	Mr. C. T. A. Wilkinson	c East, b Murdin	36	c Denton, b Thompson	62
7	Mr. P. G. H. Fender	c Buswell, b Wells	26	not out	44
8	Hitch	c Wells, b Murdin	6		
9	Strudwick	c Thompson, b Wells	0		
10	Smith (W. C.)	not out	0		
11	Rushby	b Wells	0		
		B 4, l-b 2, w , n-b 1, ...	7	B 5, l-b 1, w , n-b , ...	6
		Total	157	Total (5 wkts.) ...	263

FALL OF THE WICKETS.

1-30	2-53	3-70	4-89	5-90	6-137	7-146	8-157	9-157
1-24	2-50	3-99	4-123	5-196	6-	7-	8-	9-

BOWLING ANALYSIS.

	First Innings.					Second Innings.				
	O.	M.	R.	W.	Wd. N-b	O.	M.	R.	W.	Wd. N-b
Wells	15.4	4	30	4	... 1	6	1	22	0	...
S. G. Smith	29	12	58	3	...	29	9	69	1	...
Murdin	5	1	16	2	...	6	0	29	0	...
East	1	1	0	0	...	11	7	13	0	...
Thompson	17	3	46	1	...	37	3	124	4	...

Play commences 12 o'clock 1st day—11.30 a.m. 2nd & 3rd days.

Luncheon 2 p.m. 1st day—1.30 p.m. 2nd & 3rd days.   Stumps drawn 6.30 p.m.

Umpires—Roberts & Trott.

RESULT—NORTHAMPTONSHIRE Won by 140 runs on 1st innings.

2.   This match with Northamptonshire was Fender's debut for Surrey in 1914 at the Oval

Be that as it may, it was only when he returned to his old medium pace style that he met with success.' The batsmen dismissed were the famous rugby international, John 'The Prophet' Daniell, who had made 84, together with Nos 10 and 11, J. F. Bridges and H. Chidgey.

Fender's 140 helped Surrey to total 541 against Warwickshire, one of five occasions that season when they topped 500 runs. Warwickshire, according to *Wisden*, were a formidable bowling side and Fender's runs mostly came off F. R. Foster, Jeeves, Field and Santall. Percy Jeeves, a fast-medium bowler with an economical action, and a useful batsman, has become immortalized by P. G. Wodehouse for providing his surname for Bertie Wooster's manservant. Jeeves was killed in 1916 and was remembered by Fender and others as having been a Test-match player in the making. Warwickshire must already have been demoralized when Fender arrived at No. 7 because Hobbs had led off with 183 out of 244 in under three hours, despite Quaife's bowling down the leg side, with eight men placed there, in an effort to contain him. The situation was tailor-made for Fender's uninhibited driving and pulling. 'He ran every kind of risk with obvious cheerfulness,' one report said. Fender, who was missed at cover when 30, moved from 94 to 100 with an all-run six after eighty-five minutes and he also hit two fives and twenty-two fours. The anonymous 'Rover' in the *Daily News and Leader* noted: 'Fender though tall is rather slender and one wonders where he gets his power from. Much of it comes from correct timing and much more from a pair of strong wrists.'

On Sunday, 28 June, Archduke Franz Ferdinand and his wife were assassinated at Sarajevo; the day before, in a heatwave, a crowd of 20,000 at The Oval had watched Surrey score 502 for 6 in five and a half hours against Middlesex, who at this stage were leading the championship table with Surrey in second place. Fender slogged 44 not out in the closing minutes and prompted the *Daily Telegraph* to describe him as 'the hardest hitter on the side and possibly nearly the hardest of the day'. Precise details of this innings were not given in the newspapers but it evoked such enthusiasm among the spectators that they invaded the field, and Nigel Haig was unable to complete the day's final over. In the next game, against Northamptonshire, Fender earned the first spectacles of his career and a king pair at that, but compensation came with his selection for the following week's Gentlemen v.

Players matches. Originally he was not chosen for the Lord's match but was brought in when P. A. Perrin declined his invitation. For the second year running Fender achieved little numerically when given his chance at representative level, but once again his approach and style were commented upon favourably by the critics.

The two sides which played at Lord's in the last Gentlemen v. Players game before the First World War have been rated as strong as any two teams fielded in the series and are worth giving in batting order:

Gentlemen: C. B. Fry (captain), A. H. Hornby, A. P. Day, P. F. Warner, S. G. Smith, J. W. H. T. Douglas, F. R. Foster, G. L. Jessop, P. G. H. Fender, H. G. Garnett, A. Jacques.
Players: J. B. Hobbs (captain), F. A. Tarrant, J. W. Hearne, C. P. Mead, G. Gunn, F. E. Woolley, E. Humphreys, W. Hitch, A. S. Kennedy, S. F. Barnes, H. Strudwick.

In retrospect, the professionals look unbeatable, but the Gentlemen won a tensely fought match by 134 runs. A great deal of fine cricket on a wet wicket was played, with the individual honours going to Douglas, who took 9 for 105 in the Players' first innings. The scores were: Gentlemen: 265 (S. G. Smith 52, G. L. Jessop 45; Barnes 4—71, Hitch 4—76) and 275 (A. H. Hornby 69, S. G. Smith 50; Barnes 4—72, Woolley 3—27). Players: 256 (C. P. Mead 63; Douglas 9—105) and 150 (A. S. Kennedy 40; Foster 4—56, Douglas 4—67). Fender is our main theme and his scores of 30 and 22 in difficult circumstances, late in the order, received plenty of praise for their aggression. There is no mention of it in the newspapers, but Fender is adamant that he pulled Barnes for six into the Tavern area during one of these innings. 'Either that or it went over first bounce—I can feel it on the bat now. I remember Barnes glowering at me down the wicket —I don't think it happened to him very often.' Like all his contemporaries, Fender has always considered Barnes the best bowler he ever faced. 'His stock ball was a fast leg-break but in effect he could bowl anything.' Fender said that long after the First War they were still talking in Australia about the way Barnes had moved and turned the ball on his tours there. Barnes and Arthur Mailey were the only bowlers that he made a specific point of watching from behind the arm whenever he could in order to try and learn something.

At Bradford in 1918 during a wartime charity game involving first-class players, Fender was one of Barnes's victims in a spell which read 12—3—24—4. 'I don't think I ever learned as much about what was possible in bowling as I did that day. He never bowled two consecutive balls the same and deserved much better figures; none of us knew what on earth to do against him.' What Fender termed a 'stiff-armed leg-break' was one type of ball Fender acquired from his study of Barnes's technique. 'It sounds funny but I think of Barnes whenever there is a horse jumping on television. Very often the commentators bring in a phrase about there not being enough "bounce" in a horse's approach to a wall. Barnes had this "bounce" in his run-up. He bowled this leg-break with his arm stiff, getting turn as much from the way he bounced up and banged the ball in as he did from his wrist. I tried to copy this and like Barnes there were times when I did not get the wickets I should have done because the ball turned so much. I think I got Frank Woolley once or twice with this sort of ball.'

As the international situation rapidly deteriorated, Surrey displaced Middlesex from the top of the championship table when they completed an 8-wicket win against Hampshire at Portsmouth on Saturday, 25 July, and their position as leaders was never seriously challenged again. Middlesex suffered their first defeat of the summer the previous day when they lost by an innings to Kent at Maidstone, collapsing twice against Blythe and Woolley. Fender had an excellent game at Portsmouth, hitting a relevant 60 in seventy minutes and returning match figures of 8 for 88.

War broke out as Surrey met Nottinghamshire at The Oval. On 3 August, the Bank Holiday Monday, a crowd of 15,000 watched Hobbs make 226, which at the time was his highest score. Fender hit a brisk 40 before Surrey's innings ended the next day for 542. Nottinghamshire were 230 for 5 at the close after slow batting which inspired so much barracking that the police removed the worst offenders from the ground. During that fateful afternoon a telegram summoning Arthur Carr to join his regiment was taken out to him as he batted. 'I'll have one more over,' he said before he threw away his wicket. At midnight Britain's ultimatum to Germany about Belgian neutrality expired. Only forty-five minutes' play was possible because of rain on the Wednesday, but clearly nobody was in the mood for cricket and the hold-up gave everyone the chance to talk about what they should do.

J. B. HOBBS' BENEFIT.

Lord's Cricket Ground.

SURREY v. KENT.

MONDAY & TUESDAY, AUGUST 10, 11, 1914. (Three-day Match.)

	KENT.	First Innings.		Second Innings.	
1	Humphreys..................	b Hitch	5	b Hitch	4
2	Hardinge	c Hayward, b Smith ...	2	c Ducat, b Rushby	1
3	Seymour	b Hitch	0	b Hitch	45
4	Woolley	b Hitch	51	c Strudwick, b Hitch ...	14
5	Mr. A. P. Day	b Hitch	0	lbw, b Fender	18
6	Mr. S. H. Day	c Hayward, b Smith ...	54	c Strudwick, b Rushby	1
7	Mr. L. H. W. Troughton	c Fender, b Rushby ...	5	c Hayes, b Fender	15
8	Huish	b Fender	10	c and b Fender	7
9	Blythe	c Hayward, b Smith ...	1	b Hitch	7
10	Fielder.....................	c and b Fender	0	not out	5
11	Freeman	not out	1	b Hitch	0
		B 3, l-b 4, w , n-b 4, ...	11	B 15, l-b 6, w , n-b 2, ...	23
		Total...............	140	Total...............	140

FALL OF THE WICKETS.

1-5 2-7 3-11 4-11 5-104 6-119 7-137 8-138 9-138
1-1 2-19 3-63 4-78 5-79 6-100 7-117 8-129 9-139

BOWLING ANALYSIS.	First Innings.					Second Innings.				
	O.	M.	R.	W.	Wd. N-b.	O.	M.	R.	W.	Wd. N-b.
Smith	11	4	20	3	... ...	10	2	26	...	... ...
Hitch	21	7	39	4	... 2	19	5	39	5	... 1
Rushby	15	3	37	1	... ...	17	8	27	2	... ...
Fender	6·4	...	27	2	... 2	9	5	16	3	... 1
Abel	1	...	6	...	... ...	1	...	9	...	... ...

	SURREY.	First Innings.		Second Innings.	
1	Hayward (Capt.)	lbw, b Blythe	91	b Freeman	7
2	Hobbs	lbw, b Blythe	16	not out	26
3	Hayes	c Humphreys, b Blythe	0	lbw, b A. P. Day.........	12
4	Mr. D. J. Knight	c Troughton, b Blythe	2	not out	2
5	Ducat	c Huish, b Blythe	36		
6	Mr. P. G. H. Fender.....	c Troughton, b Blythe	48		
7	Abel (W. J.)	st Huish, b Woolley ...	0		
8	Hitch	c Woolley, b Blythe ...	0		
9	Strudwick	c A. P. Day, b Blythe...	2		
10	Smith (W. C.)	b Blythe	12		
11	Rushby	not out	2		
		B 18, l-b 6, w 1, n-b , ...	25	B , l-b , w , n-b , ...	
		Total	234	Total......	47

FALL OF THE WICKETS.

1-37 2-37 3-47 4-147 5-209 6-211 7-212 8-218 9-221
1-9 2-40 3- 4- 5- 6- 7- 8- 9-

BOWLING ANALYSIS.	First Innings.					Second Innings.				
	O.	M.	R.	W.	Wd. N-b.	O.	M.	R.	W.	Wd. N-b.
Fielder	3	2	3	...	1	4	1	21	...	... ...
Blythe	25.5	3	97	9	...					
Woolley	18	1	66	1	...					
Freeman	11	1	42	...	...	6.3	1	20	1	...
A. P. Day	2	1	1	...	...	3	1	6	1	...

Play commences 12 o'clock 1st day—11.45 a.m. 2nd & 3rd days.
Luncheon interval 1.30 p.m. Stumps drawn 6.0 p.m.

Umpires—Parris & Butt. RESULT—Surrey won by 8 wickets.

3. *Hayward's 91 when Surrey played Kent at Lord's in 1914 was the best wet-wicket batting Fender ever saw*

Fender remembers dashing between The Oval and his father's office to discuss his own position, the streets being crowded with groups of anxious people. The War Office had already made known their intention to occupy The Oval, temporarily, and Surrey had accepted an invitation to play their next two home fixtures at Lord's. These games against Kent and Yorkshire, crucial to Surrey's championship hopes, were due to start the week beginning Monday, 10 August. Fender, like his colleagues, fell in with the prevailing mood, that life as far as possible should continue normally for the moment, and that there would be time to join up later. So the Surrey players travelled to Worcester by train that evening on Wednesday, 5 August, for their next match as arranged, 'obviously disturbed and worried sick like everyone else', as Fender put it. Cricket all round the country carried on, and Surrey, in fact took part in seven more matches, Fender playing in six of them, before the first-class programme came to a halt. Inevitably the matches took place in a tense and unreal atmosphere and they were sparsely reported in the newspapers.

Surrey won convincingly both the games they played at Lord's as the home side. Crowds of around 7,000 more than once during the week were an indication, perhaps, of how people tried to cling to normality. Kent were beaten by 8 wickets inside two days, a marvellous innings of 91 by Hayward on a difficult wicket being the decisive factor. Fender was Surrey's second highest scorer as Blythe took 9 for 97 in the first innings. Fender, who was dropped first ball at mid-off, hit 48 in twenty minutes, 'driving and pulling nine fours with tremendous vigour'. Fender remembered Hayward's batting as 'The best bad wicket innings I ever saw; better even than Jack and Sutcliffe at Melbourne in '28–'29. Hayward met everything in the middle of the bat. Mine was just biff-bang stuff.'

This game was Hobbs's benefit match but, understandably, was not as rewarding for him as it might have been and he had another benefit in 1919. Yorkshire arrived, having won their eight previous matches, but were beaten by an innings after Hobbs (202) and Hayward (116) began the game with a first-wicket stand of 290. The Oval was available to Surrey for their final match against the ten Gloucestershire players. It ended on Tuesday, 1 September, with Hayward, in what was to prove the final match of his career, catching the last Gloucestershire man off Fender to give Surrey another innings win.

Surrey County Cricket Club.

KENNINGTON OVAL.

SURREY v. GLOUCESTERSHIRE.

MONDAY, AUGUST 31, 1914. (Three-Day Match.)

	SURREY.	First Innings.		Second Innings.
1	Hayward	c Board, b Ellis	1	
2	Hobbs	c Smith, b Toogood	141	
3	Hayes	lbw., b Toogood	50	
4	Mr. D. J. Knight	c Sub., b Toogood	102	
5	Harrison	b Toogood	8	
6	Mr. C. T. A. Wilkinson	c Champain, b Parker	14	
7	Mr. P. G. H. Fender	b Parker	0	
8	Abel (W. J.)	c Ellis, b Toogood	52	
9	Hitch	b Parker	17	
10	Strudwick	lbw., b Toogood	0	
11	Rushby	not out	9	
		B 3, l-b 2, w , n-b 1,	6	B , l-b , w , n-b ,
		Total	400	Total

FALL OF THE WICKETS.

1-2	2-104	3-242	4-268	5-289	6-289	7-336	8-388	9-388
1-	2-	3-	4-	5-	6-	7-	8-	9-

BOWLING ANALYSIS.

	First Innings.					Second Innings.				
	O.	M.	R.	W.	Wd. N-b.	O.	M.	R.	W.	Wd. N-b
Ellis	21		89	1						
Cranfield	27	4	89							
Parker	24.1	5	101	3	1					
Toogood	43	10	115	6						

	GLOUCESTERSHIRE.	First Innings.		Second Innings.	
1	Mr. M. A. Green	lbw., b Rushby	0	c Hayes, b Hitch	13
2	Smith	b Hitch	4	lbw., Fender	1
3	Cranfield	c Abel, b Hitch	21	c Strudwick, b Fender	2
4	Langdon	b Hitch	6	b Fender	36
5	Board	lbw., b Fender	23	c Strudwick, b Hitch	1
6	Mr. F. H. B. Champain	not out	17	run out	1
7	Mr. C. O. H. Sewell	c Hobbs, b Hitch	10	b Fender	165
8	Parker	b Fender	2	c Hobbs, b Fender	9
9	Ellis	b Fender	0	not out	4
10	Toogood	b Hitch	12	c Hayes, b Fender	2
11	A. N. Other	absent	0	absent	0
		B , l-b 4, w , n-b 1,	5	B 18, l-b 8, w , n-b 4,	30
		Total	100	Total	264

FALL OF THE WICKETS.

1-5	2-5	3-27	4-55	5-63	6-74	7-83	8-83	9-100
1-1	2-9	3-20	4-40	5-198	6-239	7-257	8-257	9-264

BOWLING ANALYSIS.

	First Innings.					Second Innings.				
	O.	M.	R.	W.	Wd. N-b	O.	M.	R.	W.	Wd. N-b
Hitch	13.3	1	44	5	1	12	1	63	2	4
Rushby	6	0	19	1		7	0	36	0	
Fender	7	1	32	3		17.4	2	83	6	
Hayes						5	0	35	0	
Abel						3	0	12	0	
Wilkinson						1	0	5	0	

Play commences 12 o'clock 1st day—11.30 a.m. 2nd & 3rd days.
Luncheon 2 p.m. 1st day—1.30 p.m. 2nd & 3rd days.   Stumps drawn 6.30 p.m.
Umpires—Barlow & Butt.   **RESULT**—SURREY won by an innings & 36 runs.

4.   *Gloucestershire had only ten men available for this final match of the 1914 summer before first-class cricket was abandoned—Dipper, the missing man, having joined up. There seems to be a possible error in the second innings dismissal of Toogood. All other sources credit the catch to Hayward, not Hayes*

Fender had an analysis of 6 for 83 and match figures of 9 for 115, both the best of his career at that point. It was to be May 1920, before Fender was able to play for Surrey again. Like everybody else similarly affected, he has often wondered what he might have achieved but for this disruption to what would probably have been the best years of his career. The next day Fender enlisted in the Inns of Court Regiment and after basic training was commissioned as a lieutenant in the Royal Fusiliers. He was not the first independent spirit to find several aspects of Army routine irksome. 'I was thankful when somebody dropped a sandbag on my foot and I could not march about the barrack square for a time.' Less than a year later he had become a trainee pilot at Norwich with the Royal Flying Corps. His transfer had been helped along by a certain Captain P. F. Warner, then a staff officer at the War Office. Flying was very much in its pioneering stages in 1915 and though the RFC had an aura of glamour and excitement, the risks involved in every flight should not be forgotten.

To present-day eyes left blasé by supersonic flight, the Maurice Farman Shorthorn and Longhorn biplanes, in which Fender and his contemporaries learned to fly, resemble nothing other than the proverbial box-kites held together by string. They had open cockpits, of course, the simplest of controls and a top speed of around 60–70 m.p.h. Fender still has his pilot's log-book. It shows that in the manner of that time he began with numerous short flights of a few minutes, in dual-controlled machines with an instructor, at about 200 feet. He still had less than four hours total time in the air to his credit when he first flew solo and for a long time after this continued, in particular, to practise landing techniques. 'It was all rather primitive, but when things went smoothly it had an exhilaration like nothing else I have ever known in my life.' On one of Fender's first cross-country training flights by himself, he became the first of his batch of trainees to see a German plane, which had been dropping some small bombs or grenades in the Great Yarmouth area.

'I was on the way home and had turned right to have a look at the sea when I saw this Hun plane. I remember I was sitting on an empty sugar crate because my seat was too low. I had a rifle strapped to the fuselage outside because we had orders to be armed, but I had never used it. Looking back it was all rather a waste of time as you couldn't shoot properly and fly at the same time. We trainees had strict instructions to avoid contact with any other planes, especially German ones, and I turned back inland. Later my CO showed me a long letter he had from some local mayor reporting that a British flier had shown gross cowardice by not protecting the population from the dastardly actions of the Germans. He laughed and assured me I had done the right thing.'

Fender was later stationed at the Joyce Green and Hounslow airfields in suburban London on stand-by alternate nights with one other pilot, to ward off Zeppelin attacks. 'We had one or two cracks at them but at this time our planes were not really good enough and there were also all sorts of problems with the guns; the Zeppelins were usually flying higher and faster and you did not often get close to them.' Early in 1916 Fender was posted to India before some of these technical problems were improved in the British aircraft. Night flying at this time was even more hazardous than in the daytime, with no means of ensuring that the plane was flying level. 'Landing was never easy; we'd fire a Very pistol when we thought we were over our airfield and they'd light cans of petrol to mark a runway for us, and it could be tricky if there was any wind. In the daytime you always flew with one eye on the ground in case you had to come down and tinker with the engine.'

Fender and a close friend, who was being posted to France, decided to share the expense of a farewell party in London after his embarkation orders for India came through. They had £150 between them and for 10s 6d a head some 300 guests were provided with a band, supper and limitless champagne, which for London's West End seems almost unbelievable today. As the night progressed, the management pointed out to the hosts, with some delicacy, that about 450 people were now enjoying their hospitality and 'perhaps the young gentlemen would kindly meet the bill for the additional numbers please?' A more than embarrassed Fender was still 'discussing' the point as his friends launched an immediate whip-round. A huge pile of sovereigns and notes was collected in a top hat and finally poured in a torrent into the manager's hands. A great deal of champagne was also poured over Fender's head and the party continued with gusto until dawn. Fender earned the nickname 'Bill' from this incident and he has always remained 'Bill' to his closest friends. To his family he was 'George' and he invariably signed autographs as 'Percy Fender'. At one stage in his cricket life, the nickname 'Mossy' Fender began to be used, but Fender never liked it and was thankful it never caught on widely.

From the moment Fender landed in India he contracted a series of illnesses, and a little more than six months later was being shipped home as an invalid. He remained a sick man, in varying degrees, for the next two years. He certainly had a virulent form of dysentery; cholera at one stage was also suspected, together with other fevers of tropical origin whose names he does not recall. Medical knowledge in these areas was not as advanced then and back in London Fender had lengthy spells in numerous clinics and hospitals with nobody being too precise about what was wrong. At one time he was written off in the medical terms of that period as 'both VDH and DAH', standing respectively for valvular disease of the heart and disorderly action of the heart. These were generalized diagnoses for anyone under care in whom, perhaps, a heart murmur had been detected, of the sort which nowadays would be considered of no clinical importance. For Fender as a normally active sportsman it was a worrying time. He was able to play in two one-day Services' matches for charity at Lord's in 1917, but was in a weakened state.

A year later Fender was stronger and, though still on light duties and in the care of the Army medical authorities, he played a certain amount of cricket in the latter part of the summer. At The Oval on 5 August 1918, in what was the first game played on the ground since 1914, Fender showed more than a glimpse of his old explosiveness in the third of a one-day series between an England XI and a Dominions XI. The South African, Herbie Taylor, was the highest scorer with 63 as the Dominions made 194 for 9 declared, between showers. Air Mechanic J. B. Hobbs, Lance-Corporal G. Gunn and Private F. E. Woolley all failed as the England XI slumped to 75 for 6 with fifty minutes' play left. Lieutenant Fender then joined Lieutenant-Colonel J. W. H. T. Douglas and, as *Wisden* put it, 'played an innings worthy of Jessop at his best'. Fender hit 70 of the next 87 runs in three-quarters of an hour before he was out shortly before the game ended. Two days later Fender made 60 at Lord's for a team against the Public Schools, but less happily was batting at the other end when an innings by Lord Harris was ended by what *The Times* described as 'an unfortunate run out'. Lord Harris, aged sixty-seven, who had first played at Lord's fifty years earlier, turned out at the last moment when 'Plum' Warner withdrew. For the Public Schools, A. P. F. Chapman (Uppingham) was their best batsman.

Fender's lengthy problems with his health seemed at last to be behind him, but in the late autumn came the football accident in which he broke his leg so badly. Further tedious months in hospital ensued, with the leg having to be reset more than once, and he spent nearly fourteen months in all on crutches. Fender, who was a goalkeeper, enjoyed the good fellowship prevalent in amateur football at that time, and preferred it as a game to the rugby he had had to play at St Paul's. At different times Fender made spasmodic appearances for the Casuals, the Corinthians and in non-League games for Fulham, and he also played for the famous Leopold club while he was working in Belgium. The highlight of these football activities was when he kept goal for the Casuals in the AFA Cup Final at White City in April 1913, when they beat New Crusaders 3–2. His chief memories were of conceding an early goal from a pass back by one of his own defenders and of the lack of atmosphere in the big stadium, which easily absorbed the attendance of 10,000.

When first-class cricket resumed in 1919 Fender was still on crutches and so missed that curious summer of two-day county matches and half-past seven finishes. Instead he tried without success to gain a place at Caius, Jack Hulbert's old college at Cambridge. Those interviewing him lost interest when they found that his leg, which was still in plaster, would prevent him from playing any cricket, and that he wished to concentrate on French, German and accountancy, in order to help himself in business.

It proved frustrating to Fender to watch cricket matches in which he should have been involved, and that summer he found more solace in horse racing. He often visited the racecourses nearest to London and, as a well-known cricketer temporarily *hors de combat*, found he had enough fame and acquaintances to receive useful tips from owners and others. Fender claimed to have finished the flat season with a small profit. He also took a holiday in Monte Carlo, where he tested at the roulette tables a system he had spent many hours working out in hospital. On one such visit to Monaco he finished some £1,800 to the good and returned shortly afterwards on the proceeds with his parents as his guests. Fender always enjoyed any form of gambling but had the willpower never to lose more than he could afford.

Early in 1920 Fender's leg was declared as sound as it was likely to be. Golf, shooting, real tennis and walking helped to build up its strength, though he could never again run far without some discomfort. He was fit, however, to take his place in the Surrey side from the start of the 1920 season when, for the first time, his mind faced the exciting new challenge of captaincy.

4. Surrey find a captain

Fender's aptitude for captaincy was unsuspected before circumstances left him in charge of Surrey for most of the 1920 season. He had virtually no experience of the job and certainly none at first-class level, but from the beginning his success in the role was startling. Surrey won ten of the first twelve matches in which Fender led them and only once was the margin of victory anything less than emphatic. Rain brought draws in the other two games of this sequence, once when Surrey were certain to win and the other time when only one day's play was possible. Miles Howell was the first choice to lead the side in both 1919 and 1920, according to the Surrey committee minute books, but for various reasons he was unable to accept. Wilkinson was officially appointed in his place each time, but in neither season could he appear regularly. Fender received his chance in 1920 simply because he was the only other amateur likely to play with any frequency.

Originally, Wilkinson was expected to miss the first three months of the 1920 programme. He was able to turn out, however, in Surrey's third and fourth matches after they had begun under Fender with successive two-day wins at The Oval against Northamptonshire and Warwickshire. In the next game Wilkinson's own batting ensured that Hampshire were beaten at The Oval by 2 wickets, but after this there came an unexpected defeat by Somerset at Bath. A leg injury then kept Wilkinson out of the side and he returned to his other commitments. By the time Wilkinson took his regular place as expected, in early August, Surrey were among several teams in the hunt for the championship. He was unfortunate that his return coincided with some perplexing inconsistencies in Surrey's cricket, and three of the next five matches were lost. Wilkinson personally could not be blamed, but it is a fact that it has seldom proved beneficial for a county captaincy to be shared. Surrey were not the first team, nor were they the last, to find that corporate skills and team spirit suffered when there was a lack of continuity in approach and thinking.

It was a tribute to Wilkinson's vision and unselfishness that he

seemed to have been among the first to recognize Fender's knack
of extracting the best from the side. Wilkinson left himself out of
the team in order that Fender could return to the helm for the
crucial match against Yorkshire at The Oval on 21 August. This
game provided Fender with a major triumph, as will be shown
later. Wilkinson came back for the next game at Northampton
and it proved to be his final appearance for Surrey. He went off
to the Olympic hockey tournament in Antwerp and it was Fender
who captained Surrey at Lord's in that most famous of all county
matches. Victory brought Middlesex the championship in 'Plum'
Warner's last match; Lancashire beat Worcestershire the same
day to finish second; and Surrey finally were third in the table.
It was a momentous ending to the 1920 programme, which had
already created a special place in the minds of cricket followers.

There were several reasons for this. The war had receded that
much further from instant and painful memory and the reversion
to three-day championship fixtures, in place of the two-day games
tried as an experiment in 1919, was an important factor. It helped
to emphasize, subconsciously or otherwise, that a return had been
made to the sanity of the 1914 summer, memories of which must
have carried so many brave young men through their ordeals in
sterner spheres. For many people the late-Edwardian way of life,
with its strict demarcation lines between upstairs and downstairs,
had still not passed away, though not many more years were to
elapse before it did. In cricket, what might be termed the country
house week-end approach still pervaded many a championship
game, and the particular method of points scoring, though not
without its imperfections, at least encouraged teams to achieve a
clear-cut result. Team placings were calculated on a percentage
basis of points obtained from points possible.

The 1920 season was also the first when Saturday and Wednesday starts became the norm for nearly all county fixtures and
attendances were generally good, despite a summer by no means
warm or dry, with July especially wretched. Playing standards,
of course, and especially the bowling, had not had time to return to
pre-war days and Sydney Pardon, in his Editor's Notes in *Wisden*,
was concerned at the disparity between the strongest and the
weakest counties. This was the year when Derbyshire actually
lost seventeen of their seventeen matches, their other fixture
being abandoned without a ball bowled. Glamorgan's elevation to
first-class status would make the problem worse in 1921, Pardon

wrote. He confessed to having no remedy to suggest, 'as it is quite clear that the Championship must be kept open to new aspirants'. An interesting quotation this, remembering that, apart from one unsuccessful approach in 1949 by Devon, there have been no applications since.

Surrey's resources had not changed greatly since Fender had last played for them six years earlier. He began his new life as captain by winning the toss against Northamptonshire on Saturday, 1 May 1920. Scoring runs remained the team's prime strength, with Hobbs still the outstanding batsman in England and Sandham filling the place previously held by Hayward. The bowling, frankly, was weak and Surrey's good record was once again achieved with Rushby, Hitch and Fender carrying the main burden. Their figures in championship matches confirm the extent to which Surrey relied on them:

	O	M	R	W	Av.
Rushby	775.1	237	1,635	95	17.21
Fender	704.4	126	2,241	109	20.51
Hitch	749.5	146	2,187	97	22.54

After these three it was G. M. 'Gilly' Reay, an amateur all-rounder who was not available regularly, who did the most work with 318 overs and 42 wickets at 18.71 each.

Fender took 124 wickets altogether in his thirty matches that summer, scored 841 runs and held 43 catches. His batting tended to be inconsistent, with four fifties in the first half of the season and virtually nothing later, apart from his thirty-five-minute hundred against Northamptonshire. It was rare, however, for Fender not to contribute something to each game and any qualms about his physical fitness were dispelled satisfactorily to himself and others. It was Fender's emergence as a captain, however, that provided the underlying story to this season though, in passing, his first significant showing in a Gentlemen v. Players match at Lord's should be noted. The Gentlemen were beaten by 7 wickets and never recovered from a disastrous start in which 6 wickets fell cheaply. Fender then made 50 in forty minutes, including three sixes, which was to remain the top score for his side in the game. In its context his batting was acknowledged as a piece of fearless cricket and it was timely, too, with MCC about to pick their team for Australia.

As a captain Fender soon instilled a remarkable purposefulness

and unity in the Surrey ranks, though his approach to the job at
this stage seldom 'threatened committee-men with heart failure',
as R. C. Robertson-Glasgow was later to describe it. If not as
controversial and daring as he afterwards became, Fender showed
imagination, tactical awareness and verve from the first moment
he held the reins. These traits were by no means common to
county captains at that time. The manner in which Surrey drove
forward with their own brand of forceful cricket under Fender's
inspiration and restless spirit was soon noticed by press and public. Surrey had their limitations, but there was rarely any need to
cavil at their approach, and the pattern did not alter greatly
throughout Fender's extended reign. Yorkshire and Lancashire,
as the 1920s ran their course, provided the supreme examples of
the triumphs which could accrue to great players and a grim
fixity of intent. Surrey were always liable to win any particular
match and they frequently provided more entertainment. But
The Oval wicket was too good, and the bowling never good
enough, to allow the consistency and efficiency of the northern
teams to be equalled.

What there was at The Oval, however, was a more obvious
enjoyment, with fun galore to be shared. Surrey always had fine
batsmen, the fielding was usually brilliant and everything possible
was always tried to atone for the other shortcomings, with
Fender—a flamboyant puppet-master—clearly to be seen pulling
the strings. Nobody ever went to Bramall Lane or Old Trafford
specifically to study captaincy, but watching Fender experiment
with varying stratagems was part of the pleasure for The Oval
crowd: not least when his ruses did not work and something else
had to be tried. Either way, Fender was a conversational topic,
both at the time and later, and few other captains have been able
to claim that. Fender admitted that long before he had the chance
to lead Surrey he felt that too much captaincy in first-class cricket
was stereotyped; he reeled off the names of a dozen county captains at that time who, in his words, 'changed the bowling by
their watch'.

Sandham, who was still in the throes of establishing himself,
watched Fender's captaincy skills evolve. His first memories of
Fender, compared with others that he played under, were of
Fender discussing with his own players before a match the opposing team's strengths and weaknesses, and that he also changed his
bowling more frequently than anybody else. 'He would switch

people round from end to end more and, if we came up against a big stand, he would suddenly bowl people at them who did not normally bowl. He would fiddle with the field placings a lot. He was always strict about fielding and you had to watch him all the time as he would move you from ball to ball, if possible without the batsmen seeing. Our own batting order would be changed; these were all things that were different from other captains. When any of this came off, the crowd loved it, even if they did not always know all that was happening. On the field we'd smile at each other watching Mr Fender; it was never dull.'

In these early days of leadership Fender did not cajole, plan and impose his will on each and every player, notably the bowlers, to the extent that he did later. He sought advice and guidance from his senior players, especially Strudwick and Hobbs, and his active and flexible mind assimilated everything he was told and put it to best effect. 'I tried to enlist everyone if they had something to say. You must remember that with our bowling problems we did not always have things going smoothly for us. As far as I was concerned it was necessary to create the best possible team spirit; a new sort of atmosphere, so that at least everything we did have was used properly. This was why I wondered about merging the amateur and professional dressing-rooms and this was the reason I insisted we all travelled together on the trains to away matches.' Fender's whole approach was obviously a far cry from one of his predecessors as Surrey captain, the famous K. J. Key, who was once quoted as saying that a captain could do nothing for his side other than to win the toss.

Fifty years after it was written, Fender's chapter on captaincy in the Lonsdale Library's *The Game of Cricket* (Seeley, Service & Co., 1930) remains as masterly an exposition of the subject as anything ever penned. It is recommended to anyone who doubts the contribution a captain can make. Fender's own aims come across in a passage on tactics when he describes the two distinct types of captain he encountered during his career. 'The one is mechanical, and the other has imagination and initiative. The first has a knowledge of the tactics and strategy of the game which is limited to the conventional theories of the Text Books. The other has the same knowledge as a basis, but, while using it as a foundation, employs his brain and his imagination, when the opportunity offers, *for the varying of the strict letter of the Text Book Law.*' (Author's italics.)

Fender confirmed that he owed more to Strudwick than to anybody else when he first led Surrey, something that was hinted at by more than one writer at the time. 'Strudwick was always a great help; if things were not going right, he usually had two, sometimes three, suggestions to make. Once I learned that the first idea he put forward was usually the best, I found it often worked.' Strudwick was remembered by Fender as one of the most knowledgeable cricketers he ever met and a man who enjoyed being involved all the time. Fender never understood the prejudice that still exists in the game against wicket-keepers as captains. 'I can think of several in my time who knew as much about cricket as anybody. They see more of the game than most people and I am not sure that it is right to assume they have enough to do without being captain.' Fender continued to draw on Strudwick's advice when the wicket-keeper had become the Surrey scorer, and Alf Gover has a good story about this. Strudwick would bring the bowling figures into the dressing-room during an interval and, if things had not gone well, Fender would ask him what he should do next. On one occasion Strudwick's answer was: 'The first thing, Mr Fender, is to take yourself off—look at these figures.' Fender roared with laughter and did not bowl when play resumed. 'Nobody could mind that sort of thing from Struddy; he was such a good man,' Gover added.

Strudwick, according to Fender, had a far keener tactical mind than Hobbs, the senior professional, who positively disliked responsibilities other than his own. 'It may have been because he was so unassuming a man. He would give his view if it was sought, but that was as far as it went. It got to the point that when I had to leave the field for a meeting or something, I would say to Jack, "All right if Struddy takes over?" and Jack would say, "Yes please" and everyone was happy.' (This compromise was not applied at Aylestone Road on 10 June 1920, when Fender had to return to London overnight on urgent business and left Hobbs in charge. When Fender returned late the next afternoon he found the ground deserted, Surrey having completed an easy win in about a day and a half. Leicestershire batted three men short through injuries in their second innings. With Rushby straining his side, there were five absentees in all by the time the match ended.)

As Fender's confidence grew with experience, he leaned more and more towards the unorthodox, but he never resented it if one or another of the senior players advised a modicum of restraint, not least in the matter of declarations. 'Once something had been agreed, though, he expected everybody to follow the path that had been decided without fail,' Sandham said. Just occasionally Fender's style of captaincy could strike an onlooker as being 'fidgety' and undoubtedly he was the first to show impatience if he felt that any given situation was, as it were, marking time. Amid the generous praise Sandham had for Fender's captaincy, he believed that Fender probably cost Surrey victory against Middlesex and Warner at Lord's in that gripping last match of the 1920 season. Fender, to his credit, also admitted that he had always blamed himself for the 55-run defeat and the story can best be told now out of sequence.

Sandham and Shepherd were sharing a promising third-wicket stand, which Fender felt was falling fractionally behind the clock, after Surrey had been left 244 to win in three hours. Fender, from the balcony, gesticulated, as he thought, for Shepherd to step up the run rate. Sandham for the second time in the match was playing a crucial innings and Fender felt he could be left to gauge his own progress best. Fender's signal, however, was misinterpreted and both batsmen tried to score more quickly. Shepherd fell to a wonderful catch by Hendren near the sight-screen and this was followed by the rapid dismissals of Fender himself and Peach, both hard hitters. Sandham, by now thoroughly put out of his stride mentally, and still mindful of Fender's signal, then gave Hearne a simple return catch from a full toss, and Surrey never recovered. 'Looking back, I don't think Mr Fender should have interfered just then, even if we did misunderstand his signal. We'd have been all right,' was Sandham's view.

Fender agreed with him. 'I think I signalled to Shepherd, as I thought, about fifteen minutes too soon. The last few runs in these sort of situations can always come quickly. Looking back I think it was an occasion to have taken chances with only the last few runs. My idea at the time was to get a little ahead of the clock. It was not really necessary to do so and I ought to have left them alone.' In this game Fender was dismissed in each innings by Jack Durston, a fast bowler whose ability, he believed, was never properly recognized. A full-length book and numerous articles were written about this particular Middlesex v. Surrey game, but they never mentioned that Durston was allowed to leave Lord's early on the Monday in order to keep goal for Brentford in an evening match against Milwall. A 12,000 crowd saw Brentford

win this Third Division game 1–0. Brentford in the first place had
given Durston permission to play for Middlesex, missing the
season's opening fixture on the Saturday. It is difficult to imagine
a county these days allowing their main fast bowler to risk injury
at football, not least in the middle of a match that could clinch the
championship for them.

Fender's special type of thrustful leadership was evident from
the first game in 1920 when Surrey were told on the second day to
hit quick runs against Northamptonshire in unsettled weather
conditions. They declared their second innings at 276 for 3 after
150 minutes; Northamptonshire collapsed, and by six o'clock
Surrey had won by 299 runs. In what seems to have been the first
comment in print about Fender's captaincy, Colonel Philip
Trevor in the *Daily Telegraph* remarked: 'Fender's declaration
was wise as well as sportsmanlike . . . to risk today's weather was
to risk a fine chance of winning.' Unlike some bowler captains
Fender never had any qualms about bowling himself. In his third
game as captain he took 8 for 66 in perfect conditions in Nottinghamshire's second innings at Trent Bridge, bowling 21 overs despite an injured hand. It was the first time Fender took 8 wickets
in an innings and Surrey won by 10 wickets.

'A gentle full toss' brought one of his wickets and the *Nottingham Guardian* thought 'his record flattered his ability'. The
Nottingham Journal was more explicit about the varied assortment
of balls that Fender delivered. 'A very easy going sort of bowler
whose bite is worse than his bark,' their correspondent wrote.
'A sensible man, he'll toss up anything likely to provoke an in-
discretion instead of "bowling a man in". And so, despite a dislocated finger, his last six overs brought five scalps for a discount
of 29. A fine example of the value of experiment.' (And a fine
account of Fender's bowling method for most of his career, too,
Fender himself conceded.)

One of the first examples of Fender's expediency with Surrey's
limited attack came when he asked Hobbs to share the new ball
with Hitch in Rushby's absences from the games with Warwickshire and Essex. At Edgbaston Hobbs claimed 5 of the 6 wickets
that fell before the close on a wet pitch, after play had not begun
until after five o'clock; at Leyton, Hobbs took 4 of the first 6
wickets to fall at the start of the match. In 1920 Hobbs actually
headed the bowling averages with 17 wickets from 83 overs, but
it was a false position, of course, compared with Rhodes, the

second man, who took 161 wickets from more than 1,000 overs. Hobbs, like Hammond, it has often been said, would have been a great bowler if he had never made a run in his life. Hobbs had a knack for swinging a ball awkwardly at medium pace, but was usually reluctant to bowl and his captains naturally fell in with his wishes.

Three Surrey wins that season, in particular, drew people's attention to Fender, and a close look at them illustrates the bearing he could bring on a result. Two of these matches were against Yorkshire, home and away, and the third against Lancashire at The Oval. In each case, too, Fender's own playing ability was a factor as well as his positive leadership. On Saturday, 19 June, Surrey scored 305 at Sheffield and Fender blatantly ordered his tailenders to throw away their wickets, setting an example with a wild stroke against Rhodes. No first-day declarations were allowed at this time and Fender whenever possible liked to try and snatch a quick wicket at the end of the day. Hitch, in fact, took 3 in the closing fifty minutes and the 20,000 crowd went home with mixed feelings. On the second day Yorkshire were dismissed for 199 (Fender 4—43 and a brilliant slip catch to end an obdurate innings by Rhodes) and Surrey began the last day 263 runs ahead with 6 wickets left. Fender, first thing, hit 56 out of 71 in twenty-five minutes, including 21 in an over off Rhodes, before he declared. Yorkshire, needing 373, made only 168, Fender having a hand in the dismissal of the three highest scorers. The *Sheffield Daily Telegraph* summed up the game's pattern: 'Fender led the way in gallant style and as is often the way, his daring met with success.'

The cricket correspondents of the national newspapers tended to travel outside London infrequently for county games in 1920, but they had the chance to pay unanimous attention to Fender as a captain on 24 July after he had conjured a victory against Lancashire. A draw looked certain after rain disrupted the first day and by the Thursday evening Lancashire, second in the table to Surrey, had made 208 (Fender 7—64) and Surrey were 138 for 4. Peach with 77 led some fast scoring on the final morning and Surrey's lead was 70 when Fender declared at one o'clock with 9 wickets down. Spooner was caught off Fender before lunch and tigerish bowling and fielding during the afternoon led to Lancashire being dismissed for 160. A googly from Fender had Makepeace (62) leg before when he threatened to bat out the day. Surrey needed 91 to win in eighty minutes and Hobbs hit freely to complete a 9-wicket win without the extra half-hour being necessary. Fender's declaration before Surrey had gleaned as many runs as possible seems to have been contrary to normal practice at that time. Though Surrey had only 1 wicket to fall, it attracted a great deal of comment, and was seen as the game's turning point.

Wisden called it 'a happy inspiration'; *The Times* noted, 'While most people were delighted, a few were rather alarmed'; the *Daily Express* said: 'Had he the power of crystal gazing, Fender could not have foreseen the afternoon's play with more clearness'; while the *Daily News* remarked: 'Surrey pulled this out of the pit and the sporting—almost impudent—declaration made by P. G. Fender . . . had no doubt a lot to do with the defeat of the Northerners.' 'Cricketer' (Cardus presumably) in the *Manchester Guardian* wrote: 'It was rather a cheeky declaration, most people thought, and one that certainly did not convey a flattering opinion of Lancashire's batting ability, but as so often happens at this greatest of all games, the clerk of luck sitting up aloft favoured the brave.' An overall summary in the *Daily Telegraph* said: 'Great praise is due to P. G. H. Fender for his admirable captaincy. His declaration of the first innings, his management of the bowling at his disposal and his own clever performance with the ball, excited the admiration of all cricketers who watched this interesting match played.'

Captaincy in this period was an aspect of county cricket which usually did not earn much notice from daily newspaper critics. These comments were significant, therefore, because they confirmed that Fender's manipulation of a match was something new. It was left, however, to the normally restrained *Morning Post* to publish what was an almost fulsome tribute to Fender. It was not written by an impressionable young reporter either, as the particular Hornby mentioned was born in 1847. After speaking of Fender as a young cricketer with vision and an infective genius, the *Post*'s special correspondent went on: 'Yes, Fender is a great captain. We have not seen a side better skippered than Surrey was in this match. We have a lively recollection of Allan Gibson Steel, of Albert Neilson Hornby, of Jack Shuter, of A. J. Webbe but none could have done better than Fender did in this match. The judgement and the persistence with which he kept his men on their toes made us all marvel. He got every ounce out of his side in every point of the game. It was an immense triumph. . . . This was a tremendous day at The Oval. Surrey forced a win against odds and it came off. Fender apart from his captainship had ten wickets in the two innings. He did not spare himself at any moment and his side backed him up at every point to a man. He has the genius of captainship which came out in the happiness of his changes in the bowling. . . .' (There was more but the writer has made his point!)

There was little chance to bask in any afterglow from this newspaper coverage as the next day Surrey were routed for 61 on an awkward Blackheath pitch and by tea-time on the second day Kent had beaten them by an innings. This was Fender's first defeat as a captain, though there was compensation the same day when he received his invitation to tour Australia with MCC. Surrey had the worst of the conditions in this match, but there was no question they played badly as Surrey invariably did at this time at the Rectory Field. Fender had another disappointment against Somerset at The Oval in the next match even if his own astuteness was not found wanting. Apart from thirty minutes on the first day, rain allowed any play in this game only on Thursday, 29 July. Somerset's first innings was completed for 138 and Surrey began their reply under threatening clouds. The forecast for Friday was abysmal and as Surrey approached the Somerset score, Fender sent out a message to the batsmen, half an hour from the close, NOT to score runs.

Fender had calculated that if there should be no play on the Friday, a 'No result' verdict would be more advantageous to Surrey's percentage in the table than it would be to gain two points for first innings lead in a drawn game. Few other captains bothered with this sort of subtlety (though the Yorkshire 'professors' did the following week against Leicestershire) and it was doubtful if The Oval spectators comprehended Surrey's defensive tactics late in the day. Surrey actually drew level with Somerset's total in the closing moments and Fender's feelings could be imagined as Shepherd, inadvertently, snicked a boundary off the edge from the last ball of the day. It put Surrey ahead and displaced them from the top of the championship table. A leader in the *Observer* a week or two later, pertinently summed up: 'The system which penalizes a strong county for being ahead on the first innings, unless it can bring the game to a conclusion, has produced some ironical performances this summer. . . .'

Wilkinson returned to take command after the Somerset match

and there is no need to delve deeply into the next three weeks. Defeats came first against Nottinghamshire and Middlesex at The Oval, followed by a victory against Lancashire at Manchester, where Fender had match figures of 9—98. Another win, more shakily, then came against Kent at The Oval before a defeat from Sussex at Hastings. It was enough to prompt more than one newspaper, with almost indecent haste, to carry articles along the lines of 'What has happened to Surrey?' without, in the time-honoured custom, providing any particularly helpful answer. On 21 August Wilkinson left himself out against Yorkshire at The Oval and Fender was once again captain, as what *Wisden* termed 'an astonishing victory' was gained by 31 runs. This match had a fluctuating third day watched by 10,000 people and one which helped add greatly to Fender's growing reputation for providing entertainment and the unexpected result.

Surrey seemed comfortably placed when they started the final day with a lead of 102 runs and 8 wickets in hand, but Rhodes and Rockley Wilson bowled them out cheaply. Yorkshire had all the time in the world to make the 185 they needed to win. Earlier suspicions that the wicket was starting to crumble were forgotten when Holmes and Sutcliffe put on 50 in half an hour. Fender bowled at this point and in his first over knocked back Holmes's middle stump as the batsman tried to pull a long hop. Wickets then fell steadily, Fender held 3 marvellous catches and Yorkshire's last seven batsmen fell for 48 runs. Fender first had to be rescued from exuberant spectators by the police and then had to make a speech from the pavilion balcony. Those were the days, indeed, for county cricket.

According to the contemporary reports, Fender switched his bowlers about cleverly from end to end, it being one of those days when a wicket quickly followed each time, but, above all, the critical moment was a catch by Fender at third slip which dismissed George Hirst. The fieldsman recalls it as 'the best, I think, I ever made that won a match'. The *Morning Post* described it as 'verging on the impossible', and Fender remembers how Hirst's downfall was plotted with the bowler. Hirst had come into the Yorkshire team after his duties that term as Eton coach had ended. He was top scorer with 81 in the first innings and for the second time looked ominously calm and controlled.

Fender brought back Reay, a tall, medium-fast bowler, and instructed him to attempt four successive straight balls pitched well up, and then to drop a shorter ball outside the off stump. The hope was that Hirst would play the first four balls carefully and then lift or slice his shot as he tried to cut the fifth. In fact Reay dropped his second ball short—and the Yorkshire scorebook confirms it was the second ball of the over—but the original intention still worked. Hirst actually hit the ball off the meat of the bat but Fender dived to his right and held the ball near the ground 'and somehow it stuck'.

It was timely for H. J. Henley to remind *Daily Mail* readers the next day that batsmen said of Fender: 'He is always up to something.' The *Daily Telegraph* felt: 'Very rightly did the crowd which assembled in front of the pavilion call first for Fender. His wonderful catch which dismissed Hirst was a factor in the Surrey victory and his clever captaincy was a greater factor in it.' After the game Fender played bridge that evening at one of his clubs. 'I felt my luck was in and I'm pretty sure it was that evening too.' Only Surrey's visit to Northampton, to which the next chapter is devoted, and the match with Middlesex at Lord's, remained of Surrey's season. The summer, overall, had proved a wonderful return to first-class cricket for Fender and that winter the Surrey committee could have had few reservations about choosing him as captain in his own right for 1921. As *Wisden* said: 'Under Mr Fender's inspiring leadership the side worked together like one man, their efforts being a constant delight to the crowds that gathered at The Oval.'

In view of the quick recognition for Fender's qualities as a captain in 1920, it is relevant to speculate what course MCC's tour of Australia a few months later might have taken if Fender had been made captain when R. H. Spooner stood down. Spooner was the original choice to lead the MCC party, but withdrew because of a knee injury. It was, in all reality, two or three years too soon, probably, for Fender to have been considered, or even to have done himself justice. Certainly it would be far-fetched to think that England would have won under Fender. The Australians proved too strong a side for that, but whether the disparity between the teams would have been so wide if England had been under a different captain from J. W. H. T. Douglas must remain conjecture. It will be disclosed later that during the tour there was a move for Fender to replace Douglas as captain in some of the Tests, though Fender himself knew nothing about this at the time. There is some interesting background to Douglas's appointment and it was, perhaps, revealing that Douglas was seldom mentioned as the possible captain for the tour before he replaced Spooner, and that several newspapers had reservations about his appointment when he was given the job.

Both before Spooner's selection, and after his enforced withdrawal, the names of more unlikely candidates than Fender were bandied about and Douglas was never among them. They included C. B. Fry, who by now was in his forty-ninth year; P. F. Warner if he could be persuaded to postpone his retirement; P. R. Johnson, a forty-year-old Somerset amateur, who had hardly played in 1920 because of a broken wrist; as well as F. W. Gilligan, A. W. Carr and the Hon. L. H. Tennyson, the captains, respectively, of Oxford University, Nottinghamshire and Hampshire. A case could be argued that none of these people justified a place in the team, it being too late in their careers for some of them, and too early for others. Among Fender's advocates was the *Star*, which devoted a leader-page feature to the subject two days before the team was selected. The article was by J.G.S. and, even if he was unable to resist telling his readers, 'You want a good fender for ashes', it contained a reasoned argument:

'Enterprise and initiative are the hall marks of a good captain. Fender has these attributes well developed and what is more he is a thorough sportsman. Brain and geniality are there. Now, is not this the man to be captain of the team which England will before long be sending out to Australia to keep those wonderful Ashes. . . . We see men put forward as possible captains who are admirable batsmen or capital this or that but where can be found one who has more presentday, practical knowledge and proved enterprise than Fender? He is the favourite of a team that is making a strong bid for the county championship. He knows the game from top to bottom. . . .'

MCC announced the team on 26 July and with hindsight we can see it was clearly one of those touring sides that might have been made up differently if it had been chosen nearer the end of the season. When changes had to be made later, the over-all balance altered more than once. The fifteen names first chosen were coupled with a statement that D. J. Knight and G. E. C. Wood had been unable to accept invitations. The names were: R. H. Spooner (captain), J. W. H. T. Douglas, P. G. H. Fender, Rhodes, Hobbs, Woolley, Hendren, Hearne (J. W.), Russell,

Strudwick, Barnes, Howell (H.), Waddington, Makepeace and Dolphin.

Parkin came in when Barnes rejected the terms of his contract in early August; Spooner's withdrawal became known publicly on 16 August and Douglas was appointed captain twenty-four hours later; E. R. Wilson was added the day after that. By the time the team left London on 18 September, MCC had decided to send an extra man, but it was still not clear whether V. W. C. Jupp would be able to accept an invitation. If not, the extra place was to be filled by Hitch and this is what eventually happened.

Lord Harris travelled personally to Southend where Essex were playing Derbyshire to tell Douglas he was to succeed Spooner as captain. That same morning the anonymous Mentor in the *Daily News* alleged that Douglas had refused to tour under any county captain other than Spooner, but the writer wondered how Douglas would feel if P. F. Warner became available. 'If Douglas or Warner stay at home, Percy G. Fender who has led Surrey for the greater part of the season, is in my judgement the only possible leader,' he wrote. After Douglas had accepted, the *Daily Telegraph* came nearer to what was probably MCC's view, when they summarized the situation like this: 'To speak plainly, it would in the circumstances have been nothing less than an affront to Mr Douglas to do anything else. He was quite willing to serve under Mr Spooner but he might reasonably have objected to being passed over in favour of someone junior to himself.' (The reader will not need reminding, presumably, that this aspect of things was never raised when Douglas was hurriedly added to the 1924–25 MCC team under A. E. R. Gilligan.)

Douglas had a curiously lukewarm press in some ways for a man who had led England to a 4–1 success in Australia in 1911–12 when he took charge after P. F. Warner fell ill. Douglas had also taken MCC to South Africa in 1913–14 when the rubber was won 4–0. The newspapers all praised Douglas's own playing ability; they recounted his prowess as an Olympic boxer; and mentioned his fine record as a soldier. More than one writer then recalled the criticism that followed the first Test in 1911–12 when Douglas had bowled himself in preference to Barnes. *The Times* commented: 'Colonel Douglas's abilities as a captain—like his ability as a player—are self-made and sound rather than brilliant. Perhaps his chief fault is lack of imagination.' The *Daily News* remarked: 'With regard to his qualifications for the cricket captaincy, opinions differ concerning the nicety of his judgement.' The *Star* said: 'It has been disputed whether Douglas has the right temperament to captain the side.' These were strong criticisms for that time and confirm for cricket historians that it is nothing new for the game in England to be at sixes and sevens with itself when it comes to selecting the captain for an Australian tour. P. B. H. May in 1958–59 remains the only unquestioned choice this century.

Fender's inclusion as a player was taken for granted by all the cricket correspondents, even if the *Yorkshire Post* (after noting originally that only three Yorkshiremen had been chosen) was less than effusive, perhaps, when it said: 'His ability to come in later and knock bowlers off their length will be as useful as his bowling, which if not first class is at all events likely to be effective when the bowling artists of the team are checked.' Fender's role in what turned out to be such a disastrous tour for England will follow. First, the game in which Fender made his world-record hundred in thirty-five minutes must be dealt with; it was an extraordinary match in many respects.

5. The fastest hundred

Fender's famed hundred so nearly failed to happen on three counts. He was not due originally to play in the match with Northamptonshire, who in 1920 were hardly the strongest of sides. Then, as soon as he went in to bat, he was dropped at cover point. Finally, if Fender had been leading Surrey in this game, he would, he thought later, have declared sooner than Wilkinson did, without waiting for his own hundred, or for Peach, his partner, to reach his double hundred. Fender's unselfish approach to his own cricket led him to disapprove of personal milestones 'getting in the way', as he termed it. Fender became angry with R. W. V. Robins on this issue in a match at the 1928 Bournemouth Festival. Robins ignored a request from Fender to stop bowling leg-side full tosses to help Leslie Townsend (Derbyshire) reach his thousand runs and complete the double. 'You've got to leave a chap feeling he got his record properly,' was Fender's view. 'With the last pair at the wicket, I went on myself in place of Robins. I didn't try to get Townsend's partner out, but I did my best against Townsend himself and he still got what he wanted.'

Fender admitted that this question of records and landmarks was difficult for captains. He remembered arguments with Lionel Tennyson and Charles Bray when next he saw them after he felt they had transgressed in this context: Tennyson for continuing in the rain to let Bradman reach 1,000 on 31 May at Southampton in 1930; Bray for 'allowing' the no-ball to be discovered that ensured the record 555 to Holmes and Sutcliffe at Leyton in 1932. Fender often found his attitude brought him criticism but that the player concerned would be less indignant than the newspapers or public. There were regrets in the press, for instance, when Fender declared Surrey's innings closed against Northamptonshire in 1921 with Sandham 292 not out. Sandham himself readily understood that a first day score of 616 for 5 was enough for Surrey. Similarly, Hendren laughed when Surrey took the new ball and he was dismissed for 199 at The Oval in 1926, but a section of the crowd barracked Fender. A disgruntled Middlesex supporter sitting in the pavilion seats called out: 'That's why you're not England captain, Fender.'

The Surrey team list for Northampton, published in several newspapers on Wednesday, 25 August 1920, did not include Fender, but among the names was D. J. Knight, who six days earlier had been injured at Hastings. It might have been Surrey's first intention for Fender to rest before the show-down with Middlesex at the week-end, or he might have had a business engagement. His plans seemed to have changed when Knight withdrew at fairly short notice. Certainly Fender travelled separately and the match had started when he reached the County Ground. This explained why a substitute held the catch to claim an early Northamptonshire wicket. Northamptonshire were dismissed for 306 and they owed much to an innings of 128 by 'Fanny' Walden, who was only 5ft 2in and better known as a masterly dribbler for Tottenham Hotspur and England. Bad light ended play a few minutes early, with Surrey 12 for the loss of Hobbs, prompting the *Sporting Life* to comment that Surrey had 'a stiff task ahead of them this morning'. What that unknown pundit felt shortly after tea, when Surrey declared at 619 for 5, was never disclosed.

Northamptonshire must have been fairly satisfied thirty minutes before lunch next day when Surrey were 160 for 4. Wilkinson, Shepherd and Sandham had all fallen to the straightforward medium pace of 'Dick' Woolley, elder and right-handed brother of Frank. Peach and Ducat were together at the interval, but Northamptonshire still had no idea what Wordsworth's 'ruthless destiny' had in store. These two went on to make 288 for the fifth wicket in about two and a quarter hours, and the bowling was slaughtered. Fender's innings that followed, therefore, was carnage among the dead and dying, but all the same it was a remarkable example of ferocious hitting. Fender and Peach shared a sixth wicket stand of 171 in forty-two minutes before Surrey declared. It converted to an hourly scoring rate of 244, something unapproached in first-class cricket before or since by any partnership lasting longer than half an hour. When the end came Fender was 113 not out and Peach 200 not out and it is only by a statistical chance, of course, that Fender superseded Peach as the day's main hero. For Fender the flogging of tired Northamptonshire bowling happened to bring a world record, but there were other more significant bouts of hitting in his career.

For Peach in his first full season as an all-rounder, this maiden hundred was to remain the greatest occasion of his life as a batsman.

Fender's record, however, must remain the prime topic. He hit five sixes and either eighteen or seventeen fours, it being impossible to compile an authentic breakdown, stroke by stroke, of Fender's innings. The Surrey scorebook disappeared in the war: only the Northamptonshire one has survived and some appalling discrepancies mar its pages. The famous Leo Bullimer was the Northamptonshire scorer in this game. He was forty-four and not yet half-way through his fifty-one-year stint as the county's scorer. Bullimer's customary neatness and distinctive copperplate writing are apparent in the photograph of the relevant score-sheet (see Plate 6). He scored with a pen; one six has been inked over heavily, as if he first wrote a four, perhaps, but otherwise not an amendment or second thought. Yet, to give only a few inaccuracies from the batting shown, Fender's strokes totalled 112 and not 113; Peach's runs totalled 195 and not 200; Ducat's 142 and not 149; and Wilkinson's 41 and not 43. These mistakes alone made Surrey's score 604 and not 619. Bullimer's scoring was normally reliable and it has to be assumed that the profusion of runs on this occasion proved too much for him.

There have been several worthy attempts by statisticians in recent years to reconstruct Fender's innings and though such matters by no means have universal interest they have a place in this account. Easily the most reasoned interpretation, ball by ball, of what happened has been put together by Mr L. T. Newell, an expert on Northamptonshire's statistics and a man familiar with Bullimer's methods. Though inconsistencies exist in the bowling analyses for this match, they were not as glaring as the errors in the batting records. It was from the bowling figures that Mr Newell worked, over by over, when he assembled the most likely sequence of Fender's hits. He published some of his deductions first in *Cricket News* on 30 July 1977, and both the article and other facts generously passed on by Mr Newell have been of the utmost help to the author. Five players from the match were still alive when this chapter was first drafted and in addition several spectators helped with eyewitness accounts.

As Fender walked out to bat just after four o'clock he flailed the air with his bat, one-handed. He was capless and had neither a sweater nor the neckerchief he often wore. To those who had not seen him before Fender looked both awkward and menacing. He faced almost every ball with the bat already raised to his shoulder, which was not a normal trait of his batsmanship. It confirmed a suspicion gleaned that this hundred came about during a light-hearted slog that could have ended abruptly at any moment. All through, a great deal of trust was placed in the eye, and the ball was usually hit in the air and in all directions. The day was sunny and warm; after lunch the crowd had grown to between 3,000 and 5,000, evenly spread around the edges of the field. There was no delay in returning the ball, as boundary followed boundary. Northamptonshire, whose four main bowlers were all medium to medium-fast, averaged around 24 overs an hour throughout the Surrey innings and they used none of the defensive or delaying tactics that their latter-day successors would have done. The County Ground varied little from its present size and shape, with tempting spaces for the pull and square drive, and the pitch was lifeless. Nearly everything, in fact, was conducive to fast scoring and both score-boards failed to keep up with what happened next.

This can best be looked at first through the local evening newspapers. There were two in Northampton at this time—they have since merged—both providing a lengthy run-of-play report until about five o'clock. It was a pity that Fender was still batting as their deadline approached. There had been so much eventful cricket already that afternoon that space was running out, even with a daily quota of some 1,500 words. Here, verbatim, is how the *Northampton Daily Chronicle* described Fender's innings:

'Fender should have had a very brief stay for after a single he skied one to a great height that Freeman dropped at cover-point. But he, too, started to revel in the bowling, and making use of his long reach, he hit away to some purpose. Eighteen were scored in one of Murdin's overs, and Fender to vary matters sent the ball alongside the ladies' stand for six. He had another life when Humfrey failed to judge a chance in the country, but he laughed at risks and proceeded to give a dazzling display of fireworks.

'The big amateur now completely filled the picture. He drove Thomas for two 6's in one over which yielded 18—17 to Fender, and from the other end he took 19 out of 20 in an over off Murdin, including another six. When an adjournment was made for tea he had hit 93 in half an hour, the score then reading 574 for five.

'Fender on his return treated the bowling absolutely merci-
lessly, and hoisted his century with a six and having been at the
crease barely thirty-five minutes.

'The Surrey captain waited until Peach had reached his 200
before applying the closure, which he did at five o'clock with the
score at 619 for five.'

The rival *Northampton Daily Echo* report was shorter and other
than that Fender reached 50 in twenty minutes added nothing
significant. There were, however, variations in minor detail, the
main one concerning the tea score. This was given as 574 in the
Chronicle with Fender 93, and as 572 in the *Echo* with Fender 91.
These differences were perpetuated next morning in the national
newspapers, who did not have their own men at the match. From
several recognizable phrases there was no doubt that both Northampton reporters, and possibly one other journalist, filed stories
to the London agencies and newspapers after their own work was
finished. There was obviously no collusion between these
reporters and it was possible that they took their facts from different scorers. The Northampton press-box layout made this
feasible: three separate cubicles, the scorers in the middle one,
flanked on both sides by press. A sliding partition allowed reporters
to communicate with the scorer immediately next to them. By
tea-time the scorers might have had different tallies: one at
least, we suspect, had already lost his way.

In the next day's London newspapers, and in the rewrites
carried by the Northamptonshire weeklies, Fender's time for 50
had shrunk from twenty minutes to nineteen and his half-hour's
batting before tea had become twenty-nine minutes. The *Daily
Mirror* used a stock picture of Fender from its library and settled
on 91 in half an hour in their caption and 93 in twenty-nine minutes
in their match report. These differences remained trivial, of
course, other than when dealing in retrospect with an historic
innings. Fortunately for posterity there seemed unanimity that
Fender reached three figures in thirty-five minutes, even though
few people at the time, and certainly the majority of the press,
failed to appreciate that Fender's time *was* a world record. Cricket
statistics were not as thorough then as they have become since.
None of the newspapers in headlines or text categorically seized
on the basic fact that cricket's fastest hundred had been scored.

Only the *Daily Sketch* specifically mentioned this and they buried it in the depths of their story. They added that Jessop's best was the 101 he made in forty minutes at Harrogate in 1897, thereby implying that this was the previous fastest hundred, as indeed it was. Broadly speaking the newspapers shirked the issue and the *Morning Post* epitomized the widespread cautiousness by saying that Fender's batting 'must approach a record in important cricket'. The *Daily Mail* showed its lack of awareness when it said about Fender's hundred: 'It was an astonishing piece of forceful cricket but by no means a record,' and went on to remind people of Alletson's 189 in ninety minutes in 1911 and Jessop's 191 in the same time in 1907. (Alletson took approximately sixty-six minutes over his first hundred runs and Jessop forty-two minutes.)

Fender agrees that it was not appreciated at the time that he had achieved a world record. He did not keep the bat he used and felt certain he would have done if he had known. In several interviews in later years Fender further confused researchers by saying that he only batted twenty-three minutes before tea. He would say that he looked at a clock as he went out to bat and it showed seven minutes past four. It was never clarified whether this was the same clock being used by either the scorers or the umpires, nor whether tea was taken promptly. There was no point in pursuing this parti-cular memory further, but it did provide one more puzzling aspect. So did Bullimer, once again, because the scorebook had Fender timed in at 4.01 with the declaration made at 5.03!

Fender was on firmer ground, probably, when he also said that he might have reached his hundred even more quickly but had held back after tea to let Peach get his double hundred. Wilkinson told Fender at tea he would declare when Fender reached his hundred. Peach was 175 not out at tea and by then had his sights set on his own milestone. Fender seems to have tried to give Peach the strike after the interval as he took two singles in each of the first 2 overs before reaching his hundred in the third over. Fender always maintained that Peach reached 200 first, but the scorebook did not bear this out. It also seems improbable that the evening newspapers would have been wrong on this sequence of events.

Fender went from 97 to 103 with a six against Murdin and scored 15 of the 16 runs this over cost. 'Merry' Murdin bowled from one end throughout the Fender–Peach stand and must have needed to draw heavily on the qualities which led to his nickname. Murdin was faster than Woolley and his stock ball tended to move towards the slips. The over by Murdin mentioned by the *Chronicle* as costing 20 runs was the penultimate over before tea. Fender did not often play back, but the first ball of this over brought him the only six in his life that he struck while playing back defensively. 'I had anticipated a bumper, but the ball never rose; I went through hard with the stroke and it cleared the bowler's head and skimmed low all the way into the football field.' Murdin was the bowler when Fender was missed at cover by Freeman, who lost a high, swirling chance in the sun. 'Ned' Freeman was substituting for Walden, who was resting a bruised leg, and was himself a footballer with Northampton Town. Fender's reported chance in the deep field at 34 might not actually have gone to hand. Neither Fender nor Stuart Humfrey, who later became a well-known ophthalmic surgeon, remembered it.

For those who wish the fullest possible detail: Fender and Peach faced only eighty-nine balls between them under Mr Newell's reconstruction. Fender arrived to play the last ball of an over by Thomas, who could swing the ball both ways and later in his career came close to being chosen for Australia in 1928–29. Fender took a single from his first ball and Murdin and Thomas then each bowled 5 complete overs before tea. Afterwards, before Surrey declared, Murdin bowled a further 2.4 overs and Woolley bowled 2 overs at the other end. Extras conceded during the stand before tea make it impossible to deduce precisely the proportion of bowling for each batsman. All that can be calculated is that Fender before tea received a minimum of thirty-three balls, and a maximum of thirty-nine balls, and scored 93 runs. After the interval he received thirteen balls and scored 20 runs, his hundred coming from the seventh ball he faced in this period.

In total, therefore, Fender needed somewhere between forty and forty-six balls for his hundred and he played between forty-six and fifty-two balls in all. Chris Old took seventy-two balls when in 1977, playing for Yorkshire against Warwickshire, he gained second place to Fender on the list of fastest hundreds. Another rapid modern hundred came from Robin Hobbs in 1975 for Essex against the Australians. Hobbs was timed at forty-four minutes and he received forty-five balls. Without decrying these efforts it must be said that both Old and Hobbs scored many of their runs against innocuous slow bowling deliberately tossed up. The ultimate speed in which a first-class hundred could be made remains open to argument, but Fender's record would not seem unassailable, as Old's time of thirty-seven minutes showed.

There have been two instances of hundreds scored in eighteen minutes in minor cricket, according to Mr E. K. Gross, who for thirty years has been an accepted authority on records outside the first-class sphere. These were believed to be the quickest hundreds ever made in a properly conducted match at any level, but Mr Gross warned there were gaps, inevitably, in this area of knowledge. He knew of a case in South Africa of a man scoring 250 in an hour, but the time for reaching 100 was not recorded. The eighteen-minute hundreds came from L. C. Quinlan in Australia in 1909–10, playing for Trinity v. Mercantile at Cairns, NSW, and from G. J. Bryan at Maresfield Park, Sussex, in 1925 for the Royal Engineers v. Royal Corps of Signals. It would be possible in theory for a first-class hundred to be reached in eighteen minutes, but seems unlikely without collusion from the fielding side.

Just over an hour remained for play after Surrey declared and Northamptonshire were 59 for 2 by the close to bring the total runs scored that Thursday to 666. The wicket remained docile and it was ten to five on the Friday before Northamptonshire were all out for 430 and Surrey went on to win by 8 wickets. The match aggregate of 1,475 runs has remained a record for the county championship. John Moss, of Nottinghamshire, one of the umpires, was probably the only man present at Northampton to have seen more runs scored previously in a three-day game. In 1904 he had stood in the Worcestershire v. Oxford University match at Worcester, which brought 1,492 runs. The score-card at Northampton in full was as on pages 94–5. (See also Plate 6.)

Seven years after this match, almost to the day, Fender became the first man in first-class cricket to take 6 wickets in eleven balls. He had the chance of a hat trick twice in one over and he was as proud of this bowling feat as he was of his fastest hundred. This one happened on Saturday, 27 August 1927, when Surrey began a match with Middlesex at Lord's, and forty-five years elapsed before anyone bettered his achievement. Then Pat Pocock, another Surrey spin bowler, and by coincidence another 'Percy' though only by nickname, took 7 Sussex wickets in eleven balls at Eastbourne. Middlesex, at 37 for 3 from 23 overs, were struggling in good light but on a damp pitch when Fender went on at the Nursery End. In thirty-three balls he ended the innings for 54 with the following spell: .4..... 11..... ..w1.2 ....w. ww.ww. 1.w .

Several newspapers mentioned that Fender's success was not

attributable to the conditions: the ball turned but not excessively. A stiffish breeze was blowing from where the Warner stand has since been built and Allom and Peach had both wanted to bowl from the pavilion end. Geary had completed an economical spell of 11 overs from the Nursery End when Fender replaced him. Hendren and Enthoven, who had come together at 10 for 3, were the batsmen.

Hendren hit a four in Fender's first over and each batsman took a single from his second over. Fender was mostly bowling spin, with a full share of googlies, but the third ball of his next over was faster and of a fullish length and Enthoven, moving out to drive, hit over it and was bowled. Mann took a single and Hendren a two before the over ended. Against Hendren in his fourth over Fender bowled brisk medium pace. 'I reckoned "Pat" knew all about my spin and he was such a good player of the twisty stuff that I thought something quicker was my only hope.' Fender's fifth ball bowled Hendren and the description of this ball in *The Times* helped to explain why. 'A ball that might have bowled anybody.' It was straight, swung away late and broke back six to seven inches to hit middle and off stumps with Hendren committed to cover drive. At the pavilion end Allom had returned for Peach. He now bowled his second successive maiden to Mann before Fender in his next over took 4 wickets.

The first ball was a googly and bowled W. H. F. K. Horton as he played forward and *The Times* noted there was no cover from the batsman's right leg. (The lbw law was different at that time of course.) Next ball, a faster delivery, 'whipped across' A. P. Powell's defensive stroke and the players went in to lunch, five minutes early according to the evening newspapers, with Middlesex 49 for 7. Durston came out with Mann after the interval and managed to play his first ball but edged the next into his stumps. Powell (J. A.) was leg before, first ball, the only wicket Fender took without hitting the stumps. Price, the No. 11 batsman, pushed the last ball of the over towards cover point without scoring. Mann hit a four against Allom before Fender began his sixth over. Price knew nothing about the first ball, another googly, but he pushed blindly forward and was dropped at backward short-leg. Holmes was the fieldsman and he was standing extremely fine; the chance was low and fast and it struck him on the wrist and yielded a single. Mann blocked the next ball but was then yorked as he tried to on-drive.

Fender had taken his 7 wickets for 4 runs in nineteen balls and 6 for 1 in eleven balls, this single coming from a dropped catch. Before half-past two Hobbs and Sandham were batting for Surrey and there was a story that a late arrival in the Lord's pavilion assumed it had been raining as Surrey could not have scored so slowly. Surrey in fact did struggle against Hearne (8–39) and were put out for 149. Fender, hitting with fine judgement, according to *Wisden*, made 42, the highest score; Sandham defended skilfully for two hours scoring 39; and Strudwick in his last game for Surrey scored 13 not out. Hearne went on to make 167 not out as Middlesex reached 322 for 9 before declaring in their second innings, but Surrey eventually won by 5 wickets. Fender took 4–71 in the second innings and on the Tuesday he made the winning hit to complete a marvellous match for him. The score-card in full was as on pages 95–6.

NORTHAMPTONSHIRE v. SURREY, AUGUST 1920

Northants	First Innings		Second Innings	
Mr W. Adams	b Rushby	3	c Hobbs b Fender	31
Mr A. P. R. Hawtin	c and b Fender	34	b Rushby	5
R. Haywood	c sub b Hitch	15	c Peach b Fender	96
C. N. Woolley	c Wilkinson b Fender	58	lbw b Hitch	42
F. Walden	c Hitch b Lockton	128	b Rushby	63
Mr S. H. G. Humfrey	b Ducat	24	b Hitch	31
W. Wells	c Strudwick b Hitch	4	c Rushby b Shepherd	71
*Mr R. O. Raven	b Ducat	4	lbw b Shepherd	28
V. Murdin	b Shepherd	15	c Strudwick b Shepherd	4
A. E. Thomas	not out	8	c Ducat b Hitch	30
B. Bellamy	c Hitch b Fender	11	not out	13
Extras (lb 2)		2	Extras (b 9, lb 6, nb 1)	16
Total		306	Total	430

FALL OF WICKETS—**First Innings:** 1–3, 2–24, 3–105, 4–115, 5–171, 6–188, 7–203, 8–278, 9–288, 10–306. **Second Innings:** 1–12, 2–54, 3–161, 4–209, 5–264, 6–288, 7–365, 8–376, 9–393, 10–430.

BOWLING	O	M	R	W	O	M	R	W
Hitch	24	6	90	2	28.2	2	137	3
Rushby	25	10	66	1	27	5	68	2
Lockton	20	5	53	1	10	0	34	0
Shepherd	6	1	17	1	13	5	27	3
Fender	21.5	1	69	3	29	1	118	2
Ducat	9	4	9	2	8	1	23	0
Peach					4	2	7	0

Surrey	First Innings		Second Innings	
J. B. Hobbs	c Bellamy b Murdin	3	b Walden	54
A. Sandham	c Hawtin b Woolley	92	b Thomas	6
*Mr C. T. A. Wilkinson	b Woolley	43		
T. Shepherd	c Bellamy b Woolley	9	not out	42
H. A. Peach	not out	200		
A. Ducat	c Bellamy b Thomas	149	not out	11
Mr P. G. H. Fender	not out	113		
Extras (b 9, lb 1)		10	Extras (b 2, lb 5)	7
Total (5 wkts dec)		619	Total (2 wkts)	120

W. Hitch, Mr J. H. Lockton, H. Strudwick and T. Rushby did not bat.

FALL OF WICKETS—**First Innings:** 1–5, 2–97, 3–127, 4–160, 5–448.
Second Innings: 1–24, 2–93.

BOWLING	O	M	R	W	O	M	R	W
Wells	31	6	133	0				
Murdin	22.4	0	162	1	9	1	37	0
Thomas	23	0	142	1	14	3	24	1
Woolley	26	3	116	3	9.3	2	26	0
Humfrey	4	0	36	0				
Haywood	4	0	20	0				
Walden					4	0	26	1

Umpires: J. Moss and T. M. Russell.   * Captain
Surrey won by eight wickets.

MIDDLESEX v. SURREY, AUGUST 1927

Middlesex	First Innings		Second Innings	
Mr N. Haig	b Allom	8	c Shepherd b Geary	11
H. W. Lee	lbw b Geary	0	c Ducat b Shepherd	20
J. W. Hearne	c Peach b Geary	0	not out	167
E. Hendren	b Fender	22	c Fender b Holmes	46
Mr H. J. Enthoven	b Fender	16	lbw b Holmes	0
*Mr F. T. Mann	b Fender	5	b Fender	7
Mr W. H. F. K. Horton	b Fender	0	b Fender	8
Mr A. P. Powell	b Fender	0	c Strudwick b Fender	0
F. J. Durston	b Fender	0	c Knight b Shepherd	37
J. A. Powell	lbw b Fender	0	lbw b Fender	0
W. F. Price	not out	1	not out	1
Extras (b 2)		2	Extras (b 20, lb 5)	25
Total		54	Total (9 wkts dec)	322

FALL OF WICKETS—**First Innings:** 1–6, 2–10, 3–10, 4–46, 5–49, 6–49, 7–49, 8–49, 9–49, 10–54. **Second Innings:** 1–26, 2–63, 3–149, 4–153, 5–167, 6–187, 7–199, 8–298, 9–308.

BOWLING	O	M	R	W	O	M	R	W
Allom	12	6	18	1				
Geary	11	7	10	2	24	3	62	1
Peach	5	2	14	0	35	11	61	0
Fender	5.3	2	10	7	44	14	71	4
Holmes					22	8	35	2
Shepherd					39	9	68	2

Surrey	First Innings		Second Innings	
J. B. Hobbs	b Haig	11	b Durston	54
A. Sandham	lbw b Hearne	39	c A. P. Powell b Durston	55
A. Ducat	b Hearne	4	c Durston b Hearne	51
T. Shepherd	b Hearne	11	b J. A. Powell	8
Mr D. J. Knight	lbw b Hearne	4	lbw b J. A. Powell	17
*Mr P. G. H. Fender	c Price b Haig	42	not out	20
Mr E. R. T. Holmes	st Price b Hearne	4	not out	11
H. A. Peach	b Hearne	6		
A. Geary	b Hearne	4		
H. Strudwick	not out	13		
Mr M. J. C. Allom	b Hearne	0		
Extras (b 6, lb 5)		11	Extras (b 9, lb 2, nb 2)	13
Total		149	Total (5 wkts)	229

FALL OF WICKETS—**First Innings:** 1–16, 2–25, 3–39, 4–55, 5–102, 6–114, 7–126, 8–130, 9–141, 10–149. **Second Innings:** 1–116, 2–127, 3–151, 4–195, 5–205.

BOWLING	O	M	R	W	O	M	R	W
Haig	23	9	42	2	19	7	49	0
Durston	8	3	12	0	19	3	59	2
Hearne	26.2	8	39	8	11	2	35	1
Enthoven	4	0	16	0	9	1	22	0
J. A. Powell	8	1	29	0	13.1	1	51	2

Umpires: J. Stone and D. Denton   * Captain
Surrey won by five wickets

6. Australia and Armstrong

Within two hours of sailing from Tilbury in September 1920, Fender knew he had been earmarked for only a minor role in MCC's tour plans for Australia. He was watching the lights of Eastbourne fade in the distance when he was joined on deck by Johnny Douglas. The two men had played with and against each other several times but were still little more than acquaintances. As they smoked their pipes and talked, Douglas said: 'You know Fender, there is no man in England whose bowling I would rather bat against than yours; and there is no batsman in England I would rather bowl against either.' It was a teasing, if heavy-handed remark, made in the context of a discussion about the way opinions of cricketers could differ from person to person. Fender, inevitably, was deeply hurt. Like many outwardly brash and confident people, he was less sure of himself than he seemed at this stage of his career. As his first tour got under way, he could have done without the knowledge that his captain obviously considered him fortunate to be in the side.

Fender grew to like Douglas as a man when he came to know him, far more than might be imagined from this unpromising start. They were always to remain poles apart in manner and outlook, but numerous personal duels with bat and ball during Essex–Surrey matches brought a mutual respect over the years. Fender admired the determination that Douglas applied to his cricket, which often brought him greater success than others with more natural gifts, and he had a high regard for Douglas's ability to swing the ball in helpful conditions. At the same time Fender, like many other people at the time and since, was very conscious of Douglas's limitations as a captain. Douglas was an immensely strong man of inexhaustible stamina. He seldom appreciated that others were physically not as hardy. Many of the criticisms of his captaincy seemed to have stemmed from overbowling himself or others. Fender claimed to have heard George Louden more than once, in Essex matches, pleading unsuccessfully with Douglas to take him off. Neither does Douglas seem to have been an adaptable or quick thinker where field placings and other tactics were concerned, and he was sometimes reluctant to amend preconceived notions.

To Fender it appeared on this tour that Douglas was imbued with memories of 1911–12 when Barnes, Foster and Douglas between them had obtained 81 of the 95 wickets taken by England's bowlers in the Test matches. 'This time there was no Barnes; Waddington was no Foster; and Douglas was nine years older,' Fender said. It was unfortunate that this particular MCC tour produced no full-scale book by a dispassionate observer. Fender's own *Defending the Ashes*, mostly put together on the voyage home, was the only one published and, as a means of trying to establish what went wrong, it has proved the least satisfactory of his books. A reviewer in the *Cricketer* in July 1921 wrote: 'Without Mr Fender's views on controversial matters, the book has the appearance of a censored letter from the front.'

Reading between the lines, however, one cannot avoid the suspicion that in some ways this was not one of the happier touring parties, even leaving aside the unfortunate results in the Tests. Australia, of course, proved far stronger than had been anticipated, with the crucial factors being their host of run-getters, Gregory's all-round cricket and Mailey's—then—record haul of wickets. England's catching was often poor and as can happen to a team being outplayed, there were other disappointments. These included Hearne's illness, numerous injuries, and frequent failures by the best players to find their proper form in important games. E. W. Swanton in Volume II of the 1962 edition of *A History of Cricket* (Allen & Unwin) aptly ended his summary of the tour: 'In 1920–21 Douglas was surrounded, as it happened, by several men of unusual cricket intelligence, and it is not hard to suppose that the frustration they felt was ultimately reflected in their performances.'

Some years later Fender was amazed to learn from Fred Toone, the MCC manager, that after England lost the first two Test matches, Toone had asked Douglas to consider standing down to allow Fender to lead England in the third Test at Adelaide. Toone, the Yorkshire secretary, who managed two further tours to Australia and was subsequently knighted, seemed himself to have been the prime mover behind this suggestion. It had the support of Hobbs and Woolley, but it was indicative of the lack of unity in the party, perhaps, that Rhodes did not appear to have been

1. *Early school groups: (a) Fender aged twelve is second from the left in the back row in this 1905 picture of the 3rd XI at St George's College Weybridge; (b) Fender, seated right, is a member of the 1908 St Paul's XI*

2. *Fender's father and mother*

*3. (a) Fender in 1913 when his
performances for Sussex first
brought him recognition
outside the county
(b) Fender on crutches in
1919 when he was unable to
play cricket*

4. (a) Fender kept goal for the Casuals when they won the English AFA
Cup in 1912-13. Standing (l. to r.): R. W. Dower, a linesman, M. H.
Clarke, K. C. Raikes, P. G. H. Fender, A. W. Foster, H. Rimmington,
P. Harrower (referee), a linesman. Seated (l. to r.): M. Woosman,
R. C. Cutter, C. D. McIvor (captain), F. H. Mugliston, T. Dodd

Twenty-three years separate these two pictures of Fender on war service.
(b) In Royal Flying Corps uniform in 1917, and (c) when he rejoined
the Royal Air Force in 1940

5. (a) *Fender with the Surrey players he led in 1920 for the first time,*
when chance brought him the captaincy for most of the summer. Stand-
ing (l. to r.): Hitch, Ducat, Sandham, Peach, Rushby, Harrison,
Shepherd, Boyington (scorer). Seated (l. to r.): Strudwick, Hobbs,
P. G. H. Fender, M. Howell, G. M. Reay
(b) *Johnny Douglas and Fender both hold pipes in this team group of*
the MCC touring party to Australia in 1920-21 but the two men had
little else in common. Standing (l. to r.): Dolphin, Hitch, Parkin,
F. C. Toone (manager), Woolley, Russell, Waddington. Seated
(l. to r.): Strudwick, Rhodes, E. R. Wilson, J. W. H. T. Douglas,
P. G. H. Fender, Hobbs. On ground (l. to r.): Howell, Hendren,
Hearne, Makepeace

Match Played at *Northampton*
Northamptonshire v. *Surrey*

Date *August 25·26·27*

First Innings *Surrey*

BATSMAN	TIME IN	TIME OUT	RUNS	HOW OUT	BOWLER	TOTAL
1 *Hobbs*	6·15	6·20	2·1	c *Bellamy*	*Murdin*	3
2 *Sandham*	6·15	1·0	12·12·3·42·1||||4|2·3·4·4·3||42·1|4·4||4·42· 12·4|32·4·2	c *Hawtin*	*Woolley*	92
3 *C.T.Wilkinson*	6·21	12·19	1|4·4||||||4·2·3|4|4·11	*Bowled*	*Woolley*	43
4 *Shepherd*	12·20	12·45	1431	c *Bellamy*	*Woolley*	9
5 *Peach*	12·46	5·3	4·4|||||·4·3·112·2·4·1|4 4·4·4|2||·441·4·5|3·11·4·4·13|1·62·1·3·6·2 ||1·3·||4·1|3·1·6·1||||1·22·4·1||4·4·1|6·4·11|6·1|4·1	*N.a.*		200
6 *Ducat*	1·1	4·0·5	3|||·4·4·3||1·4·4||14·62·|1|2·1·2·4·4|||4|4·2·1·43· 4·2·1|4·1||4·4|4·1||2·11|||||·4·4·11·2·142·	c *Bellamy*	*Thomas*	149
7 *P.G.Fender*	4·1	5·3	1|4·4·4·4·4·11·6·4·6·4·||4·4·6·4·3·6·4·1·4·4||6·4 |4·1		*N.a.*	113
8						
9						
10						
11						

Umpires ... *Russell* *Moss*

Scorers ... *Wethimer* *Boyington*

Byes ... 4|4	... ...	9
Leg Byes... 1	... ...	1
Wides ...	... ...	
No Balls ...	... ...	

TOTAL ... 619

	One	Two	Three	Four	Five	Six	Seven	Eight	Nine	Ten
Fall of Wickets ...	5	97	127	160	448					

---

6. *Fender's famous 35-minute hundred as it was recorded in the Northamptonshire
    add up to 112 and there are several other mistakes in the details of other players'*

BOWLING ANALYSIS.

BOWLER	1	2	3	4	5	6	7	8	9	10	11	12	13	14	15	16
Wells																
Murdin																
Thomas																
Woolley																
Humphrey																
Haywood																

	BOWLER	Overs	Maidens	Runs	Wickets	Wides	No Balls
1	Wells	31	6	133	0		
2	Murdin	22.4	0	162	1		
3	Thomas	23	0	142	1		
4	Woolley	26	3	116	3		
5	Humphrey	4	0	36	0		
6	Haywood	4	0	20	0		
7							
8							
9							
10							
11							

scorebook on 26 August 1920. The discerning reader will note that Fender's strokes
performances. The Surrey scorebook has been lost to posterity

7. *Back from Australia in 1921: (a) Fender bowls at the nets in late April; (b) a forceful stroke against Essex in May. (c) Warwick Armstrong and Fender when the Australians played Surrey. Fender learned more from Armstrong than from any other captain*

8. (a) and (b) Two different strokes as Fender hit 185 in 130 minutes for Surrey against Hampshire at The Oval in May 1922. This was the first time Fender wore glasses in a first-class match. Livsey is the wicket-keeper

9. (a) *Fender at third slip in his 'starting blocks' position. The picture was taken at Lord's against Middlesex in 1922, and contemporary newspaper captions say that Peach was bowling*

(b) *Fender, wearing one of his famous elongated sweaters, and Sandham, going out to bat in the mid-twenties. By 1980 these two were the senior Test-match cricketers alive in the world*

(c) *Fender and other Surrey players being congratulated by spectators after beating Kent in 1923 at Blackheath, the first time Surrey had won on the ground for many years*

10. (a) *Fender and his fiancée, Miss Ruth Clapham, at The Oval a few days before their wedding in 1924. The future Mrs Fender is wearing the monocle that was often mentioned in newspaper stories.*
(b) *Fender hitting H.J. Enthoven for four against Middlesex at Lord's in 1928. Price is the wicket-keeper*

11. (a) *The caption to this agency photograph of Surrey v. Nottinghamshire at The Oval in 1926 said: 'Fender delighted the crowd with a swipe to the boundary off Barratt's bowling'*
(b) *This pull earned Fender six against Peach in the 1931 Surrey trial game*
(c) *Fender bowling in a practice game about 1930*

12. (a) *Fender and Douglas Jardine in relaxed mood as Jardine leaves for India for MCC's 1933-34 tour*
(b) *As well as being a bridge expert, Fender also reached a high standard as a billiards player when he was relaxing from cricket*

13. (a) *Fender always enjoyed playing against Arthur Carr, the long-serving and controversial captain of Nottinghamshire. This picture shows Fender, the bowler, parrying a hard return hit from Carr, when their counties met at The Oval in 1932*

(b) *A 1934 Surrey team picture. Errol Holmes is now captain and it was Hobbs's last season. Standing (l. to r.): Gregory, Barling, Squires, Watt, Gover, Brooks, Wilson, Strudwick (scorer). Seated (l. to r.): Hobbs, P. G. H. Fender, E. R. T. Holmes, H. M. Garland-Wells, Sandham*

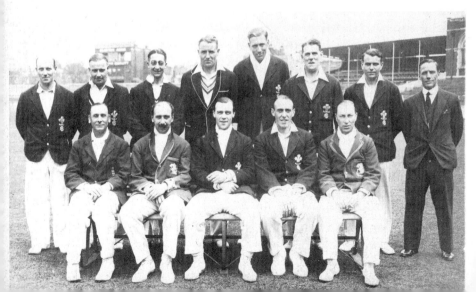

14. (a) *Fender introduces the Old England players to King George VI at the Surrey centenary match at The Oval in 1946 (l. to r.): B. A. Glanvill (Surrey president), the King, Fender, Jardine, Tate, Hendren*
(b) *The night before this match Fender took a party of cricketers to the musical* Here Come the Boys *at the Saville theatre (l. to r.): Jack Hulbert, Bobby Howes, Fender, Donald Knight, Sutcliffe, Maurice Allom, Sandham*

15. Fender, wearing an old wartime flying jacket, in his study at Horsham, where, though almost completely blind, he continued to run his wine business

consulted about the suggested change. The tour selection committee was Douglas, Hobbs and Rhodes with Toone attending, too, but all the team were aware that this committee seldom met in the early part of the trip. Douglas had his parents travelling with him and the other players did not see a great deal of him away from matches. Hobbs, according to Fender, did not think it mattered a great deal whether the committee met or not and it was usually Rhodes who would nag Douglas for a meeting so that plans could be discussed.

Fender stressed that Toone's proposal to Douglas arose from the need to change the make-up of the Test side, more than any desire to unseat Douglas, temporarily, from the leadership. 'You must remember that Douglas had not done a great deal on the tour up to this point though his own form got much better from then onwards. Douglas had certainly not been able to fathom Mailey and coupled with this was a feeling that it was time my wrist spin was given a chance. I honestly had no idea that all this was being talked about by Toone to Douglas. I don't think I would ever have figured in Wilfred's thinking, but I know I had Woolley's support. He told me long afterwards when I talked with him about it that he had grumbled to Toone because Douglas would not let him have the field he wanted. As for being captain, that would have come to me as the only amateur. Rockley Wilson was the vice-captain but the intention was that only one of us would play and I was the wrist spinner and also, I suppose, I might get more runs than Rockley.' (Fender had hit an attractive hundred in a country game at Ballarat immediately prior to the discussions between Toone and Douglas. Wilson's batting by that stage in his career had fallen away.)

Douglas refused, indignantly, to consider dropping himself, though Fender was still brought in to make his Test debut. He took the place of Hearne, who had fallen ill during the second Test and did not play again on the tour. Fender had a poor game at Adelaide in several respects but kept his place for the last two Tests, bowling much better in these games. He took 5 for 122 in Australia's first innings in the fourth Test at Melbourne and thought it was in this game that the barrackers first started to shout in unison: '**P**lease **G**o **H**ome **F**ender.' It was a chant taken up wherever he played on the rest of the tour and Fender, being Fender, often 'conducted' the shouting. In the fifth Test at Sydney, Fender took 5 for 90 in Australia's first innings and he actually headed the England Test averages for the series with 12 wickets at 34.16 each, figures that indicate England's struggle. Fender found he stood up to the immense heat that marked this Australian summer better than most of his team-mates though the hard grounds jarred his injured leg and made running painful for him when he fielded away from the wicket.

According to newspaper reports, Fender alone of either side approached Mailey for his ability to turn the ball, though Fender admitted his length was often erratic. 'Macartney was among several of the Australians who thought my control would improve with more experience. Macartney told me in 1926 they were pleased at the time when I was left out of the 1924–25 side.' When Fender was in Australia reporting the 1928–29 tour, he played some club cricket with Mailey and other former Australian Test players. Fender and Mailey would vie with each other for turn and their team-mates were astonished that Fender had not been chosen for the MCC team ahead of Freeman, whose limited value in Australian conditions had already been shown in 1922–23 and 1924–25.

Fender, like all his type, benefited in the later part of the 1920–21 tour from the increased amount of work he was given. At the time when Toone was advocating Fender's inclusion for the third Test, starting on 14 January, Fender had bowled 71 overs in Australia and only 42 of these were in first-class matches. 'I needed far more work and in my first Test I hardly knew where the stumps were,' he said. Wilson at the same stage had 75 overs (51 in first-class games) and neither he nor Fender had played an important match since Brisbane six weeks earlier. Toone arranged special net facilities for the two amateurs before the Adelaide Test and for two days solidly they bowled and batted to each other, alternately an hour at a time, morning and afternoon. Fender remembers Wilson, a gifted coach, always credited with instilling Douglas Jardine's batting technique at Winchester, helping him with advice about his batting, too, at that time.

Even if the tour policy had leaned more towards slow bowling early on and been less obsessed with the quicker men, it would never have been easy for Douglas and his senior professionals to decide which particular players should have been used. The problem arose from what, in theory, was almost an embarrassment of choice. In the previous English summer Rhodes had taken 161 wickets at 13.18 each, Woolley 185 (14.23) and Hearne 142

(17.83) and all three were assured of places in the Test side as batsmen. As it happened none of them proved all that effective as bowlers but, even with limited use, their very presence tended to militate against the claims of Fender or Wilson. 'White and Verity had not yet "happened" and to be fair to Douglas there was not a great tradition of English slow bowling in good weather in Australia,' Fender pointed out. Parkin, who played in all five Tests, had the advantage over Fender and Wilson with his variety in method. In retrospect, several critics believed Wilson might have proved the best choice, but until Hearne's illness it was not feasible to provide him with work. When Wilson finally played in the fifth Test his accurate and studious skill astonished the Australians. Fender particularly remembered that Wilson put a brake on Macartney (170) and Gregory (93) for an hour or so when they had been in full cry.

With Douglas closeted with his family, Fender, Wilson and Toone were thrown together a great deal during the seven-month tour. Fender, on the outward voyage, shared a cabin on the *Osterley* with the manager. Their relationship even managed to survive Fender's spilling a breakfast tray, including a particularly moist omelette, down a new pair of white ducks, which Toone had proudly put on for the first time. These two visited Pompeii when the ship called at Naples, and heavy traffic made them late back. Toone hired a tender and they caught the ship as she was leaving the outer harbour. The captain told them he would not have heaved to and lowered a gangway if he had not recognized the vivid MCC hatband on Toone's trilby. One of Wilson's contributions to the tour, Fender recalled, was a series of fluent and witty after-dinner speeches, a task Douglas happily delegated. The example Fender cited in his book, though, makes one wonder if Wilson's wry humour was always understood. At a drinks party, when MCC changed trains at Kalgoorlie, Wilson likened the two mayors of the host mining townships (Kalgoorlie and Boulder) as they sat at the top table, to the twin kings of Moab—Jehoshaphat and Ahab. Not many audiences, least of all gold miners of that period, perhaps, had the necessary biblical knowledge for the period 850 BC to grasp the allusion.

Like every other cricketer who has toured Australia, Fender has the happiest memories of the hospitality and kindness he received. In those times MCC would be greeted by cheering crowds at stations and along the streets to their hotels. During long journeys they would have to show themselves at wayside stops made by their train in the remoter parts. It could be wearing, but at least there was more time between matches to get to know the country and its people than is allowed by modern itineraries and air travel. Just occasionally Fender found the almost thrustful friendship and interest of the average Australian hard to accept. He remembered one host at a poolside party near the sea becoming truculent over Fender's refusal to have a swim. Fender was batting the next day and had a theory that salt water was bad for his eyes. At the same time, Fender realized in later years that his traditional English reticence more than once had made him less forthcoming than he should have been. In this context Fender enjoyed later visits to Australia as a pressman and Second World War serviceman more, in some ways, than he did when he was being lionized as a player.

'I think, too, when you are younger you find it harder to sort out the difference between liking and disliking opponents, who on this tour were beating us heavily and deservedly. Like every series it had its little incidents. There was for instance plenty of short-pitched bowling from Gregory and there were other irksome things, but there was less publicity than there would be today. There is a lot of talk now about everything on the field being forgotten afterwards over a few beers. Well I'm not so sure it always *is* forgotten though these irritations become easier to accept as you get older. At that time I found it difficult to mix with several of the Australians.'

Fender was the unwitting cause of a fight on a tram as he made his way to the ground to play in one Test match and was ordered off the vehicle by the conductor. He thought it was in Melbourne during the fourth Test match. Fender was standing at one end of the crowded tram when a furious fist fight broke out at the other end. Soon several other men on the tram were exchanging blows. The tram came to a halt and the conductor separated the two main combatants and then pushed his way back to Fender. With the conductor's expletives suitably deleted, something like the following dialogue ensued:

Conductor: 'Off, you'll have to get off.'
Fender: 'What do you mean?'
Conductor: 'Off you get. They are fighting about you.'
Fender: 'Me?'

Conductor: 'Yes. One says you are a Pommie cricketer and the other says that nobody that looks like you could be a cricketer.'

Fender: 'But I *am* a cricketer and I'm playing in the Test.'

Conductor: 'Yes, I know. But you've got to get off. If you don't they will start fighting again.'

Fender got off amid loud cheering and waving from everyone as the tram resumed its journey. You may be wondering why Fender was on a tram in the first place. Fender was never a rich man and as an amateur he often had to pay for his own local transport and the tram was cheaper than a taxi. His hotels and main travelling expenses, of course, were covered, but he estimated that minor incidentals which he could not avoid had cost him about £400 in Australia. That sum has to be multiplied several times to get its equivalent sixty years later. Fender and Wilson raised this, individually, with MCC when they returned home and the club were sympathetic. Fender found the amateurs were helped far more with out-of-pocket expenses when he toured South Africa two years later, though the trip still cost him a great deal.

The expense often prevented many leading amateurs from touring abroad before the distinction between them and professionals was abolished in 1963. It was an effort to defray some of their expenses that induced Fender and Wilson to accept sundry journalistic contracts during their visit to Australia. Fender wrote for the *Daily News* and several magazines and Wilson's articles appeared, primarily, in the *Daily Express*. For once it was not Fender who bore the brunt of the criticism that ensued. Neither man, in fact, wrote anything especially controversial by modern standards. Wilson, however, did once or twice manage to offend Australian susceptibilities, something very easily done to this day, as any cricket journalist will confirm. A motion was passed at MCC's next annual meeting which deprecated cricketers who reported matches in which they were playing and most tour contracts since have forbidden the practice.

This was an ill-starred tour for MCC in more ways than just its results. A passenger on the *Osterley* died of typhus at Colombo and the team spent a week in a quarantine station when they reached Fremantle, reducing the time available for the Western Australia match to one day. Later a shipping strike prevented them from fulfilling their Tasmanian fixtures. With limited opportunities,

Fender's only cricket worth noting in the early weeks came at Sydney against New South Wales, who included nine of the 1921 Australian side in England, as well as Kelleway, who declined his invitation to tour. MCC made 236 and on a good wicket dismissed the opposition for 153, which was regarded as a fine achievement. Fender took 4–26 in 9 overs and hit 54 of MCC's 250 in their second innings. MCC fully expected to win as New South Wales set out to score 334, but a foretaste of the Australian batting strength in the Tests was given when the state won by 6 wickets. Macartney (161) and Collins (106) began with a first-wicket stand of 244 in three hours. Fender and six other MCC bowlers were completely mastered.

Macartney had first impressed himself on Fender's mind with the century in each innings he made against Sussex in 1912 and, as far as Fender was concerned, he remained the outstanding Australian batsman of his time. Fender never saw Trumper and he retained personal reservations about Bradman. 'Macartney had a brilliance that was unique to him alone; easily the sanest hitter of a ball I ever saw. He used to "pick" the ball up early and so surely. Jessop was an exception to every generalization, but Macartney hit the ball sanely without any stupid extravagances. Macartney's footwork was so quick he overcame the disadvantages of being a shortish man and hit hard and in an orthodox way. He was marvellous to watch unless one was bowling to him.'

Macartney and Mailey were the closest friends Fender made on the Australian side and they spent a lot of time together when the 1921 Australians travelled to England on the same ship that took MCC home. 'I always remember bowling to Macartney for Surrey in 1921 or 1926 and failing miserably. I knew he'd be our main worry and as the pitch was "doing a bit", I thought even he might be on his guard. I was bowling when he arrived and first ball decided to try and bowl him a fast yorker on his leg stump, or at least as fast as I could. Charlie shuffled back towards the square-leg umpire and cut it for four past second slip. I thought to myself "He won't expect another one", so I repeated the performance. Again I managed to do what I was trying to do, and again he played the same stroke, and got another four. Then he looked up and grinned: "I knew you'd have something special for me you old —." They were good yorkers, too,' Fender said wryly.

Fender was England's twelfth man in the first Test at Sydney, being left out of the side for Waddington just before the toss.

Mailey sketched a telling cartoon of a dejected Fender immediately after he had heard of his omission. Fender used the original drawing captioned 'The Twelfth Man' as the frontispiece for his book of the tour and it is similarly used in this one. Fender had been told to change, but heard from Douglas in the corridor outside the dressing-room just before the toss that Waddington's batting had decided the issue. Fender was naturally disappointed at the time, but a study of his figures and the lack of work he had been given makes it unlikely that he would ever have played. Waddington, who usually batted 'No. 9 or later' (as Fender put it) for Yorkshire had made 51 not out against an Australian XI at Brisbane in the late stages of a 'dead' match ten days earlier. More relevantly Waddington had taken 8–33 in a two-day match against New South Wales colts just before the Test and he probably justified a Test place on the same ground. Waddington played in the first and fourth Tests without success, but regularly took wickets in the lesser matches and headed the tour averages for all games with 58 wickets at 12.29 each.

Fender's 106 against a Ballarat 15 in a two-day game prior to his selection for the third Test was a typically spirited innings by him against bowling reportedly stronger than was sometimes met in matches against odds. Douglas stood down from this game, but acted as scorer for part of the time, according to the *Ballarat Star*, and as Fender walked out to bat, warned those within earshot that they would now see some remarkable strokes. Fender and Woolley (159 not out) shared a fifth-wicket stand of 190 in eighty minutes. One of Fender's three sixes, which soared over a tree on the square-leg boundary and out of the ground, was the biggest hit local spectators had seen, he was told. The other two sixes, according to the newspaper, were from consecutive hits, enormous pulled drives sending the ball across the street next to the ground to land in a fowl yard within a foot or so of each other. Fifty-six years later, when Fender was in Melbourne for the Centenary Test celebrations, he had a letter from a man who had witnessed these hits and had never forgotten them. Local legend still claimed that a Fender six had killed a duck; the writer did not know whether it was true but he had told his own grandchildren the tale. For the Ballarat side, a certain twenty-three-year-old schoolmaster, W. M. Woodfull (spelt Woodfall in Fender's book) made 50 in the first innings, showing all the defensive strength which brought him so many runs later in Test cricket.

A week later, at Adelaide, Fender's first Test-match appearance was made in a game that lasted six days and brought 1,753 runs and six centuries. It was also the match when E. A. McDonald was brought in to join Gregory for the first time in the Australian attack, a batsman making way for him. At this time it was by no means a regular practice to open the bowling with a really fast bowler at each end—presumably a ploy that should be credited to Armstrong—and Fender had a clear memory of discussion of the tactic's merit in the English camp. Already 2–0 down in the series, the England players knew they had little chance of retaining the Ashes and Fender recalled that thinking was equally divided on whether Australia had strengthened their hand or not. Fender himself had no doubts that Australia were stronger, even if McDonald, on paper, was hardly the force he was to be in England a few months later, and for Lancashire later still. Fender never thought McDonald was as fast as Burns or Larwood, but he put him ahead of Gregory in terms of ability and threat.

Up to a point England did better in this Test than in the first two matches of the series. Australia began with an innings of 354 (Collins 162) and when England scored 447 (A. C. Russell 135 not out), they had gained the first innings lead for the first time in the rubber. Australia scored 582 in their second innings with Kelleway making 147 in seven hours and Armstrong (121), Pellew (104) and Gregory (78 not out) nailing down the coffin lid. Even so, England did not entirely discount the possibility of making 490 on a perfect wicket but, apart from 123 by Hobbs, nobody stayed long enough. Australia won the match by 119 runs and the series with it. Fender's bowling analyses were 1 for 52 and 1 for 105 and he scored 2 and 42 with the bat. At least he helped to make the losing margin smaller than seemed likely at one time and was last out, caught by Ryder at long-off, against Mailey. Fender's blackest moment in this match, however, concerned a catch he dropped in the second innings from the first ball Kelleway faced: one of the most dreadfully expensive misses of all time.

In the mid-1960s Fender sat next to Rhodes at a cricket dinner. Rhodes, by then eighty-nine and blind, when told his neighbour's identity, remarked: 'Ah yes, Mr Fender, you're the chap who dropped the catch that lost us the Test in Adelaide in 1921.' True, possibly, if a little harsh: this chance by Kelleway seemed to have been one of those created partially by the fieldsman's great attempt to catch it, though Fender admitted that, having got so near, he should have held the ball. The Adelaide newspaper, the *Advertiser*, described the incident as follows: 'He [Kelleway] cut his first ball breast high to Fender at first slip and was dropped.' This description is shown to be patently wrong by a photograph in Fender's book of the dropped catch and the picture confirmed Fender's own memory of the chance.

The ball was edged off Howell close enough to Strudwick's right hand for him to dive optimistically, but it was always falling well short of first and second slip, who were Woolley and either Douglas or Russell, a positive identification being hard to make from the photograph. Fender, at third slip, had been in his 'starting blocks' position. He had made two or three steps forward and across before reaching out with his left hand. The ball struck the top of Fender's shortened fingers and was parried but not held. It was one of the few times in his entire career that Fender remembered dropping a catch because of the lack of flexibility in the fingers he damaged years before in his factory accident. 'I didn't grasp the ball properly and don't want to make excuses, but it would have been the best catch of my life if I had been able to complete it.'

Fender pulled his weight as an all-rounder far more .in the fourth and fifth Tests as Australia completed their 5–0 win in the series. Their strong batting and Mailey's bowling ensured that there was no let-up to their utter dominance. Amid all this, Fender's chief memory of the closing weeks of the tour was the relative success he gained as a batsman against Mailey, whose prodigious spin and experimentation were so akin to Fender's own ambitions. Fender had been annoyed as he made his 42 in the third Test by the number of times he played firm strokes against Mailey's leg-breaks, only to find the ball going straight to a fieldsman. It was Hobbs who advised him to stop trying to find the gaps and to aim his strokes direct at a fielder so he would then find that the ball's spin would take it into a gap. Fender bore this in mind and had several duels with Mailey as he scored 59 in the second innings of the fourth Test, 60 and 27 in the return game with New South Wales, and 40 in the second innings of the fifth Test. These runs brought Fender some small personal pleasure, and coupled with the wickets he took, prompted more than one commentator to wonder why he had not been given more opportunities earlier in the tour.

It was meagre compensation, overall, for what was clearly an unsatisfactory tour for both Fender and MCC. As an intensely competitive person, Fender, more than most people, always disliked being beaten; he positively loathed it if he felt that not everything possible had been done to avoid it. The general disenchantment with cricket common to all losing teams on tour was probably responsible for Fender's hardly remembering that he took 12 wickets against South Australia at Adelaide just before sailing for home. His match analysis of 12–184 was the best return of his career, numerically, though he wondered, with typical humour, if he might not have been the only English bowler still willing to bowl at that stage. For several reasons South Australia were below strength and in plumb conditions they were dismissed for 195 after batting first. Fender's figures were 24.3–4–75–7 and as a fielder he was also responsible for a run out.

Feelings still ran high about criticisms of Australian crowd behaviour and umpires by Fender and Wilson in their press cables during the fifth Test. As still happens, these had been 'quoted back' from London to Australian newspapers and both players, at times, were barracked by the Adelaide crowd. When the state's innings ended, though, Fender was 'heartily cheered' as he left the field and the *Advertiser* also mentioned that 'one wag called out "now you've got something to write home about".' When MCC batted they scored 627 (Rhodes 210, Russell 201, Douglas 106 not out), this being the first time that two touring MCC players had made double centuries in the same innings. (Only Graveney and Watson at Georgetown in 1953–54 have done this since.) South Australia made 369 in their second innings and so were beaten by an innings and 63 runs. Fender, mixing spin and pace this time, was even given the second new ball and his figures were 30.1–3–109–5.

Three days later the Englishmen boarded the *Osterley* once again; the Australian side to England joined the ship at Fremantle and during the voyage beat their rivals at the various deck games as heavily as they had been beating them at cricket. Most of the MCC players disembarked at Toulon and travelled to Paris to pick up the Calais boat train. They arrived at Victoria Station at ten o'clock at night on Sunday, 17 April, seven months after leaving London, and were given a rousing reception from a huge crowd. As Fender wrote at the time: 'Judging by the warmth of our greeting, one would hesitate to guess what would have happened had we come back a winning side. . . .'

Fender was destined to play in only two more Test matches with Australia, the unsatisfactory drawn fourth and fifth games of the 1921 series, and it is appropriate to deal with these matches in this chapter. Fender, like all his generation, tended to link the 1920–21 and 1921 rubbers as one series, partly, no doubt, because the pattern and players involved in the ten Tests over a nine-month period were mostly the same, and partly because of the massive and contentious figure of Warwick Armstrong, the Australian captain. (It is a shame, incidentally, to knock down a famous legend, but Fender had no knowledge, and thought it highly unlikely, that Armstrong shovelled coal in the *Osterley*'s stokehold on the journey to England in a bid to trim his reputed twenty-two stone.)

Armstrong has remained in English cricketing minds as the ogre to end all ogres. It was a reputation founded on numerous rows at the time about the playing hours of an ill-planned itinerary for the 1921 tour. It also owed a great deal to some romanticized but exaggerated writing in numerous books since. Fender found Armstrong a far kinder and benevolent individual than the grim despot that has come down to posterity. He retained an enormous respect for Armstrong as a tough, shrewd captain, and, of course, as a fellow sparrer against authority. In later years in press boxes, they were firm allies and their conversation on the tactics being used, or more possibly not being used, would enthral those within earshot.

Fender believed that he learned more about handling bowlers in the field from Armstrong than from any other captain he ever watched, a tribute that lost nothing in significance even remembering the splendidly equipped attack that Armstrong had in his charge. In eight successive Tests England were overwhelmed and crushed in a manner not even matched entirely by Bradman's teams in 1946–47 and 1948, though Armstrong's sides in Australia, of course, were playing timeless Tests. Military similes quickly came to mind among cricketers whose First World War days were not far behind them and Fender always likened Armstrong's methods to those used by successful Army commanders.

Gregory and McDonald were the shock troops; Kelleway, Ryder, Collins, Hendry and Armstrong himself, at different times, were the troops of the line, stabilizing a position gained; Mailey was the mining section. He was allowed a free and unpredictable hand to explode when appropriate, with the runs conceded not mattering, if the wickets came. 'Never in my life did I have bowlers like Armstrong had, but the way he shuffled them about, the "thrust" at a new batsman, the "holding" operation if required, the field placings for different batsmen, these were the sort of things Armstrong showed me were possible and which no other captains seemed to think about in the same way. I know he did some silly things when he was bored, but when it mattered I don't think anybody ever got the better of Armstrong.'

This is a book about Fender and so it is no part of the brief to try and follow the collective thinking of the England selectors in 1921, which led to the use of thirty players in that summer's Test matches. The selectors had an impossible task, but many of their desperate changes bewildered people then and still do so. Fender began the season by no means well but started to take wickets in June and early July. It was a fiercely hit 101 at Lord's in a losing cause for the Gentlemen against the Players which finally led to his inclusion in a party of fifteen players for the fourth Test at Manchester, starting on Saturday, 23 July. By then Australia had retained the Ashes and Douglas, though keeping his place in the side, had been superseded as captain by Lionel Tennyson, later to be a fellow director in Fender's wine firm.

At the risk of repeating a theme already set down in these pages, it must be put on record there had been several advocates for Fender to be England captain in 1921 and three newspapers pursued the point when he was included in the party for the fourth Test. *The Times* said it would 'set many people wondering whether it would have been the best policy in May to choose him straightway as leader. His value on a side is appreciably diminished when he is not captain. However it is too late now for speculations of this kind. . . .' The *Morning Post* praised Fender's various all-round skills and commented: 'It is a belated choice for perhaps the best captain amongst the counties. He should have been given the leadership of an out-and-out new side in the first of the Tests at Trent Bridge. But that is an old story. . . .' The *Daily Express* was slightly more compromising than its august rivals but, looking ahead, pleaded for Fender to be made official vice-captain. 'Why not? We want the best brains at our disposal on the field to counter-balance the almost uncanny ingenuity and resource of Armstrong. Also we must keep our eyes on the next series of Test matches— and Fender still has youth and enthusiasm on his side.' Years later William Pollock looked back in *The Cream of Cricket*

(Methuen, 1934) and wrote of Fender at this time: 'In my opinion, the Jack to Warwick Armstrong's Ace—but never given the chance to come down on him.' It is fair to ask after all this time, were they all wrong?

There was no play at Manchester on the Saturday, drizzle leaving the field extremely wet. Any chance of starting was not finally abandoned until half-past five, by which time the crowd was sufficiently restless to need dispersal by the police. It was also noteworthy that this was one of the first times at a Test ground in England that the disappointed spectators were given pass-out tickets for Monday as compensation, despite the presence of the usual notices that no money would be refunded in the event of there not being any play. On a sodden, slow pitch, England on the Monday and Tuesday had the best of what play was left in this Test, which has become remembered only for Tennyson's illegal declaration and for Armstrong's bowling two successive overs. Fender was closely involved in both these incidents as he was batting with Ernest Tyldesley when they happened. Tennyson won the toss and England, led by Russell (101), scored consistently, if at times none too briskly by the standards of that time.

The conditions were all against the Australian bowlers and several catches, too, were put down. Immediately after tea Mead, with the total 260, was caught at cover trying to force the pace and Fender was promoted to No. 6 to increase the run rate. In fact Tyldesley cut loose the more effectively, though one report speaks of Fender being severe on Gregory, thereby forcing Armstrong to bowl himself to slow things down. At ten to six Tennyson came on to the field and waved in his batsmen, with England's score 341 for 4. Neither umpire nor some of the Australians followed Fender and Tyldesley off the field straight away, though eventually they did so. Meanwhile Armstrong, prompted by 'Sammy' Carter the Australian wicket-keeper, had gone into the English dressing-room and, equipped with a *Wisden*, had objected to the declaration. He pointed out that the match had become a two-day game. Under a law passed in 1914, the Australians were entitled to not less than one hour forty minutes batting on the first day of a two-day match if there was a declaration.

Fender had stripped and was snatching a quick bath before going out, as he thought, to field when Tennyson told him he had to continue his innings. Just over twenty minutes had elapsed when England resumed batting and there was another minute or two's delay while a section of the crowd barracked Armstrong, until Tennyson and A. E. 'Jim' Street, one of the umpires, went across and explained what had happened. Amid the hubbub nobody noticed that Armstrong, having bowled the last over before the stoppage, then proceeded to bowl the first over on the resumption. England added a further 21 runs before the end and finished the day 362 for 4 (Tyldesley 78 not out, Fender 44 not out). There was, as the *Daily Telegraph* put it, 'a comic interlude ere stumps were drawn'. Armstrong in the final fifteen minutes bowled two feet outside the leg stump to a predominantly leg-side field and Fender, switching hands on the bat, pulled one ball left-handed for 2 runs on to the vacant off-side. More rain fell overnight and next day Australia batted defensively—Collins staying almost five hours for 40—and the match ended tamely. Fender took 2 for 30 in 15 overs, having Andrews caught at mid-off from a full toss and soon afterwards bowling Taylor with a quicker googly.

The 1922 *Wisden* referred to Tennyson's forgetting the changed law and added: 'It was strange that no one in the pavilion remembered the existing Law sufficiently well to save him from such a blunder.' The next day's newspapers also assumed it was Tennyson's mistake and that everyone quickly recognized that Armstrong was right, as undoubtedly he seemed to have been. Fender believed, however, that a great many people claimed to have known better than Tennyson only with the benefit of hindsight. He had a distinct memory that the English dressing-room at the time was full of the most senior and experienced administrators in English cricket, all arguing the pros and cons. At that particular moment Tennyson was far from alone in not realizing he was mistaken, whatever line people took later. It was, after all, a relatively new law that did not need to be invoked often. English officialdom at that stage of the summer, too, was in the mood to bristle, or at least to be on its guard, at any view put forward by Armstrong. Fender pointed out that if the issue had been clear-cut and simple, it would never have taken twenty minutes to get everyone back on the field.

For once Fender, as he himself said, 'had the good sense not to stick my oar in, though I protested to Lionel that he was right and I have never been one hundred per cent happy about what was ruled. Don't run away with the idea that the arguments did not go on. It may sound a bit abstruse all these years later, but in my case I even wondered if the fixture was still a Test match after we lost Saturday's play. Tests were stipulated as being of three days' duration; nowhere that I could find did it specify that a Test could become a two-day or a one-day match if rain prevented it starting on time, whatever the laws of common practice decreed about other first-class matches.' Fender to his knowledge never saw this argued in print, but said that it came up that week-end in conversation among some of the players. At that time the only previous Test in England to have lost its opening day had been at Manchester in 1884 when the implementation of any two-day regulations had not arisen. Fender said: 'If it was to be a two-day match could it be a Test? Or putting it another way, if it was a Test, was not the Monday the second day and Lionel, therefore, entitled to declare when he wanted?'

Fender and Armstrong subsequently discussed the events that afternoon at Manchester during a train journey between Brisbane and Sydney they made together while reporting the 1928–29 series. Fender knew that the Australians, distrustful of the conditions, had not wanted to bat that Monday evening, and Armstrong confessed to Fender that his protest against Tennyson's declaration had been 'a try-on'. Carter had been convinced Tennyson was wrong; Armstrong had not been so sure but was willing to see 'to use up some time'. Fender also taxed Armstrong with having bowled 2 overs consecutively to provoke further discussion and to waste even more time. 'He would not answer this, but smiled and looked away.'

Fender at the time did not notice that Armstrong had bowled 2 consecutive overs. He did notice the almost unseemly haste with which Armstrong first tried to resume bowling as if anxious to gain his point that England had to continue batting. Some of the Australian fieldsmen were not in position when Armstrong attempted to resume bowling, though he stopped when the crowd shouted and yelled. Not all the newspapers next day even mentioned the 2 consecutive overs Armstrong delivered and some that did, suggested the crowd had spotted what the umpires missed. When Tennyson and Street quietened the noisiest section, Armstrong bowled as soon as the demonstration stopped, before Street could get back to his proper position.

Just over a fortnight later at The Oval the teams played another rain disrupted draw and again there were some unruly crowd scenes about the fitness of the ground for play after a hold-up.

Fender did nothing with either bat or ball in this match but earned a place in its story by being caught by Armstrong, who by that stage was in between whiles reading a newspaper in the outfield. It was Armstrong's final protest at the futility of travelling 13,000 miles to play three-day Tests in English weather conditions. Some three hours were left after each side had been able to complete an innings. After a brief onslaught from Gregory and McDonald had been withstood by Russell and George Brown, the Australians in their own so apt phrase, 'gave it away' and only Mailey was used of the front-rank bowlers.

The Times reported: 'Mr Armstrong took up his position on the farthest boundary by the Vauxhall entrance and declined to move either at the end of an over or when the ball came his way. But he did once run quite fast when Mr Fender hit "a balloon" off Mr Mailey. He got under the ball and brought off a distinctly good catch.' Frank Thorogood in the *Daily News* noted: 'Like the crafty alligator who basks with apparent indifference, the Australian captain always keeps one eye open, and it was a delightful incident to see him running nearly 20 yards from long-on to make this catch.' Fender, sent in at No. 3 'to give the crowd some fun', had been trying for a six. He regarded it as a compliment from a kindred spirit that Armstrong bestirred himself to take the catch. 'We enjoyed playing against each other and I suppose he felt he could not let me get away with anything.'

Fender played four other matches against the 1921 Australians. He was in Mr L. Robinson's XI, that had the better of a drawn match at Attleborough in early May, and Surrey lost both their games with the touring side, the only times Fender and Armstrong led opposing teams. The Australians won the first match in May by an innings, with Armstrong taking 12 wickets and Fender hitting hard for top score of 57 in the second innings as Surrey went down. The second meeting in mid-June threatened to bring the Australians their only defeat against a county. On the third morning Surrey, with 9 wickets standing, required 162 to win. The London newspapers, full of praise for Fender's handling of his team, were convinced Surrey would succeed. They urged people not to miss the finish, but Gregory's speed proved too much and, in something of an anti-climax, Surrey were beaten by 78 runs on the stroke of lunch.

Finally Fender played for Mr C. I. Thornton's XI at Scarborough in September as the Australians lost the last match of their tour. It was a game that brought Armstrong the first 'pair' of his career: 'Target for once of the ironies rather than their ruthless manipulator,' as Ronald Mason wrote in *Warwick Armstrong's Australians* (Epworth Press, 1971). This 'wry conclusion to his great campaign', came about when Fender caught Armstrong off Rhodes in the second innings. Fender revelled in the closing details as the accounts were read to him of how Woolley, Rhodes and Jupp brought victory with barely a minute or two to spare. Douglas was captain of Thornton's XI and Fender agreed it must have been pleasing for him to beat Armstrong's team at last. 'And you notice he did it with slow bowling, too,' Fender said. As already shown with Rhodes and the catch Fender dropped, cricketers have long memories.

7. In sun and shadow

The years 1921 to 1925 brought Fender's career to its zenith both as resourceful captain and brilliant all-rounder. In these five seasons Surrey finished second, third, fourth, third and second in the championship, the nearest they ever came under Fender to winning the title. His own contribution could seldom be measured in figures, but two summers in particular are worth noting. In 1921 Fender became the first man to take more than 50 catches in the same year that he performed the double, something that only Peter Walker (Glamorgan) in 1961 has done since; in 1923 he had his best all-round year with 1,427 runs, 178 wickets and 47 catches. From the start of this period, too, Fender staked his own special claim on the public consciousness and not only on followers of cricket. It was an aspect of Fender's life which must be explained if his stature as a celebrity is to be appreciated. He did after all become famous to a degree which, strictly speaking, came close to exceeding his merits as a player and the echoes lingered long after he left the game.

Right into old age Fender's name (and initials) still possessed that aura of newsworthiness which, though hard to define, lifts some people into the foreground and keeps them there. It is a question of personality as well as achievement, with chance and circumstances helping to decide that others as worthy, or even worthier, should pass unnoticed. In the early twenties ordinary people had few outlets for their enthusiasm and leisure time. It helped to explain why thousands would line London's streets to gape at a visiting child film-star from America, like Jackie Coogan, or wait for hours to watch a society wedding at St Margaret's, Westminster. Cricketers more than most sportsmen reaped their share of this sort of adulation and Fender benefited, too, from the fact that the national press then was so metropolitan orientated. Fender would always have been an outstanding cricketer, but his career would never have been spent in a ceaseless glare of publicity if he had played for Northamptonshire or Derbyshire and lived in Wellingborough or Buxton.

Instead, as we know, Fender exercised his flair with Surrey in
an era when an Oval crowd might be 20,000-strong, while away
from the game he was the proverbial man about town in London's
West End. There were always many reasons other than cricket,
therefore, for the endless column inches totted up by Fender.
There was Fender at first nights and Fender at dances; Fender at
the races and Fender at shoots; Fender taking part in the amateur
billiards championship and Fender refereeing international
bridge matches. Then there was Fender the wine merchant,
prominent at city functions and in club circles; and later the Fender family at presentations and royal garden parties. It was Fender
who was chosen to give one of the earliest radio talks on cricket in
the 2LO days at Savoy Hill; and it was Fender the part-time journalist who wrote so provocatively in the glossy magazines and the
London evening newspapers. Fender the godsend to cartoonists
has previously been mentioned; in this age it was both daring and
typical of Fender the amateur cricketer to use these drawings in
advertisements. The product was the brand of cigarettes he had
made specially for himself, another individualistic touch.

Three times Fender rejected Conservative offers to stand for
Parliament; another tentative approach from a Kent constituency
was hurriedly withdrawn after the local association's president,
Lord Harris, vetoed it. Fender was sufficiently well known to be
satirized in several London revues; a new MP wrote an article
claiming it was as hard to catch the Speaker's eye in the House as to
hold a hit by Mr Fender, and he did not have to explain who Mr
Fender was. All these activities and events were widely reported
in the press, and London alone at that time had nineteen morning
newspapers and five evenings, albeit of varying merit, to say
nothing of the two or three newspapers in each main provincial
city. A lot written about Fender was no doubt trivial but he
became one of the most easily recognizable people in public life.

Fender had a certain style about him and the English public
have always welcomed this in their heroes. It was the Charleston
age for the privileged and Fender had his share of the giddy
times, though in his case he had to work hard as well. What
would now be termed his image was different in every respect
from most other ex-public schoolboy cricketers of the period.
He had the knack of communicating his enjoyment. Above all he
seldom lost the common touch; nobody in circles less fortunate
ever begrudged Fender the pattern of his life. There was, of

course, no doubt that eyebrows were collectively raised sometimes in cricket's hierarchy, but the suspicion that Fender was a martyr to some undisclosed whim of authority did nothing to detract from his popularity. Taken together it accounted for why Fender's name loomed so large then and why old men remember it with gladness and a smile to this day.

Enough of Fender's approach has already been shown to make a game-by-game look at his cricket needless. His form was too often transient to provide the sort of statistics that justify a detailed breakdown. Those who want to examine Fender's performances in such a way are first recommended to read Louis Palgrave's excellent Surrey history *The Story of The Oval* (Cornish Brothers, Birmingham, 1949) and then the relevant daily accounts in the newspaper files and *Wisden*. It is the intention in these pages to touch upon the more special feats and controversies of his cricket life. The previous chapter mentioned a hundred made by Fender in the Gentlemen v. Players match at Lord's in 1921, that restored him to the England side. It was as fine an innings as he ever played at the highest level, despite earlier in the day having been prevented from fielding by a gastric upset. Fender (101) and J. C. White (21) added 112 in forty minutes for the ninth wicket against Parkin, Durston, L. Cook, Woolley, Hearne and Rhodes. The first 89 runs of this partnership were scored in thirty-five minutes on the Thursday evening and averted an innings defeat for the Gentlemen inside two days.

Facing arrears of 231, the Gentlemen were 160 for 8 when White joined Fender, who, according to *The Times*, had been unusually quiet for some time. 'But when the slow bowlers were replaced by Durston and Cook, he let himself go. He hit Durston for six in front of square-leg, broke his bat in on-driving Cook, borrowed Mr White's and hit the next ball into the pavilion. In ten minutes or so he went from 25 to 61.' The crowd protested with shouts of 'Play it out' as Rhodes began to lead the Players from the field at half-past six, but after a signal from Tennyson on the balcony play continued until 6.45. By then Fender was 84 not out and had ensured that the Players would have to bat again. They eventually won by nine wickets but as *The Times* put it: 'All who saw his innings will now be able to talk for the rest of their lives of "Fender's Hundred" and compare it with one Mr. Jessop made on an historic occasion at the Oval.'

Fender always enjoyed the Gentlemen v. Players fixtures. 'At

Lord's they were invariably hard-fought games. In my time it used to be a point of honour among the professionals that no amateur got a hundred without deserving it and the records show how few Gentlemen did make a hundred in the series. I know in this game one or two of their bowlers were thoroughly irked by what I had managed to do. I suspect they felt I was not good enough to get a hundred against them. That is why they wanted to finish promptly at half-past six. It meant they lost their chance to win that evening but I would have been interrupted in full flow earlier than I was.'

This match was played on a fast, dry pitch of irregular bounce and two descriptions of Fender's method bear repetition. *The Times* noted: 'Mr Fender aimed at some extraordinary places on the boundary and sometimes hit places more extraordinary still. But his cutting was beautifully orthodox and good cutting is essential to a first-class hitter. Mr Fender's performance in saving the innings defeat on such a wicket was veritably great.' H. J. Henley in the *Daily Mail* wrote: 'Hitting flat-footed, with that quick, semi-circular swing of the bat of his, he treated the professional bowlers as if they were third-rate club men. It was a triumph for eye and wrist—and audacity. Balls of perfect length he treated as though they were long hops or half volleys. He thumped them through the covers and pulled them severely to square-leg or lifted them high into the outfield.'

Surrey's second place in the county table that year was achieved without Hobbs, who was able to play only one championship game because of injury and illness, and they also had seven men picked by England at least once. It was a summer of great heat and hard wickets and several of Surrey's fifteen wins were nail-biting affairs that stemmed from shrewdly timed declarations by Fender. At times even his resilience was taxed by the excitement and the physical strain. After Middlesex were beaten by 19 runs at The Oval, Fender felt so exhausted that he slept for three hours on a pile of towels on the floor of the amateurs' dressing-room. He was finally woken by a club attendant wishing to lock up. Kent were beaten by 75 runs on the stroke of time and the newspapers reported that the crowd rushed in front of The Oval pavilion and 'cheered themselves hoarse for 15 minutes'. This was Hitch's benefit match and 58,000 paid for admission, in addition to members.

A good win against Leicestershire in the season's last home

match led to arguments which lasted in the newspapers for several days. Tom Sidwell, the Leicestershire wicket-keeper, had gone in as night-watchman on the second evening, but he lost his way on the Underground next morning and was not present in time for the start. Fender declined to let him resume batting later after the umpires sought guidance from Lord's at Fender's request. MCC ruled that as Sidwell had not been kept away by illness or accident, and was not present, he had to be regarded as out, *unless the opposing captain consented to let him bat out of order*. Fender, for all his own manœuvrings inside the laws, was a stickler for the proprieties and could be intolerant if he felt the other person or team had only themselves to blame.

His decision in this instance was thought harsh in some quarters but the great majority of newspaper opinion supported him. The correspondents pointed out that Fender had already taken a big risk in declaring late on the second day and leaving Leicestershire plenty of time to make the 335 they needed on a pitch playing better than any previous time. Sidwell had gone in to suit Leicestershire and it was not fair for him to resume when the Surrey attack might no longer be fresh, was another point of view stressed.

The other side of Fender's character in this sort of incident was seen on the first day of Surrey's game with Sussex in 1924. Fender himself was late this time and in his absence Jardine tossed with Arthur Gilligan. By the time Fender arrived, torrential rain had stopped play after 4 overs from Tate and Gilligan. Sussex had recalled Robert Relf to their side after a two-year absence and during the hold-up it was realized that Relf was no longer qualified for Sussex. He had interrupted his qualification by playing for Berkshire, his native county, the year before. Once again Lord's was rung for guidance.

As the match had started, MCC suggested that Sussex, though in the wrong, should continue to play Relf; alternatively they should play with only ten men and Gilligan decided that this was what Sussex should do. Fender, however, would not hear of it and, as Gilligan said, 'generously and sportingly' told Sussex to send for a replacement. A wire was sent to Haywards Heath for one Parks (J. H.), which was how this famous player earned his first chance in the Sussex side. Fender this time was censured by the newspapers because the matter was pursued at all, but Gilligan strongly defended him. In his book *Sussex Cricket* (Chapman & Hall, 1933) Gilligan wrote that the Sussex oversight was entirely their own fault. Criticism of Fender and the Surrey committee was 'extremely unfair in every way'.

Surrey's only defeats in the championship in 1921 were against Nottinghamshire and Middlesex and both contained points of interest. Fender persuaded the Surrey selectors to include a lob bowler, Trevor Molony, aged twenty-three, at Trent Bridge in mid-May and it was not Molony's fault that Surrey were beaten by 7 wickets. Molony, to date, remains the last lob bowler to be picked specifically by a county to bowl underarm. Fender's family connection with lob bowling has been mentioned and it was fitting for him to be the last English county captain to use one. Molony took 3 for 11 in 7 overs as Nottinghamshire made 201 in the first innings. According to the *Cricketer* of 21 May Molony bowled leg theory with an inner and outer ring of four men apiece, with only a mid-off on the off-side. He was accurate, varied his flight and bowled 'exceedingly good full tosses at an awkward height' and caused batsmen to lash out in desperation.

The magazine went on: 'The attempts of the last few batsmen in the Notts side to play him were ludicrous and evinced much laughter from the crowd.' Payton and Barratt were both caught on the leg-side boundary and Whysall, who took guard outside the leg stump, was held at mid-off as he tried to swat the ball through the empty covers with an overhead tennis shot. Fender enjoyed the fun more than most, but he hardly used Molony in the other two matches he played. Molony disappeared from first-class cricket as suddenly as he had emerged, and his death in Cannes in 1962 went unreported by *Wisden*. It was always rumoured in later years that it was Strudwick as much as anyone who had objected to Molony's bowling because of the dangerous way that batsmen swung round violently as they aimed their hits. The *Nottingham Journal* on 16 May commented: 'The lob always was and is a stratagem. Its weakness is its strength because it is unconventional. What would cricket be like if all bowlers adopted the underhand style? Well, batsmen would learn to score without falling readily into simple traps.'

For the second season in succession Middlesex and Surrey met in the summer's final game at Lord's in a fixture that would settle the championship and again it was Middlesex who won both the match and the title. Surrey this time would have been champions if they had won, and for much of the game they were well placed. Surrey scored 269 and dismissed Middlesex for 132. Nigel Haig and Durston were mainly responsible for Surrey's being restricted to 184 in their second innings and Middlesex set out to make 322 to win with fifteen minutes left on the second evening. A second wicket stand of 229 between R. H. Twining (135) and Hearne (106) effectively won the match on the last day; a chance by Twining at 59 to first slip from the first ball Fender bowled after lunch was the only blemish by either man. Middlesex won by 6 wickets at five past six as Fender shuffled seven bowlers without success. As Louis Palgrave wrote: 'No-one could begrudge Middlesex their splendid win after everything seemed lost but P. G. H. Fender was unlucky in failing—right at the last hurdle—to secure the championship for his county in the first year of his leadership.'

In 1922 Fender played three of the most spectacular innings of his life. He hit 185 out of 294 in 130 minutes against Hampshire at The Oval in his second match of the season. Then in early June came the unbeaten 91 in fifty minutes which brought defeat to Leicestershire after they misjudged a declaration. This was the match mentioned in the first chapter when Fender allegedly 'conned' the opposing captain. Finally Fender scored 137 out of 217 in ninety minutes against Kent at The Oval in late July. The statistics from the sort of aggressive stroke-making shown in these innings can never convey its brilliance, and though discrepancies abounded in the newspaper reports, some of the facts claimed justify a mention.

Against Hampshire, wearing his new glasses, Fender arrived in mid-afternoon with Surrey 161 for 4. Kennedy forced him to go carefully at first before he slogged 154 in little more than ninety minutes. Fender reached his hundred in eighty-five minutes just before tea, surviving difficult chances at 22 and 94 to deep extra cover and long-on, the fielders losing the ball each time in the sun. After tea, Fender took 52 from fourteen consecutive balls bowled to him. When he was finally caught in front of the pavilion, he had struck three sixes, three fives and twenty-five fours. Vigorous drives, cuts and pulls brought most of his runs. Several reports mentioned that the wicket was pitched well towards the left, looking out from the pavilion, and that many of Fender's strokes carried over 100 yards on the other side of the field and would have earned 6 runs on most grounds.

Against Kent at The Oval, the *Sporting Life* reported that Fender made 50 out of 74 in forty-seven minutes and reached 100 out of 135 twenty minutes later. When he was bowled by Woolley he

P. G. H. FENDER'S DAY AT THE OVAL

5. *Fender's first match in glasses was, inevitably, noted by the famous cartoonist Tom Webster in 1922*

had hit three sixes, one five and eighteen fours and had made no errors. Fender had come in half an hour before lunch on the second day and it was not until after the interval that he cut loose with 51, coming from 5 overs by Ashdown and Woolley, as Miles Howell contributed a single. When G. J. Bryan bowled from the Vauxhall end, Fender hit his first ball on the rise for one of cricket's most famous sixes. A slashed stroke against a widish half volley sent the ball over extra cover's head and it sailed out of the ground towards the gasworks. Gerald Brodribb in *Hit for Six* (Heinemann, 1960) wrote that E. H. D. Sewell had the shot measured later and it was 132 yards from the wicket to where it went over the wall. It reputedly hit the gasworks gates across the road, still on the full pitch. Bryan's next ball was on-driven for 5 and Fender and Peach took 38 from Bryan's first ten balls, despite a ten-minute rain stoppage in his first over.

This was the first summer that Fender was forced to use himself as both Surrey's principal attacking bowler and as the side's stock bowler. Rushby had finished playing and neither Hitch nor Peach was as successful as usual. Fender's 1,100 overs seem to have been split in rough proportion, four to one, between leg-spin and medium pace. In both styles he consistently took wickets: the first ten matches of the season brought him 71, including 10 wickets in a match once, 9 on three occasions and 8 on another. There was no falling away in his slip fielding and as *Wisden* said: 'Over and above all this he was, by general consent, by far the best of the county captains, never losing his grip of the game and managing his side with a judgement that was seldom at fault.'

Sydney Pardon, *Wisden*'s Editor, wrote an article in *The Times* as early as May that year claiming that if England had needed to select a Test team in 1922, Fender was the only amateur whose inclusion would mean that a better-qualified professional had not been omitted. Pardon and other good judges modified their view of amateur standards after the University and Gentlemen v. Players matches, but Fender was certainly unfortunate that in 1922 and 1923 there were no Test matches in England in which he could have shown his mettle.

Early in August 1922, Fender and Lord Harris were involved in a controversy that, for once, was nothing to do with Fender personally and neither were the two men in direct conflict. In an almost bizarre episode Kent suddenly queried the residential qualification of Alfred Jeacocke, the Surrey amateur batsman, and

MCC upheld their objection. Jeacocke's offence was that two years earlier he had moved to a house on the Kent side of the Forest Hill Road marking the boundary between Surrey and Kent. There had been a housing shortage in 1920 when Jeacocke married, and his father lent him the accommodation concerned rent free until he found a property that suited him.

To Fender as Surrey captain and spokesman fell the task of defending Jeacocke and explaining to the newspapers why Jeacocke had to miss the rest of the season. The *Evening Standard* of 15 August quoted Fender: 'Mr Jeacocke has now been back in Surrey for some time. But the fact he broke his qualification is considered sufficient, in spite of the circumstances, to keep him out of first-class cricket for two years—that is until about the middle of 1924. I repeat that it is absolutely through no fault of his own, but the strict letter of the law is that he should not be allowed to play. It cannot be too often repeated that the reason why he lived "out of Surrey" was the housing difficulty over which he had no control.'

Lord Harris, earlier that season, had brought about W. R. Hammond's removal from the Gloucestershire team because he was not properly qualified. The story which quoted Fender carried the following statement from Lord Harris: 'The Kent committee does not conceive it to be its duty to hunt about the country for cases on suspicion but where it knows the facts it does think itself bound, in loyalty to its comrades, the first-class counties, to ask for an inquiry through the committee of MCC. I am glad to say that my conscience does not prick me, and I am not aware that my colleagues of the Kent committee are suffering from any contrition because we have done our best to secure respect for the rules laid down by the counties.' The whole incident caused quite a furore at the time. (Defending his actions in the *Cricketer* later, Lord Harris was to write: 'Bolshevism is rampant and seeks to abolish all laws and rules, and this year cricket has not escaped its attack.')

Fender, though angry, was thoroughly restrained in everything he said publicly, but others were far more forthright and felt that Kent had behaved badly. Prominent headlines like 'Fender's defence of Jeacocke' and 'Surrey Captain replies to Lord Harris' probably did Fender no good, though, in NW8. There was a happy postscript to this affair when Jeacocke was able to return for Surrey in 1923. The regulations were changed to allow any cricketer who had played for a county for three years—as Jeacocke had for Surrey—to be deemed qualified for that county for the rest of his career. Jeacocke used to start work in the family business at Smithfield Market at 3 a.m. before getting a taxi to The Oval in time for the start of play. He would tease the Surrey professionals that they did not know what it was like to do a day's work.

This year also saw the start of another episode in Fender's career, which quite unintentionally, was to incur a frown in due course from authority. Fender was mainly instrumental in launching a short-lived Royal Air Force Festival in late September to raise money for the RAF Club, which had just moved from Bruton Street to its premises in Piccadilly. Senior cricket administrators at first welcomed these games and lent their names to the organizing committee. The leading players took part from 20–26 September at Eastbourne in fixtures between North v. South and ex-RAF v. The Rest of England. In 1923 the programme was switched to Hastings where the Capped met the Uncapped and Lord Cowdray's XI played the Rest. It did not prove ideal to play cricket so late in the English autumn and attendances barely covered expenses, but the weeks proved enjoyable social occasions.

In 1924 the RAF Festival gained in status when the South Africans played the South of England in the first match, followed again by Lord Cowdray's XI v. The Rest, but that year the week had been advanced to 3–9 September, mainly because of MCC's impending departure for Australia. The changed dates meant a clash with the Scarborough Festival, which was deprived of several leading players. Some of these, according to Fender, preferred the RAF Festival anyway because they stayed at the best hotels with the amateurs and were included in the accompanying functions more often than was the case at Scarborough. After 1924, Fender gathered it was made clear to several professionals that Scarborough was to have prior claim on their services and this contributed to the decision to allow the RAF Festival to lapse. Once again there had been no open rift between Fender and the Establishment but, to put it no higher, he had been associated with something which cut across officialdom's own preferences.

MCC included six amateurs at South Africa's request in their side to tour there in 1922–23. Hobbs and Hearne decided to conserve their strength by wintering at home, but it was still a strong team with Fender, of course, an automatic choice on everybody's list. There had been plenty of newspaper advocacy for him to be captain or, failing that, for Tennyson, England's captain the year before, to be appointed. Several newspapers openly expressed their disappointment in the choice of Frank Mann. They queried his right to a place in the team and saw his selection as bias towards someone with strong associations with Lord's. Mann's appointment, in fact, was in keeping with MCC's approach to this sort of tour at the time and he had enormous success in ambassadorial terms. The goodwill and popularity Mann inspired in South Africa have only been approached in that country since, among MCC captains, by his son George Mann in 1948–49. Mann appointed Fender vice-captain during the voyage to Capetown, but did not miss a match himself so Fender never led the side on tour.

Fender found the South Africans among the most lavish hosts he met in his life, but the tour had its share of frustrations for him. He seldom enjoyed playing cricket on matting wickets; many of the matches outside the main centres were against opposition too weak to make for a proper contest; and there was often less time in each place compared with an itinerary in Australia, so the players grew weary of the ceaseless train travel. There were also, it appears, one or two personality clashes among the MCC party. These were never allowed to interfere with the cricket and the team brought great satisfaction to their supporters at home by gaining England's first Test successes since 1913–14 in the same country. The London newspapers were in despair when South Africa won the first Test by 168 runs, but England won the second by 1 wicket: the next two were drawn and England won the fifth by 109 runs.

Like others before him, Fender was continually amazed by the way matting wickets could vary from ground to ground according to the type of surface on which the mat was laid—grass, sand, gravel or ant-heap. Its tautness had an important bearing on the mat's behaviour: some were merely pegged at the corners and others stretched by nails all along the edges. Common to most matting wickets, however, was a far higher degree of bounce than on turf wickets: as a batsman Fender found it harder to play the ball in attack or to keep it down defensively; as a bowler he found the ball often turned too much or rose over the top of the stumps. South Africans, similarly, had big adjustments to make outside the Union as it then was. Fender found Blanckenberg's brisk spin on the mat as difficult to play as any he ever met in his life. Blanckenberg was never anything like as effective in England in 1924, but it still gave Fender enormous satisfaction to make a hundred against him for Surrey. Blanckenberg lost all touch with the cricket world after he stopped playing. He was understood to have moved to Germany and in South African reference books and in *Wisden* he is listed as 'Presumed dead'.

Fender began the tour well with aggressive innings of 96 and 89 against Western Province at Capetown and Eastern Province at Port Elizabeth, both helping MCC to recover from poor starts, but after this his best score was 60 in the third Test at Durban. It was the first use of Kingsmead, Durban, as a Test venue—six months earlier the ground had been part of a swamp. That was one of the few times when Fender, by his standards, was considered to have adopted a stonewaller's role. He batted three hours for his 60, helping to add 154 with Mead (181) after England were 71 for 4 on the first day. Fender, who hit only three fours, was finally held at short mid-on from what he claimed was a bump ball. The *Daily Mail*, commentating on the Reuter cables, said of this innings: 'He curbed his natural inclination. He shelved his wide array of strokes. . . . an unrecognisable Fender, surely!'

In all matches on the tour Fender, with 79 wickets (average 17.89), was second to Kennedy (82) in terms of wicket aggregate, but he was expensive in the Tests with his 10 wickets costing 41.80 each. On paper Fender's best return was the 7–55 he took against Orange Free State at Bloemfontein in the tour's pen-ultimate game, but his most significant bowling came at the start of the second Test at Capetown. The Newlands mat was laid on grass and Fender found he had more control of the ball there than anywhere else; he also made clever use of a cross-wind that was blowing. Less than three hours after the Test began, South Africa had been bundled out for 113 and Fender was involved in 5 of the first 6 wickets to fall. At the start he caught George Hearne at slip from the first ball Macaulay delivered. The total was 22 when Fender bowled. His first ball had Catterall caught behind by Brown and soon afterwards he bowled Taylor with one that came straight on.

In Fender's first over after lunch he had Nourse leg before. Brann at the other end was bowled by Kennedy before Fender struck again. This time Ling lifted a ball behind the bowler and Mann ran across from mid-on to hold the catch. South Africa were 67 for 6 and Fender was rested soon afterwards, finishing the innings with 14–4–29–4. He remembered it as one of the best pieces of bowling of his life. According to South African newspapers he bowled slower than usual with a low trajectory and obtained both turn and lift. The Reuter cables quoted the other English players as saying they had never seen Fender bowl better and that his swerve was 'phenomenal'. All through it was a fluctuating match. England finally needed 173 to win and they were 86 for 6 before Mann and Jupp, both surviving chances, added 68 for the seventh wicket, although 5 runs were still required when Macaulay, the last man, joined Kennedy. Macaulay's only scoring stroke was the winning hit.

Fender spent a lot of time with Arthur Carr on that tour. Carr, an outstanding driver of the ball, had a miserable time on the mat. Fender and Carr often practised at the nets together trying to work out their problems, Fender experimenting with different types of delivery and Carr trying to master the ball's steep rise. Fender had long believed that Carr would be an even better batsman if he improved his cutting. 'Arthur could drive like a team of runaway horses but he couldn't cut and I was always on to him to improve his cutting. My theory was that it helped to unsettle a bowler's length if you hit through the covers as early as possible. To this end I would stand outside my crease, the bowler would drop the ball shorter and shorter and, hey presto, you could take advantage with a cut. They did not know what to do next. Arthur's batting was better built to do this than mine, but he never did learn to cut properly, to my mind.'

Carr kept wicket at Kimberley when Brown and Livesey were both injured and Fender 'enjoyed' bamboozling his friend as much as he did the batsmen. Fender took 3 wickets in four balls early in the match and Griqualand West were beaten in two days. It gave Fender the chance to accept an invitation to go trekking with two friends for a few days. During the trip they 'panned' for diamonds and between them secured some minor stones which earned them £78. 'Enough to pay for the hire of my horse,' Fender said. Another memory came in the next match against East Rand at Benoni when play was ended prematurely by a dust storm, frightening in its intensity. Without warning a fierce wind raised the dust on the sandy and gritty ground within a few seconds and with such force that from the stands the players disappeared from sight. The newspapers reported that both the

cricketers' flannels and the white muslin frocks of women spectators were quickly clothed in brick-red dust as if they had been in
a tub of dye. Canvas tents and the luncheon marquee were
shredded to ribbons by the wind's force, and the match was
abandoned.

One other aspect of this South African tour concerned Fender's
work in the wine trade. In following his cricket career, the story
has moved ahead of developments in his business life. Like most
other servicemen returning from a war, Fender's experiences in
uniform had changed him: he was older, of course, and had
matured in many ways. In 1919–20 he found that work with his
father's firm was limiting, and he had his full quota of the restless-
ness common in those circumstances. Mr Fender recognized the
signs and accepted them. There was no acrimony, but Fender
broke away and, using his own contacts and friends, he began his
own wine business in High Holborn with his brother, Robert,
and another friend. Simultaneously he founded another company,
Fender Brothers, to look after his paper-merchant interests,
though not many years passed before he relinquished his connection with this firm. Fender gave his shares to his brother as a
wedding present: Robert Fender was later to move to the West
Country and in 1968 became High Sheriff of Gloucestershire.

Fender continued to work part time with his father at Crescens
Robinson and in 1922 became a director, eventually succeeding
his father as chairman in 1943 and holding office for twenty-five
years. His wine business flourished from the start, initially as
Herbert Fender & Co. and later as Fender, Tennyson, Yetts and
Mills, and Fender himself remained chairman and managing
director until 1976. From High Holborn the firm moved to premises at the old police court in Marylebone Lane where, for
some years, the former cells proved ideal as wine cellars, and later
on to Grosvenor Street until after the Second World War. In
Grosvenor Street they were surrounded by the London fashion
houses and this particular section of London business life formed
a large part of their clientele, though by no means all. Fender's
own interests and friends spilled into many different professions
and trades, and Fender boardroom luncheons, both for the ex-
cellence of the food and wine, and for the variety of the guest
lists, established a special reputation of their own.

Part of all this was the carefree and genial presence of Lionel
Tennyson, who was invited by Fender to join the board after

Tennyson returned, out of pocket, from leading S. B. Joel's private tour to South Africa in 1924–25. Anyone wishing to get a glimpse of the jovial and rumbustious character that made up the third Baron Tennyson should read his own books *From Verse to Worse* (Cassell, 1933) and *Sticky Wickets* (Christopher Johnson, 1950). John Arlott once wrote that Tennyson, as gambler, drinker and trencherman, was a Regency Buck born out of period. Fender knew both Tennyson's faults and attributes: they complemented each other splendidly in the wine business and the firm prospered.

'Lionel was a great friend; he knew everybody and had the knack of bringing in business. He was a bit of an extrovert and some people thought him irresponsible at times. But he certainly never let me or the business down and we had some wonderful times.' Their association carried over into cricket, of course, and Surrey–Hampshire matches definitely tended to be enjoyable affairs for everyone. 'Neither team was usually contending for honours,' Fender said, 'and nothing involving Lionel could ever be dull.' Both men shared a liking for Bournemouth, its hotels and other social assets, and during the winter were always urging their respective committees for Surrey's match in Hampshire to be played there. They did not always succeed in this, but the story gives an idea of the atmosphere in which the fixture was played.

Like all private wine merchants at that time, Fender had his own brand of whisky, a mature blend, bottled in Scotland, of course, and labelled P.G.H. In due course there followed the L.T. label, a younger liqueur type of whisky with a blue coronet on its label, which remains especially popular to this day in Spain, among other places. Fender took several cases of P.G.H. with him to South Africa in 1922–23 and secured an agent in Durban; it proved extremely popular. Numerous hotels and clubs began to stock P.G.H. over the years, but eventually the larger distilling companies objected, and threatened reprisals to Fender's clients. Some years later Fender had to ship several cases of P.G.H. back home. 'It was a sales war we lost, frankly, but it was good experience and had been profitable for a time.'

When Fender, at the age of eighty-four, went out to Australia for the Centenary Test in 1977, he investigated the possibilities of exporting whisky once more under a P.G.H. label. There was even talk that the label should carry a mention of his thirty-five-minute hundred, but the scheme fell down because the Australians wished to import in bulk. Fender had insisted that his whisky had to be bottled in Scotland. 'I am as proud of my own whisky as of any of my cricket records and I was not going to run any risk of it being blended with Japanese or anybody else's brands.'

There was a touch of irony about Fender's selling whisky in South Africa during MCC's tour because, among the duties allocated to him as vice-captain by Mann, was the job of ensuring that one of the amateurs in the side did not touch whisky. After all this time the story does not harm anyone: the player concerned could drink any amount of champagne and other wine or beer and remain perfectly sober, but after a couple of whiskies he became thoroughly disagreeable. 'I met a number of people like that over the years, where spirits were concerned,' Fender remembered.

He was also asked more than once in his life how, as an active sportsman, he could reconcile this with making his living from selling alcohol. 'I could only fall back on the clichés, I'm afraid: there has to be moderation in all things. If you have too many glasses of wine or anything else you don't enjoy them; you merely drink them.' Fender was different from most cricketers in that he loathed beer or shandy, irrespective of how hot the day had been. He enjoyed a whisky and soda during a match or after it, but he preferred to take a warm bath if he had sweated a lot. Often he would even take a bath during the lunch or tea intervals and The Oval dressing-room attendant got to know by instinct when the captain would want a bath and would have one ready for him.

In 1923 Surrey at last beat Kent at Blackheath and Fender had a lot to do with the success. It was Surrey's first win in Kent since 1897 at Beckenham, and ten defeats and three draws had been Surrey's fate since 1906, when they had regularly played Kent at the Rectory Field. In good weather Surrey batted first and were 114 for 5 before Fender hit judiciously for the top score of 73 (ten fours) and Surrey reached 272. Kent were 42 for 4 by Saturday's close, after a fine opening spell by Hitch, and they were all out for 125. Fender, with 67 not out, again had the best score as Surrey made 262 for 7 in their second innings before declaring, and Kent needed 410 to win. On Monday evening Seymour and Woolley made 73 without being separated and the total was 135 for 1 next day, when Woolley had to retire hurt after being struck on the arm by Sadler. Kent's batting then collapsed and they were dismissed for 187, which gave Surrey victory by 222 runs.

Fender took 4–51 and held 2 catches in the closing stages, his all-round form, the *Morning Post* said, 'lending weight to the clamour for his appointment as an England captain'. The end of what they felt was a Kentish hoodoo meant more than can be appreciated to every member of the Surrey team from Hobbs downwards. Fender, after Surrey's customary defeat at Blackheath the year before, had inadvertently offered the non-smoking Strudwick a cigarette as they left the ground in 1922. 'No thank you, Mr Fender—I'll have my first when we beat them here,' Strudwick said. Fender remembered this as he went out to the Surrey charabanc, but he found Strudwick already smoking and the Surrey team laughing about it. 'I decided not to wait for yours, Mr Fender.' The Kent committee presented a ball used in this match to Fender. In turn, he gave it as a ninetieth birthday present to Strudwick in January 1970, only a fortnight, as it proved, before the wicket-keeper died.

Fender's figures for 1923, in the Appendix of this book, confirm why *Wisden* commented: 'The amount of work he got through was astonishing but he kept fresh to the end.' Surrey scored runs galore, but nobody other than Fender could get enough wickets and their record included thirteen draws. Yorkshire were champions, the second of four consecutive titles they won, and it was one of their greatest seasons—twenty-five wins in thirty-two matches and the championship assured by 17 August. Surrey's 360 in a rain-ruined game at The Oval was the highest total all summer against Yorkshire, and Surrey also came quite close to beating them at Sheffield. Needing 184, Surrey were 127 for 3 at tea, but afterwards Kilner took 5 wickets and Surrey lost by 25 runs.

Other than first innings points, there was no reward for a drawn match at this time and a cheeky declaration by Fender at Bath in early May epitomized his approach on many occasions over the years. Surrey, who had trailed on the first innings, declared soon after Hobbs reached his hundredth hundred. They left Somerset 168 in even time to win, but victory went to Surrey by 10 runs at 6.50 p.m. As Hubert Preston wrote in the *People*: 'Such boldness seems to sterilise the opposition. . . . Fender had everything to gain and nothing to lose, and by giving his opponents plenty of time to get the runs, he brought off a triumph when the chances seemed all against him.'

Some critics noted that Fender seemed to have acquired a

modicum of restraint when it was necessary this season, but it was
a relative term. Against Gloucestershire at Bristol Fender batted
two and a half hours to save Surrey from defeat. The reports said
he sacrificed many runs to keep the bowling, but still hit brilliantly
and finished 124 not out. When Nottinghamshire came to The
Oval, the 25,000 August Bank Holiday Monday crowd saw Hobbs
make 105 in his best style, but Surrey were still 101 runs behind
with only 4 wickets left. Fender then made 50 in thirty-three
minutes and 103 in seventy-five minutes. He hit nineteen fours,
including five in one over against Flint's medium pace.

Fender took part in thirty-six matches between 2 May and
25 September, the most he ever played in one summer, and in only
five games did he not have to bowl in both innings. His best
figures came at Edgbaston where, in 14.5 overs, he captured
Warwickshire's last 7 wickets for 34 in their first innings. Quaife
(W. G.) made 33 not out and eluded him, but Fender bowled Mr
B. W. Quaife for 0. Reporters were just starting to comment on
Fender's habit of coming on to the field through the same gate as
his professionals. Several linked this with comments on the
anomaly of having a father and son with different status in the same
side.

For the first time Fender played against the West Indians this
year and Surrey at The Oval were thrashed by 10 wickets. George
Challenor scored 155 not out and 66 not out and Fender was in-
trigued by the way the West Indian deliberately and safely played
the ball over the top of the slips on several occasions. He had never
seen this done with such certainty before and in time added this
unorthodox stroke to his own repertoire. 'I found this upper cut
pretty effective to anything that was rising on or outside the off
stump, whatever the textbooks might say. Sometimes one edged
the ball, but I never remember being caught playing this shot.
In effect you were helping it on its way; it saved you having to
pull the ball round to leg off your face.' Fender's virtuosity always
made him willing to dabble in unusual stroke-making, not least
if there was nothing at stake and the crowd needed a diversion.
Late in his career he occasionally played the 'draw' stroke which
had gradually become obsolete in the second half of the nineteenth
century. The batsman had to angle his bat so that the ball was
glanced between his legs and the stumps towards long leg. 'It
would amuse the fielders as much as the crowd,' Fender said.
In the same season Fender also played against the West Indians

at Scarborough for a strong side raised by Leveson-Gower. This was the famous match when Leveson-Gower's XI were left 28 to win and lost Hobbs, Stevens, Tyldesley, Rhodes, Chapman and Mann with 19 on the board before Douglas and Fender won the game 'with some lucky snicks', as Fender put it.

Fender took part in both Test trials in 1923 when, amid the inevitable press discussion, the sides were led by Mann and Carr after many people expected Fender to be one of the captains. Fender turned in a match-winning performance in the first trial at Old Trafford on 23 June when the South beat the North by 38 runs. Fender held 4 slip catches off Tate in the first innings and, late in the game, hit 49 crucial runs and then took 6–44, including 5 for 17 in 12.2 overs to end the match. Before the second trial at Lord's on 18 August, between England and The Rest, the arguments in print became even more numerous about Fender's position. G. A. Faulkner in the *Westminster Gazette* wrote: 'I cannot help saying that Fender has every cause to feel that the Selection Committee have been more than unkind to him in so blinding themselves to the good work he has put in for the last few years as captain of Surrey. . . . To have made Fender captain of The Rest was the least the Selection Committee could have done for him. He has thoroughly earned the right to a trial in this capacity and I cannot help feeling that people are beginning to wonder if Fender isn't rather being "Convicted without a trial".'

An article, signed Tityrus, in *Athletic News* at this time said: 'It has been said that ever since the armistice was signed that cricket is in dire need of attractive personalities. That may be, but no sooner does a man of this calibre forge his way to the front by ability and fearless self-assertion than he seems to be much criticized. . . . Possibly Fender is the kind of captain who insists on the rigour of the game, on the observance of the law, who never yields a point to any rival captain or player and is too exact, precise, and unyielding for the tremendous majority of his brother amateurs. Gentlemen who play cricket are as a rule very casual kind of persons. There is nothing casual or lacking in definiteness about Fender. He is not, I understand, deferential, or excessively modest, or mild-mannered, or any of the other cardinal virtues so often attributed to the successful player of a national game. Fender is just himself and apparently does not try to be anybody else or all things to all men.'

A leader in the *Pall Mall Gazette* commented: 'There is far too much "politics" in the quarter where this decision has been taken and, it is to be feared, more than a spice of snobbery. Mr Fender is a modern cricketer and understands how the game should be played if it is to flourish today. There are some people at Lord's who don't understand and who resent anyone else understanding.' These kinds of article, and there were many more of similar ilk in most newspapers, can hardly have made enjoyable reading at certain breakfast tables. Once again cricket officialdom had no cause to feel well disposed towards Fender, even if the player himself could hardly be blamed for what was being written.

Fender was again in the headlines that summer when he pleaded for fewer first-class fixtures in an after-dinner speech at the House of Commons when Welsh MPs entertained the Glamorgan team; then when he put forward a scheme to the Advisory County Cricket Committee for a two-divisional championship with promotion and relegation. Fender continued to advocate this latter idea for the championship for the rest of his life and his scheme had not changed greatly when he put it forward yet again in the *Cricket Quarterly* in July 1963. He was not the first man to propose two divisions, nor has he been the last. To help boost the second-division counties financially, Fender suggested that first-division teams could play away friendlies against them on an expenses-only basis. Nothing came of Fender's plan, but it was interesting to note that even in 1923 it was by no means derided by either the popular newspapers or the more serious ones.

The *Observer* pointed out that the championship as it stood was 'fraught with all kinds of inequalities'. Their special correspondent said Fender was as modern in his views as he was in his methods on the field and went on: 'For some reasons, not always easy to understand, there has been long standing antipathy to anything in the nature of a league associated with first-class county cricket, but exactly what harm would be done has never been altogether satisfactorily explained. It is not sufficient to say that the adoption of a league system would be harmful to the game generally; it requires something more than that to prove that the game would be detrimentally affected. When all is said or done, the fact cannot be disguised that first-class cricket is a commercial proposition.'

There was a great deal of merit in Fender's proposal, the *Sporting Life* said, but they felt self-preservation would stop the leading counties from voting for it in case they were relegated. The article, written by Cover Point, concluded: 'Mr Fender is a little in advance of the thought of the time in his proposals. Cricket legislators and administrators are not yet sufficiently broad-minded to accept his views. . . . But sooner or later they will form the basis of a revised championship.'

In 1924 Fender's own form was distinctly uneven and this, coupled with the ruinous contrariety with Lord Harris, detailed in the first chapter, made it a wretched season for him. It was primarily in his bowling that the chief set-backs came. For a time in mid-summer Fender lost his ability to spin the ball and his control also suffered. At times he became almost reluctant to bowl himself and in round figures he delivered 600 fewer overs and took 100 fewer wickets, in all games, than he had the year before. Most cricketers have a disappointing year sooner or later when everything goes wrong. There was no one obvious explanation in Fender's case, but several factors, singly or in total, could have been responsible.

It was a cold, wet summer and Fender always preferred sunshine and hard wickets; it might have been the accumulated if hidden strain of several seasons' heavy work; in July, too, he had a rare injury when he wrenched a back muscle and could not bat in the Gentlemen's second innings at Lord's. He carried on for Surrey but the injury 'stayed' with him for several weeks. Fenley, another leg-spinner, in his first and best season for the county, helped to fill the gap as Fender struggled. But Surrey still missed their captain's versatility though they were beaten only once in the championship in a match when Fender and Hobbs were absent.

Above all there was the deep-rooted disappointment Fender felt at losing first his Test place and second the opportunity to tour Australia again. It has already been said that fundamentally Fender did not think he would be given the captaincy for the 1924–25 tour but he had originally expected to be included as a player. Initially, most of the cricket writers assumed that his inherent flair and past record made him a certain choice, irrespective of the lean patch he was going through. Fender was still in the England Test side when most of his colleagues received the first-availability letters sent out by MCC and he suspected the worst when he did not receive one. Nor did he have to wait too long before his fears were realized. By then the press seemed to have accepted that his omission, though unfortunate, was to be expected. It may have been that word had percolated on the cricket grape-vine that Fender had been blackballed and that any propaganda on his behalf was wasted effort. There were also several unpredictable selections to discuss at length, together with other happenings connected with the tour party.

As with the 1920–21 selections, the story became something of a serial over several weeks and was not without interest. The first bombshell came on 19 July when several newspapers reported that Hobbs would not be touring Australia and, less importantly, that G. E. C. Wood, England's amateur wicket-keeper, was also unavailable and that Hearne had not yet made up his mind whether to go if chosen. Various explanations involving his health, business interests and family were given for Hobbs's absence. To the ordinary person the mystery deepened when it became known that Hobbs hoped to go to South Africa with Solly Joel's private side. The first ten names announced by MCC for the tour were in the newspapers of 23 July. There were three amateurs in A. E. R. Gilligan (captain), A. P. F. Chapman and J. L. Bryan, with Strudwick, Woolley, Hendren, Sandham, Sutcliffe, Tate, and Tyldesley (R.), who filled one of the spin-bowling places. The newspapers said that by agreement with Australia the party would be limited to fifteen, so five places remained to be filled.

Almost in passing, the newspapers also mentioned that Mann had been asked first to captain the side but that he had declined for business reasons. What was not made clear was whether Mann was invited before or after Gilligan led England in the first three Test matches in 1924 against South Africa. All three of these matches had been won convincingly and criticism of the captain has never been a simple matter in these circumstances. It was true, however, that one or two aspects of Gilligan's tactical thinking had not escaped adverse comment. Fender, of course, was almost certainly ruled out by now. If a more mature leader than Gilligan was felt to be needed in Australia, it would have been understandable if MCC had settled on Mann; once he was unavailable Gilligan had no serious rival. MCC did, however, waste no time in seizing the chance when it arose to add an experienced amateur to the touring side's composition.

Within forty-eight hours of the emergence of the first ten names, came Douglas's return as England captain when Gilligan had to stand down from the fourth Test match. In what seems to have been a leak during the game at Old Trafford, Douglas's addi-

tion to the touring side as vice-captain became common knowledge. Hearne's availability also became known at this time.

On 30 July, the day after the fourth Test ended, MCC announced the party had been increased to sixteen and that Douglas,
C. H. Gibson, Hearne, Freeman and Kilner had been invited and
that only the deputy wicket-keeper's place remained open. The
selections of Gibson, the former Cambridge University medium-
pace bowler, who had been in the Argentine for two years, and to
a lesser extent Freeman, caused plenty of debate. Three of the
team, Gibson, Bryan and Chapman, were not playing regularly
in the championship at the time. The saga was still far from
finished. On 12 August it became known that Hobbs was willing
to go after all, the deciding factor apparently being that MCC had
given permission for his wife to accompany him. Meanwhile
Gibson had found that his commitments would not allow him to
leave South America.

Finally, on 20 August, came the news that the team had been
increased to seventeen, the largest number MCC had ever sent to
Australia and that Hobbs, Whysall and Howell were the late three
additions. Lord Harris was quoted as saying that Hobbs's health
had originally been in doubt but that MCC did not wish Hobbs's
Australian admirers to be disappointed. Whysall, though not a
regular wicket-keeper, had scored a lot of runs for Nottinghamshire and was an excellent short slip. Howell's inclusion was seen
as adding much-needed pace to the team, not least in case Gilligan's health let him down. Fender was on a motoring honeymoon
when MCC left England, but had arranged for some wine for the
team to be sent to their ship. He still has a thank-you letter for
this from Strudwick in which the wicket-keeper discusses the
prospects for the tour. Strudwick felt they had a good side and
added: 'But we all wish you were with us.'

Fender had made a fine start to 1924 before his batting and bowling form ebbed away. Only his slip fielding remained constant
throughout the summer: he took 39 catches, more than anyone
else, and they brought his total to 223 in five consecutive English
seasons. He began the summer at The Oval with an innings of
52 (twelve fours), match figures of 8–82 and 5 catches against
Glamorgan, followed by a score of 107 for Surrey against the
South Africans, spread over Saturday and Monday. Fender came
in at 82 for 5 and scored his runs out of 133 added in eighty-five
minutes, but rain spoilt the game completely. During the match

6. *A typical Tom Webster cartoon at Fender's expense when Surrey met the 1924 South Africans in a rain-disrupted match*

Fender and Lord Harris were the speakers when the Surrey Club entertained the South Africans to dinner at Skinners' Hall. Their clash was only a fortnight or so away.

At Nottingham, Fender had a good Test trial: though he was missed twice his 81 out of 108 in 100 minutes rescued the England XI's first innings. He did not accomplish much in the first two Tests he played before being dropped. South Africa lost both games by an innings and 18 runs. Fender contributed 36 as England chased quick runs at Edgbaston before Gilligan and Tate dismissed South Africa for 30; at Lord's Fender did not bat as England amassed 531 for 2 declared. His bowling was disappointing. When Macaulay replaced him for the third Test, the press took the line that Fender would soon recover his form and that Macaulay's inclusion brought variety to England's change bowling.

Just before the third Test match Fender and Parker each did the hat trick for their sides in the Surrey–Gloucestershire match at The Oval. Fender's victims were A. G. Dipper, caught at short-leg, M. G. Salter (at mid-off) and F. G. Rogers (bowled). Another curiosity came when he took 6–91 against Cambridge University. R. J. O. Meyer was given out, bowled, when he glanced a ball from Fender that brushed his wicket on its way to the boundary. The bail did not fall, but it so swivelled that it was left balancing at right angles to its proper position, on top of the leg stump. Nobody on the field was clear how the regulations then stood on this freak incident. After a lengthy consultation the umpires ruled Meyer out because the bail had to be replaced in its groove before play could continue. It caused a lot of discussion and the umpires were later criticized. Towards the end of the summer, Fender began to put his bowling problems behind him. In late August Sadler (10–71) and Fender (8–52) brought Surrey an exciting win by 109 runs against Yorkshire at The Oval in the extra half-hour. Yorkshire looked to be saving the match until Fender unexpectedly switched Sadler to the pavilion end and the young fast bowler took 4 late wickets.

On 17 September Fender's wedding at Frinton-on-Sea Parish Church was attended by numerous cricket celebrities and the Essex batsman the Revd F. H. Gillingham, as he then was, helped the local rector to officiate. His bride was Miss Ruth Clapham, the daughter of a Manchester jeweller and silversmith; the couple had met the previous winter in Monte Carlo. Mrs Fender was frequently pictured in society magazines because she was one of the few women to wear a monocle. In her case it was not a fashion gimmick but, in layman's language, it served to prop open a lazy eyelid. Mrs Fender was to die with tragic suddenness in 1937 from Bright's disease, leaving her husband with a young son and daughter.

Fender was kept fully occupied in the winter of 1924–25 with settling into a new home, expanding his wine business and writing a lengthy weekly analysis of what was happening in Australia for the *Sunday Express*. These articles from long range were always complimentary to Gilligan and his men and invariably optimistic in their tone. There could have been no objection to them from anywhere. Less tactful, possibly, was Fender's forceful rebuttal, in January 1925, of Lord Hawke's celebrated, if misunderstood, remarks about praying to God that no professional would ever captain England. The *Daily Herald* gave enormous prominence to an interview with Fender in which he said: 'Everyone is entitled to his opinion provided he expresses it in reasonable terms and chooses the time and place with discretion but to go out of one's way to express an opinion in unnecessarily strong language is apt to place a stigma upon those about whom the opinion is expressed.'

He went on to accuse Lord Hawke of offering an opinion which was tantamount to being 'a gratuitous insult to the main body of professional cricketers'. He said it was nonsense to suggest that it would be a disaster if England or a county played under other than an amateur captain. 'My experience of professional cricketers does not teach me that cricket would necessarily go to the dogs if a professional should happen to be in charge. . . . It does not seem to me to be "playing the game" to allow the publication of such an expression of opinion in such strong terms in a case where the professionals themselves have never for one moment presumed, or in anyway deserved to be stigmatized. I, personally, have played under a professional captain before [Tom Hayward] and should not hesitate to do so again, if it were in the best interests of the side.'

Fender was back to his best form in 1925. He did the double for the fourth time and Surrey seldom got anywhere without fast runs or useful wickets from him. Fender always enjoyed matches against Sussex, where he still had many connections, and this year he dominated both Surrey's fixtures with them: at The Oval he scored 61 and had match figures of 10–112, at Hove he hit 80 not out in seventy-five minutes, including 24 in an over off Tate,

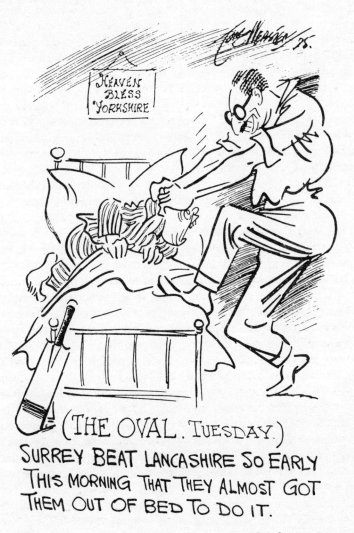

7.   *Tom Webster's reaction when Surrey completed an unexpected win against Lancashire in 1925 by half past twelve on the third day*

and took 5–45 in the first innings. Another good all-round performance came at Gloucester with 58 (four sixes and six fours)
in half an hour and match figures of 8–127. Surrey, having laid
the bogey, were now enjoying games at Blackheath, and Kent
were beaten by an innings (Fender 9–163).

On Saturday, 18 July, the first day of this match, Fender at
10.10 p.m. gave the radio talk from Savoy Hill mentioned on p. 117.
His main themes were the need for a smaller first-class cricket
programme and for regular series of trials to help the evolvement
of an England side. The next day Fender spent his Sunday at
Stamford Bridge playing in an exhibition baseball match. Clearly
his zest for life and appetite for hard work had returned, but this
particular cricket season, of course, really belonged to Hobbs,
with his sixteen centuries.

The wonderful story of Hobbs in 1925 and particularly the
game at Taunton, where he scored 101 and 101 not out to pass
W. G. Grace's career record of 126 hundreds, has been told so
often that it need not be described again. Apart from Hobbs's
brilliance the chief memory of this summer for Fender was the
dreadful pressure on Hobbs from the newspapers as they followed
him around waiting for the record to be broken. Fender confirmed
that it *was* ginger ale in the champagne glass he took out to the
wicket for Hobbs when the record was equalled in the first
innings. At the time Fender would not divulge the contents.
The temperance bodies earned considerable publicity from *The
Times* downwards with their qualms that they had been let down
by a national hero they believed to be a total abstainer.

Fender, unusually for him, quarrelled with some journalists
in Surrey's following match at Cardiff. Fender gave Hobbs the
game off to recover from the strain he had gone through and was
strongly criticized in the Welsh press for doing so. Glamorgan
were in financial straits and Hobbs would have helped the gate.
Thousands attended anyway after one newspaper stated that
Hobbs would definitely play, having checked with him by wire.
Fender angrily told newspapermen: 'It is not Hobbs's fault that
he is not in Cardiff; it is my fault. He wanted to come and I told
him he was not to come. Why I did that is my business. I am
captain of Surrey.' Rain restricted the match to four hours on the
second afternoon, but the South Wales *Evening Express* said:
'Surrey, or Mr Fender, has missed a unique opportunity of doing
a real good turn to Glamorgan.'

Nearly all Surrey's matches in August were disrupted by wet weather, the historic visit to Taunton being almost a lone exception. They finished runners-up to Yorkshire in the table but were never serious contenders themselves. The 1925 season, in fact, was to prove the last in which Surrey's strong batting, allied to Fender's ability as captain and all-rounder, was to prove sufficient to keep them near the top. For the fifth successive year Surrey did not lose a championship match at The Oval; only eight times in that period had another county beaten them. Fender led Surrey as the official captain for six more years, but the age of miracles had passed in the prosaic terms of championship placings. In 1926 Surrey were fifth, the next two years sixth, in 1929 tenth, and finally, in Fender's last two years as captain, they were eighth. The desperately needed strengthening in attack never came about.

In December 1925, Fender sailed to America to travel with a musical revue he had backed. A lot of pictures of him were taken as he sailed from Liverpool, because his arm was in a sling after an operation to remove a lump from his spinning finger. The talking point of the moment was a proposal from the Hon. F. S. G. Calthorpe, captain of MCC in West Indies that winter, that the county championship should be scrapped in 1926 to help the preparation of England's Test team against Australia. The idea had Fender's support and was widely argued. That winter, too, Fender dabbled briefly in spiritualism under the guidance of Dennis Bradley, a leading West End men's tailor, whose followers included several famous names in the legal, stage and literary worlds. Fender never became convinced enough to maintain his interest but kept an open mind on the subject.

As Herbie Collins's 1926 team assembled for the voyage to England, Fender found himself being pilloried in the Australian newspapers for an alleged attack on Australian sportsmanship, and the English press reported the row with glee as interest in the tour built up. Fender, in a speech to the Junior Imperial League at Caxton Hall, tried to convey how much more intensive and thorough the Australians were compared with Englishmen in their approach on the field. He cited Armstrong's leg theory, the way a new batsman was attacked or how a well-set player would be contained. All legitimate ploys, but things about which recent English captains had not had the same fetish. 'We are going to see certain things in the Australian game which are not to their detriment but *which are not in our game. We are up against a lot of things which*

we don't do but which other people do.' (Author's italics.) Condensed
and cabled to Australia these remarks were taken as a slur on
Australian behaviour and Collins, together with several politicians
in Melbourne and Sydney, all hit back at Fender in speeches.

At this distance it seems to have been a typical case of Australian
sensibilities having been bruised too easily, but Lord's could not
have been particularly pleased that the tour was beginning with
this sort of dispute. All winter Fender and Carr had been the only
names bandied about whenever the choice of England captain for
1926 was argued in print and elsewhere. Fender, in reality, was
never a candidate in the eyes of those who had to make the decision.
Even Carr, one suspects from this distance, was never everyone's
ideal choice in the same quarters: he seems to have been used only
to keep the seat warm until Chapman was ready. Fender never
played in the series at all, though there were justifiable reasons,
perhaps, for his inclusion ahead of Stevens. With Fender's
England career now recognized as finished, and Surrey no longer
in the hunt for championships, the moment is right to depart
from a strictly chronological account of Fender's career.

8. Bodyline—and an era ends

Contrary to what some people suspected, Fender rejected the notion that he was the master-mind for the bodyline bowling tactics used by Jardine's MCC side to Australia in 1932–33. Fender, of course, must have had more than an inkling of what was afoot, remembering his closeness to Jardine, who replaced him as Surrey captain. There was also Fender's long-standing friendship with Carr, who had directed the careers of Larwood and Voce from their start and on occasions had never hesitated to remind them of a fast bowler's ultimate weapon. These links, coupled with Fender's widespread recognition as the sharpest cricket mind in England, made it inconceivable that he had no role in the matter. By his own insistence, though, it was a minor one. He denied any suggestion that the original scheming was his and he certainly was not present at that legendary dinner in the Piccadilly Hotel grill-room when the plans were supposedly laid. He was unable to confirm a story, which H. M. Garland-Wells heard in later years, that Carr, Jardine and Fender once discussed methods of keeping Bradman quiet. 'You could try bowling at his leg stump,' Fender was alleged to have said. 'You won't get him out but he might not score quite so many runs.' Fender's denials should be accepted because he never wavered from his belief that Jardine's tactics were acceptable and he undoubtedly would have taken the responsibility for them if they had been his idea.

The extent to which Fender influenced Jardine's thinking, however, was less certain. Fender's first contribution may have come in 1930 as a journalist. He was one of the strongest critics of Bradman's jittery batting against Larwood on a rain-affected pitch at The Oval in the fifth Test match. Some historians have pinned bodyline's conception to that moment. Fender had his own explanation for its origins, which stemmed from the Australian habit of moving across in front of their stumps. Fender had kept in touch with a number of Australian journalists he had met while covering the 1928–29 series in Australia. Early in 1932 he received several letters from them with a common theme: it was expected that fast bowling would be the basis of England's attack in the forthcoming series and the feeling among several Australian batsmen was that they would have to eliminate the riskier off-side shots. It would be best to move across the wicket and nudge, deflect, pull or hook, according to temperament, rather than to off-drive or cut. It was an approach to batting confirmed by several reports Fender heard of how some of the Australians had played against West Indies in 1930–31 and South Africa in 1931–32.

Fender had no idea what stage Jardine's planning for the tour had reached, but he took these letters from Australia with him when he spent a week-end with Jardine at Walton-on-Thames. They discussed at length the implications of the Australians trying to play the ball where there were normally fewer fieldsmen positioned. Jardine was slightly sceptical at the idea that any bats-man would deliberately avoid the off-side strokes, as it seemed so contrary to accepted practice. Jardine did not need to be reminded by Fender that Larwood's natural ball was something of an in-swinger, or breakback, to the right-hander and that in Australian conditions it was essential to bowl straight and make certain every ball was played. When he and Fender talked at Walton, Jardine held a great respect for Australian on-side play but he also had reservations about their ability against fast bowling. Fender left Jardine still musing on whether a chink could be found in the Australian armour between these strongest and weakest points, and Jardine now had the contents of Fender's letters to bear in mind as well. It was possible that the pieces did not finally fall into place fully for Jardine until early in the tour. By then, as Jardine later wrote in his book *In Quest of the Ashes* (Hutchinson, 1933), a hitherto unsuspected weakness on the leg stump had been dis-closed by several leading Australians.

Jardine wrote to Fender from Australia shortly before the first Test match and referred to the letters Fender had showed him. He said how right Fender's informants had been because the ball, especially against Larwood and Voce, was being played far more than usual to the leg side. Fender lost the entire corres-pondence in the Second World War blitz, but he remembered Jardine's phrase: 'I find I now have to have four or five men on the leg side and if this goes on I shall have to move the whole b— lot to the legside.' Fender offered the original letters and Jardine's own letter for use in Jardine's defence when he returned home. At that particular moment Jardine was in the mood to let people think what they wanted and had no wish to justify himself. Fender always felt the tour's events left Jardine thoroughly disenchanted, to an extent not properly realized, and he seldom spoke about them in later years. Jardine had not wished to tour again and Fender was among those who persuaded him to lead MCC to India in 1933–34, pointing out that MCC's invitation represented a gesture of support for him and that it was important he should accept.

Whether Fender would have changed his opinion about body-line's validity if he had witnessed the 1932–33 series in person can only be conjectured. Enough emerged in later years, both from the players involved and from the diplomats in the back-ground, to suggest that bodyline contravened the spirit of cricket despite its legitimacy as the laws then stood. Fender was a just man and a realist. He might have gone through an agonizing dilemma had he covered the tour for the *Star*, as he had done four years earlier and had hoped to do so again. Instead, the newspaper decided to send Hobbs, accompanied by a ghost writer, and neither in their articles, nor in their book later, did they do body-line justice as a subject. There was, in fact, an unfortunate absence of informed comment and criticism about this tour for the English newspaper public for reasons set out in detail by E. W. Swanton in his second autobiography, *Follow On* (Collins, 1977).

Bodyline has remained a sore and disputatious subject. Those with first-hand knowledge have mostly been reluctant to discuss the matter and it has stayed a perilous and tactless topic to raise in Australia. Opinions still vary to an extraordinary degree. The very word 'bodyline' was anathema to Fender, who considered its use was provocative Australian journalism. Larwood, he claimed, bowled leg theory, something always permitted in the game, albeit that Larwood bowled it faster, more accurately and more success-fully than anybody else ever had. 'The fact is that the Australians often stood in front of their stumps as a deliberate policy,' Fender said, 'and a lot of what happened came from this. They were still doing it on the 1934 tour when several of them were bowled behind their legs more than once.' On the other hand Jack Fingle-ton has been among the Australians who pointed out that the ball followed them wherever they stood. Ray Robinson, in *The Wildest Tests* (Pelham Books, 1972), in a typically vivid simile said that bodyline was as different from traditional leg theory 'as an inter-continental missile from a boy's paper dart'. In *Cricket Between*

Two Wars (Chatto & Windus, 1942), 'Plum' Warner wrote that the difference was 'not at first generally recognized in England, nor is it still in some quarters'.

Leaving aside the ethics of bodyline, Fender's loyalty to Jardine, allied to his fierce patriotism, always left him grieved by several other aspects of the matter, and he was far from alone. 'For the first time in my cricket career England had appointed a determined and resolute captain; a man cast in the toughest Australian mould, *à la* Armstrong if you like, with the character and vision to plan for victory and the will-power and players to see it through. And what happened? It all went wrong and was followed by the climb-down when the counties thought the 1934 Australian visit was in jeopardy. It was as big a tragedy in sport as I ever knew and, if you remember, it was a long time before we found another captain to beat the Australians. I don't think the Australians would have been so conciliatory if things had been the other way around.'

On a less contentious note, Fender has never forgotten the first occasion that Jardine batted against Larwood. It was on August Bank Holiday Monday 1925 and the 34,000 crowd (31,524 paid) encroached badly on The Oval's playing area. Larwood, who had played one match for Nottinghamshire in 1924, came into the side in mid-June and was being nursed along carefully by Carr. Fender knew of Larwood's potential and the speed that Larwood could reach in short bursts was starting to be talked about on the county circuit. 'Is this chap as fast as they say he is?' Jardine asked Fender between innings. 'Yes,' Fender replied. 'He does not look so fast to me,' Jardine said, as Hobbs and Sandham played 3 overs from Larwood when the Surrey innings began shortly before lunch. Surrey were 179 for 5 when Fender joined Jardine and hit 46 in twenty-five minutes. When Fender was out, Larwood was brought back for his second spell and Jardine faced him for the first time.

Fender continued: 'Larwood's first ball was being returned by the wicket-keeper Lilley as Douglas completed his stroke; the second ball was on its way through to Lilley when the stroke was completed; the third ball Douglas finally made contact. He immediately turned round to the pavilion and raised his cap to me.' Larwood took 4–15 in 6.3 overs and the Surrey innings rapidly ended. Jardine (53) was last out, his stumps shattered by Larwood with the batsman beaten by sheer pace, though he told Fender he thought he had possibly played on. Another example of Jardine's dry sense of humour was the time when Surrey had undergone a particularly gruelling day's fielding in blazing sunshine. As Fender flopped into an armchair in the amateurs' dressing-room, he asked the attendant to get him 'twenty Player's please'. From across the room Jardine added: 'And make most of them bowlers.'

Larwood was the best fast bowler Fender ever saw, though he believed the Englishman did not take his wicket as often as E. A. McDonald. 'I suppose I had to bat against Larwood on average about six to eight times a season during the short time he was at his peak. Like everyone else I had my own ideas about what to try and do for the best. My method was to let him "see" the stumps. I would take guard on leg stump or outside it; he always bowled straight and I just pushed forward with no back lift and hoped. Sometimes I just managed to stop the ball; sometimes I got runs on the off-side.' The fastest ball Fender ever received in his career did not come from Larwood but from Voce. 'It was the only time in my whole life that I think I was frightened at cricket. I did not like Burns and Burrows in 1910 as you know, but I got over that and others like Gregory or Larwood never actually scared me. But this ball from Voce I never saw. It was a new experience and not a pleasant one.'

It happened at The Oval in 1933 when once again Nottinghamshire drew a huge holiday crowd and Fender for the second time that season hit a hundred from their bowling. These were the last two centuries Fender scored in first-class cricket. Larwood's foot injury prevented him from bowling that summer, but in both games Voce went flat out and Fender punished him severely. At The Oval Voce used fast leg theory amid hooting from the crowd. Hobbs, aged fifty, was struck several times on the hip and thigh as he made his 196th hundred and his last at The Oval. Near the end, Voce tired and Fender was caught off guard in Voce's final over of the day, when a ball rose sharply off a length at him. Fender never saw the ball but instinctively held his bat in front of his face and the ball struck the handle and flew over the wicket-keeper's head for 4. Fender made an unbeaten 100 out of 137 inside two hours. At Trent Bridge on Whit Monday it had been 106 at No. 9 in even time. (When play ended an 18,000 crowd cheered rapturously as Jardine presented Larwood and Voce each with gilt-edged security certificates worth £388, the proceeds of a shilling fund organized by Nottingham newspapers, to mark their deeds in Australia a few months earlier.)

Fender had a great admiration for Jardine as a cricketer and man. 'I don't think I ever met such a studious batsman. He had a wonderful instinct for "reading" the bowling. It was rare indeed for a bowler to deceive Jardine. He might be out, having made a mistake, but he would know what the bowler had done and where he, the batsman, had gone wrong.' Jardine was an example, Fender felt, of what could be achieved by good coaching and a player's own determination. Jardine never had the innate natural skill that many good ball-game players possess, but he became a defensive batsman of the highest calibre and was a difficult man to dislodge. 'He loved a challenge and was one of the few amateurs to play irregularly for Surrey who would deliberately choose the tougher matches to play in; he never avoided Yorkshire or our other hard games, like some of the part-timers.' At Bradford in 1928 Fender (177) and Jardine (157) shared a partnership which put on 294 for the sixth wicket in a shade under five hours. Fender remembered they were a little fortunate in that Macaulay, who had taken 3 early wickets, could not bowl for a time. 'Early on, I cut a ball straight to Macaulay at gully and it hit Macaulay in the wrong place for Macaulay, poor chap!'

Fender, unbeknown to many people in the game at the time, offered to stand down as Surrey captain early in the 1931 season in order to let Jardine take charge. 'It became obvious that Jardine was the front runner to be captain in Australia eighteen months later. I thought he was by far the best choice for the job but he had not had much experience of captaincy since his Winchester days and I thought it would help him.' Fender suggested the change in a letter to Leveson-Gower, the Surrey president, that he also showed Jardine, who was willing to take on the job. A day or so afterwards, Leveson-Gower told Fender the committee had rejected his offer. In later years, when Fender was on the Surrey committee himself, he learned from several long-serving members that not everyone had been consulted. Surrey, of course, if they had acted on Fender's proposal, would have been spared much of the rumour and adverse newspaper comment which accompanied the change in leadership when it was eventually made the following winter.

Fender said the widely accepted stories, that for years he had tutored Jardine in captaincy during Surrey matches, were untrue. 'Certainly Douglas was often at gully and I might be at outside slip and I would tell him what I was trying to do. We might exchange ideas, too, in the dressing-room, but I never deliberately set out to teach him anything. He had his own ideas and you must not forget that our approach to most things was very seldom the same.' The 1934 *Wisden* discussed this point: 'The ideas of Jardine and Fender—two captains of vastly different methods, especially in their placing of the field—seldom met in a common line of practice.' Garland-Wells, whose county career began shortly before the change, said: 'In the simplest terms Jardine was a very good captain, but Fender was a genius.' To the Surrey players the difference was deducible from the two men's own play and personalities. Jardine was never anything other than canny, careful and withdrawn, always sound but always thrifty: Fender gambled, plotted and could be extravagant with runs and wickets if it served a purpose.

Gover and F. R. Brown both considered Fender the cleverest captain they played under. Gover said: 'Jardine never gave a thing away, but with Percy George, for instance, it was always understood that we conceded a single if a new batsman came in to the non-striker's end. Nothing would be said, but everyone surreptitiously went back a few yards. That way the bowler could get at the new man before he got used to the light.' Gover always had the feeling that the scope of Fender's thinking was far wider than Jardine's. 'It wasn't too important, I suppose, but Fender was the only captain I knew who regularly rang the Air Ministry Roof for the weather forecasts. That was the place to go before the days of TV weather centres; they were often wrong, but Percy George would make allowances for that too.' Brown did not know of another captain who schemed almost every ball so constantly as Fender did. 'He would be at my elbow all the time: "bowl him this, bowl him that." As a spin bowler himself I felt he understood me better than Jardine. Fender did not mind if I got hit for four. It's an exaggeration, of course, but one boundary hit and Jardine might take me off.'

Some of the background to Fender's being deposed from the Surrey captaincy in January 1932, has never been properly clarified to this day. Even Fender's recollection of what happened was at slight variance with the Surrey committee's rather meagre minutes and the newspapers. Fender was rung at his office and asked if it was convenient for him to drop in at The Oval office after work for a meeting at about half-past five. On a bitterly cold Thursday evening he drove to Kennington and found two embarrassed committee members warming themselves in front of a log fire. They told him the committee felt it was time for a change of captain and that Jardine would lead the team in 1932. Fender, whose ear was always close to the ground, was not greatly surprised. There had been whispers that this might happen, in fact, the previous autumn. Fender, far more at ease than the two committee men, immediately confirmed his wish to continue playing whoever was captain. Any disappointment he felt was offset by the fact that Jardine was the best possible choice and, that, in any case, the committee were only doing, belatedly, what he had suggested some months earlier.

Unfortunately, the Surrey Club's public relations seem to have been rather bad, even by the standards in cricket at that time. Three weeks later, Fender's sacking leaked to the press and it appeared that Surrey had not yet settled on his successor. Furthermore the reports hinted that pressure had been put on Fender to advise the club that he would be unavailable in the coming summer. The old Pardon's Agency (who in those days provided cricket reports direct to newspapers) seem to have had the fullest version of all this on 19 February and their copy was heavily drawn on by most newspapers the next day. Fender, inevitably, was approached and was quoted as saying that Surrey's decision to make a change in the captaincy had been communicated to him on 28 January. 'It is not for me to comment,' Fender said discreetly. Both Leveson-Gower and R. C. N. Palairet, the Surrey secretary, denied the Pardon's story. Leveson-Gower was quoted: 'I have nothing to say at all. I cannot confirm the rumour and I have not even seen the report. I do not know if the matter will be discussed at the next meeting of the Surrey committee nor do I know when the committee will meet.' Palairet had been in office throughout Fender's captaincy and was himself in the throes of resigning and leaving The Oval. He claimed that no decision had been taken about the captaincy.

There was naturally a great deal of speculation in the next day's newspapers. The *Daily Telegraph*'s special correspondent remarked: 'The manner of his going has surprising features', and went on to recall that a year earlier Surrey had set up a special committee to examine why the team had not been more successful. 'I understand they issued a private report to the general committee in which it was stated that insufficient use was being made of the wealth of amateur talent available.' This had been one of many bones of contention between Fender and Leveson-Gower for

years. Fender, unlike some captains at that time, always objected
to dropping a professional to make room for an amateur unless he
was fully convinced the amateur was the better player. On a
broader front, it was a difficult time at The Oval financially and
the professional staff was being trimmed, with Ducat and Peach
among those prematurely released. Economies were being made
in several areas, and Fender remembered what he maintained had
been the illogical attitude of the secretariat to some expenses, he
claimed for a game at Old Trafford. 'Three of us amateurs stayed
privately, I think with Peter Eckersley. When we left I gave a fiver
each to the cook, the chap who laid out our clothes and the maid,
and claimed £15. Surrey would not pay it, though if we had stayed
at our usual Manchester hotel it would have cost over £50.'

Fender's departure had been badly handled, wrote H. J. Henley
in the *Daily Mail*. Henley was always a well-informed journalist
and came closer to the mark, probably, than some writers, when
he went through a number of reasons why Fender might have lost
the captaincy. He recalled rumours from the previous two seasons
that a change was going to be made. Fender had been criticized
for accepting a newspaper assignment in 1930 to report the Tests
and had missed important Surrey matches. As an amateur,
Henley wrote, Fender was a free agent, but in some quarters it
had been felt he should have resigned the captaincy. It was also
known that Fender had not seen eye to eye with his committee
on other issues, such as team selection, and Henley said that
Fender's attitude to freak declarations had also not met with
approval at The Oval. (Fender and Maurice Turnbull in the
Surrey–Glamorgan match at Cardiff provided one of several
instances in 1931 when both captains agreed to declare their first
innings closed after one ball, in order to make up time lost by rain.
Lord Hawke led officialdom's disapproval with references to
'authority being flouted'. Fender and Bev Lyon, in particular,
were notably unrepentant, with Lyon, in one public speech,
comparing Lord Hawke to Nero!)

There was little let-up in the gossip columns to the comments
about Fender's sacking, with the issue clouded for outsiders by
the fact that his own form had been good in 1931. (Surrey's two
games with Somerset helped illustrate that he retained his zest
and skill. At The Oval he hit 139 not out in eighty minutes; at
Taunton he claimed 7 for 58 in Somerset's first innings, in between
keeping wicket while Brooks was off being treated for an injury.)

Every avenue to the story was explored with Trevor Wignall wrongly, as it turned out, telling his *Daily Express* readers that Hobbs was finishing with Surrey in 1932 and quoting Hobbs as saying that he had hoped to end his career under Fender's leadership. Five days after the original leakage, Surrey held a special committee meeting and the minutes recorded: 'After discussion it was decided to issue to the press a statement.'

Most of the newspapers carried this statement in full on 26 February without comment, and it read as follows:

'Owing to conflicting statements which have appeared in the press with regard to Mr Fender and the captaincy of the Surrey XI, the committee of the Surrey County Cricket Club desire to state that nothing has been decided except that the committee are of the opinion that the time has come when a change of captaincy is desirable, *provided a suitable successor to Mr Fender can be found.* [Author's italics.] It has never been suggested that Mr Fender should not continue to play for the county. Recognising Mr Fender's long and valuable service to the county, the committee thought it proper to let him know at the earliest possible moment that the matter was under consideration.'

On 3 March Surrey's cricket committee met and recommended that Jardine be appointed captain and M. J. C. Allom vice-captain and on 17 March the full committee approved these choices and their decision was immediately passed to the newspapers. Surrey's annual report in April stressed the captaincy change had been made 'after the most careful consideration' and paid Fender a handsome tribute for all he had done. In due course the club presented him with a magnificent silver tray, inscribed with the signatures of every cricketer who had played under him, together with a gold cigarette case.

Jardine and Allom all along had been discussed in print as the most likely successors, together with S. A. Block, a Cambridge Blue in 1929, whose candidature was mooted, presumably, because of doubts surrounding the regular availability of Jardine and Allom. Jardine, though always successful when he played, had only appeared in twenty-two championship games the five previous seasons. The discrepancy between Fender's being told in late January that Jardine was his successor and the appointment's being recorded in Surrey's minutes in March was slightly puzzling. Did Surrey get rid of Fender without being certain they had a qualified successor available or was it merely that Jardine did not give them an answer for several weeks? Would Surrey in certain circumstances have re-appointed Fender after all? It might seem improbable, but the implication was there in that rather curious proviso in their statement about 'a suitable successor' having to be found. The full story seems unlikely now to be uncovered. Fender never held an official appointment with Surrey again, though he led the side on numerous occasions through the absences for different reasons of his successors. Jardine and Allom, as had been feared by some members, made only infrequent appearances in 1933, when Surrey used seven different captains, and in 1934 E. R. T. Holmes was appointed with Garland-Wells vice-captain.

Once Fender was stripped of office, Ronald Mason was to write: 'Reduced to subordinate rank, he looked forlorn and fettered, a great Prince in prison lying', which had a certain truth for many onlookers. Fender remembered it hurt much less than when he finished playing completely five years on. He had his fortieth birthday in 1932; business and family commitments were increasing; and there were moments, undoubtedly, when he was glad to be able to play a little less frequently and to shed responsibility. Including 1920, when he deputized for Wilkinson so much, Fender led Surrey for twelve seasons, a term that outlasted all his contemporaries with the exception of Tennyson and Carr. Fender had already sensed an impending change in the climate between county captains and their committees and he did not entirely agree with the new trends. It may not have been purely coincidence that Tennyson and Carr also finished within the next three years, the one so light-hearted and the other a sombre soul in many ways. Different in character and outlook they were, but they shared Fender's almost autocratic approach to the county captain's job. They, too, believed in the need for the captain to be the supreme, lone authority; like Fender they were always willing to stand or fall by whatever they did and Fender, as we have seen, duly fell.

Fender's loyalty to those who followed him was impeccable, it need hardly be said, but it could never have been easy for him from 1932 onwards. Jardine, during his brief, spasmodic term of office, consulted Fender a lot; the others a little less. A close study of Surrey's matches in the immediate post-Fender captaincy period disclosed several instances when opportunities were not seized in the same rapacious way they would have been with Fender at the helm. 'Life at The Oval without Fender in charge will be much duller,' was the theme of another Wignall column in the *Daily Express*. This time he was one hundred per cent right.

9. Captain controversial: legends and facts

Incidents attached themselves to Fender like barnacles to a ship and the majority have lost little in the telling as the years have passed. In some ways the most outlandish episode in which he was concerned took place at Leyton in 1925 when he and Jeacocke were for a few minutes the only Surrey players on the field. They bowled in turn as the other kept wicket and the Essex batsmen made no attempt to score runs. Almost unbelievably this was not reported in the newspapers, national or local, and the story is told with some hesitation. Fender and three other survivors of the match—all well into their eighties—swore positively to the author that the incident happened even if their accounts varied in minor ways. The gist of the affair has been passed down over the years by word of mouth and parts will not be completely new to older cricket circles in Essex where there have always been unsubstantiated rumours about it. Fender himself first wrote a watered-down version of what occurred in the *Illustrated Sporting and Dramatic News* of 16 June 1928, without identifying the match, and drew no contradictory letters. This alone justified its inclusion in his biography. The account that follows has been put together from several sources with caution. It may not be entirely correct, but it remains an extraordinary tale, worth recounting in detail, and there is no doubt that something close to it actually happened.

There was, it appeared, an effort by the authorities in a circular before the 1925 season to standardize the time of lunch intervals. When Surrey arrived at Leyton on Saturday, 24 May, J. W. H. T. Douglas asked Fender if they could adhere to Leyton's usual late lunch-time or if the interval should be taken at the time recommended by Lord's. 'I think we'd better stick to MCC rules,' Fender replied, to Douglas's annoyance. The spark for disagreement had been kindled. It was possibly fanned as Surrey batted all day for 431 for 8 declared and by Monday evening Essex had made a rather laborious 333 for 7. Shortly before the start on Tuesday, Harry Butt, the old Sussex wicket-keeper and one of the umpires, came to the amateurs' dressing-room and told

Fender his professionals had not arrived. Douglas looked up from lacing his boots and said: 'Strict MCC rules, Fender—the side refusing to play loses the match.' Douglas declined to postpone the start; Fender said there was no question of Surrey's yielding the match and he told Butt he would be ready to begin at 11.15, the agreed starting time.

Only a few spectators were present but their bewilderment must have been considerable when the umpires came out followed by Fender and Jeacocke, the other Surrey amateur playing. These two had driven to Leyton together and Fender knew by now that the charabanc bringing the Surrey professionals from The Oval had been delayed by traffic. The umpires and Fender and Jeacocke waited in the middle but the overnight Essex batsmen did not appear. They were C. J. Treglown and R. H. Sharp, two Army captains who, with Jeacocke, had been embarrassed witnesses of the earlier scene in the amateurs' dressing-room. Eventually Fender asked Butt to return to the pavilion and remind Douglas that under MCC laws he would be entitled to claim the match under the two-minute rule if Essex did not resume their innings. Treglown and Sharp then came to the wicket but merely kept the ball out of their stumps as Fender and Jeacocke bowled at opposite ends. Within a few more minutes the rest of the Surrey team straggled on to the field with Strudwick, ever the dedicated professional, making the classic inquiry: 'Have there been any byes yet?'

The Essex innings soon ended and Surrey batted out the match and were 318 for 8 at the end. By then Fender was at the wicket and being barracked for not declaring by the crowd, who were ignorant of the climate between the two captains by that stage. It was Treglown who filled in an important part of the jigsaw by remembering that the incident had been kept out of the newspapers by 'Peter' Perrin, who was also playing in the match and who, incidentally, was celebrating his forty-ninth birthday on that eventful day. Perrin was an influential figure in cricket and later served as an England selector. He was understood to have made a specific plea to the press not to mention the episode in the day's opening minutes for the sake of cricket's good name, to say nothing of the reputations of Douglas and Fender. Whether he succeeded, or whether the reporters were unaware of some aspects of the story, was not known. Most onlookers may have assumed the players were only passing the time, waiting for the latecomers, as

Fender and Jeacocke bowled. No evidence could be found, it has to be said, that these 'mock' overs were recorded by the scorers. Jeacocke never bowled in the match, according to *Wisden*, and the Essex scorebook, the only one available, bears no signs of them, nor of any erasures.

Yet four players in the match remain adamant that these overs were bowled, with Fender believing that about four or five in all were delivered by Jeacocke and himself. (This would tally with the newspaper reports that the match started about fifteen minutes late.) In addition, Jeacocke's son, Mr Bryan Jeacocke, a good club cricketer himself, also confirmed that his father had told him the full story in later years as described. The press did not let Perrin down, but some writers went perilously close to implying that something unusual had happened. The Surrey charabanc's late arrival was reported, which was fair enough, it being variously stated that it had broken down, lost its way, or been delayed by traffic going to the Epsom Derby meeting. Some newspapers, notably the *Daily Mail*, specifically mentioned that Fender and Jeacocke waited alone in the field when play resumed, but the *Mail* writer, H. J. Henley, omitted further precise detail about the start. At least these newspaper references confirmed the year, the match and the day that this whole affair did or did not happen. Several of the other versions handed down have the incident taking place in 1923 and on the first day of the game whichever year it was.

Douglas entertained several of the Surrey team at a National Sporting Club boxing dinner on the Monday night, according to the newspapers, and Fender emphasized there was far less atmosphere between Douglas and himself than might be imagined. Fender's memory was that Douglas was 'a bit out of sorts' that Tuesday morning and that what started as a leg-pull had got out of hand. Fender had not been sure what to do once Douglas refused, in front of Butt, to wait for the absentees. He felt that he and Jeacocke had to go out once the umpires did. Sandham remembered the incident but was unable to recall any details that take the story further, and anything he could have added would have been secondhand at best because he was on the delayed charabanc. Treglown said he had not wanted to go out to bat but Douglas had ordered him to do so and he remembered being criticized by two of the Essex professionals later for not taking advantage of the situation to score runs. It would have counted, they argued, if Treglown had been dismissed. Jimmy Cutmore, another member of the Essex team, remembered that Fender and Jeacocke bowled well wide of the off-stump and that the batsmen hardly had to play a ball.

It was made clear from the start that the complete veracity of this incident was not unchallengable, but what might be construed as a postscript was carried by the *Sporting Times* on 20 June the same year. On its famous pink newsprint, a gossip paragraph noted, after Essex had been beaten by 188 runs in the return game at The Oval: 'These days when Essex and Surrey meet there is generally a bit of a dog fight. I wonder why?' (Perhaps it was not altogether coincidental that Fender achieved the best all-round match performance of his career the following season at Leyton when he hit 104 in eighty minutes and had match figures of 10–124 as Surrey won by an innings.) Alf Gover, who had a trial with Essex at about this time, had no doubts the episode happened and he confirmed the curious mixture of antipathy and respect that Douglas and Fender held for each other. 'I once hit Douglas on the body a couple of times on an awkward pitch. It was all accidental but Douglas said to me down the wicket "That's not bowling, Gover" and straight away Fender from first slip shouted "You captain your side, Douglas, and I'll captain mine."'

Fender had a good reputation among the Surrey professionals for supporting them and for being more considerate than many another captain. Fender would equate a self-sacrificiary nought with a fifty for talent money if it had been in the interests of the team. 'Go out and get your noughts,' was Fender's phrase when instructing his tailenders to throw away their wickets if he wanted Surrey's innings to end and their opponents to have some batting before the end of the first day. More than once Gover and Allom wanted the same end because of the wind and as Gover put it: 'To my surprise at first, I usually got it—the side came first with Percy George, not your status, and that sort of thing was appreciated.' Gover could not recall that Fender ever ticked off a professional in front of the rest of the team. 'He would take you to one side and explain where you had gone wrong and you could never find fault with his thinking on technical grounds.'

Nobody was better qualified to assess Fender than Gover, whose own career with Surrey lasted twenty years from 1928 before he became one of cricket's finest coaches and a perceptive writer on the game. 'The finest cricket brain I have ever come across in over fifty years in cricket. Everything I have done I owe to Percy George; he taught me so much. A fine player and the greatest of captains, of course, but pitches, people's technique, the lot: he knew it all.' Gover added wryly: 'And I'm not saying all that because he was the only decent "slipper" I ever had with Surrey!' From his earliest days Gover remembered that Fender dinned into him: '"My side does not need your batting Gover; I want you to think bowling, day and night, all the time, think bowling; always think you are better than any batsman because you are." That was his philosophy and he instilled it in me.' As Gover matured he came to realize when Fender was 'working' on him, but it was impossible to object. 'If things were going badly he'd say "Can you manage one more over?" and perhaps you'd get a wicket and then you'd want to stay on. He would go through the motions of saying "I only asked you for one" and you would end up pleading to carry on. You then felt you had to deliver the goods. All along, of course, that was the frame of mind he wanted to get you into.'

Fender was no longer captain in 1933 when he asked Gover a special favour and the story illustrates the respect in which Fender was held. Gover had taken 6–17 as Essex were dismissed for 66 at The Oval on a rain-affected pitch. Between innings Fender asked him to ask Jardine if he could switch ends: Fender had spotted a worn patch that was even more suited to his own bowling. Gover said: 'I wouldn't have done it for anybody else. I don't think he even explained what he had in mind, but we all trusted his judgement. Anyway, I asked Jardine as we came out again. He couldn't think why on earth I wanted to bowl from the opposite end after doing so well and he said so. He let me do it, though, and Percy George used my end and took 8 cheap wickets as we won by an innings.' Fender's analysis was 25–13–29–8; there were only fifteen scoring strokes off him and Thomas Moult in the *Daily Telegraph* described Fender's bowling as 'a triumph of brain and craft.' (This spell came close numerically to being the best bowling in one innings of Fender's career. It was bettered, marginally, by his figures of 21–11–24–8 on a drying pitch against Warwickshire at The Oval in 1928.)

Someone who was aware of Fender's faults as well as his attributes was E. M. Wellings, the discriminating and forthright cricket correspondent of the London *Evening News* for so many years. Wellings, in a long letter from his retirement home in Spain, conceded that Fender was the most astute captain of his time, almost too much so, as he felt Fender could be exaggeratedly finicky over field placings. 'Something more than astuteness is needed in the England captain and I feel sure Percy George was too abrasive to have made a good Test skipper. His astuteness was sometimes closely akin to what is now politely called "gamesmanship".' Wellings remembered a match when Fender convinced the umpires that the ground needed longer to recover from rain than was the case. Instead of having a 'dead' pitch on which to bowl, Surrey eventually skittled their opponents on a 'sticky'. (Always a bone of contention this—but surely most captains over the years have taken the view best suited to their side in these cirumstances?) Wellings went on: 'For all his faults, though, Fender did a great deal for cricket: in addition to his cunning as a captain, he was a grand entertainer, a vast hitter with the bat, a leg-break bowler of much more than average skill and a splendid slip fielder. It was not his fault that Surrey never won the championship under him.'

Wellings's reservations about Fender make it right to acknowledge that Fender, like many innovators and nimble-witted people, had his detractors. Their main concern always revolved around whether his captaincy ever crossed the narrow borderline between permissible strategy and sharp practice. There was never any firm evidence that it did, and the issue was possibly clouded in people's minds by the disputes in which Fender was involved. His own sportsmanship was irreproachable and often praised, but it could never be denied that Fender and incidents were frequent associates and this was a separate matter. Fender never flouted the laws of cricket, but he certainly used them and the regulations at that time were seldom so precise in certain areas as they are today.

Nor should Fender be condemned for what was often his shrewd and unconventional thinking. It might be unpalatable, but far more has always gone on in the middle, from Hambledon onward, than dreamt of in the philosophy 'it's not cricket'. Legislators still find that no sooner do they introduce new regulations than the players find loopholes to exploit. Fender was cleverer than most of his contemporary captains; he could become impatient if his flexibility produced no response; he could also get angry with himself if things went wrong. All this had a hand in the incidents which the newspapers reported and which his committee abhorred but they were never proof in themselves that Fender over-reached himself.

In 1931 Wellings played four matches for Surrey under Fender when the Oxford season finished and in three of them Fender provided the main talking point among the players. Against Lancashire, Fender got the Surrey fieldsmen between wicket-falls to tread down marks on a wet Oval pitch, late on the Saturday. These would have left the wicket difficult on the Monday if the week-end had been sunny enough to bake the ridges. Lancashire protested and Fender challenged them to produce anything in the rules to stop him from repairing the damage and the umpires backed Fender. At Bournemouth Fender bowled lobs against Hampshire with a widely scattered field when he felt Giles Baring had been tardy in declaring. Mead was batting with a right-handed partner and one over took twelve minutes to complete. After every single, Fender insisted on the fielders changing completely over to the same position. When Sandham, at deep square leg, tried to run across the field, Fender roared at him to walk. 'The crowd were flummoxed,' Wellings said. 'They had been barracking for a declaration and now they did not know whether to hoot at Baring or at Fender.' In the next match Surrey were left a target by Kent: Fender opened with Hobbs and was immediately run out. 'He returned seething and the chase was called off.'

These memories were less controversial than Yorkshire's visit to The Oval later the same year when Wellings did not play. Despite a soaked field Yorkshire were persuaded to start for the sake of the Saturday crowd. Frank Greenwood had the heavy roller used when he won the toss and chose to bat. Fender, who had not looked too closely at the conditions beforehand, returned to the pavilion after 3 overs and suggested to Greenwood they should come off as his bowlers could not get proper footholds. Greenwood, in the circumstances, felt that play should continue, but Fender appealed to the umpires and they agreed the field was too wet. The mystified spectators protested loudly at the stoppage and about 200 people demonstrated in front of the pavilion. When Frank Chester, one of the umpires, returned later from making an inspection, he was kicked on the leg by a spectator who disappeared before the police could catch him.

The Surrey committee, according to the newspapers, were concerned at the prevailing mood and asked the captains to resume playing, which they did. An unusual statement was issued by the officials, confirming that both umpires and Fender still considered the conditions unfit. Bill Bowes remembered how angry the Yorkshire professionals were about the eighty-minute hold-up. Yorkshire might not have batted if they had known Fender would change his mind after starting and they were conscious that the effects of the roller might have worn off. The match was eventually drawn but as Bowes said: 'I have no idea what went through "Mossy" Fender's mind but there was an understandable determination among us: "Don't indulge in anything not covered by the rule book against Surrey."'

Bowes had another memory of Fender, also involving Wilfred Rhodes, from one of his own early Yorkshire–Surrey matches. Not wishing to tamper with an instructive tale, Bowes can tell the story verbatim: 'Yorkshire were doing fairly well when P.G. put himself on and his third ball was a high, slow, full toss down the leg-stump area. The batsman pushed it out to the vacant forward square-leg position for an easy single. P.G., like a contortionist, began to massage his right shoulder blade, implying that he was very stiff. In the second over he bowled another of these slow, full tosses and again the proceedings were as before. A fleeting smile appeared on the face of Wilfred, who was sitting on the players' balcony. Addressing no one in particular, he said: "Aye. In't next over yon fieldsman [he nodded in the direction] will go to mid-on and there'll be no more slow, full tosses. He's a shrewd 'un." Sure enough in the next over, a man at three-quarter deep mid-on and wide, went up to mid-on and there were no more slow, full tosses. They had been bowled deliberately in the hope of a mis-hit or rush of blood by the batsman and not to give him a simple run. If Wilfred said he was shrewd, that he was.'

Fender and Rhodes, like Fender and Douglas, shared a plentiful respect for each other, but they could equally spark each other off. Fender remembered when Surrey struggled on a wet wicket at Headingley in 1924. Six wickets were down when Hitch joined his captain. 'There's no room for all thirteen of us on this field,' Hitch was told, to his initial bewilderment. 'Let's hit them out of the ground.' Fender led the way with two sixes against Kilner and 77 were put on in forty-five minutes. During this stand Rhodes appealed for obstruction against Hitch as the batsman swung at a ball and the wicket-keeper, trying to take a catch, fell over the stumps. 'That was not obstruction and you know it, Wilfred,' Fender said at the bowler's end. 'I thought it was, Mr Fender,'

Rhodes replied. 'You better say that to Bill outside the ground later,' Fender answered and Rhodes did not reply. Fender, who never found Rhodes as difficult to play as J. C. White, said: 'Wilfred like myself could get a bit cross if things weren't going his way.' Gover recalled that Fender convulsed everyone with laughter in Surrey's second match with the South Africans in 1929. Five successive googlies beat a South African batsman all ends up, and from the sixth ball he was dropped at slip by Shepherd. Fender raised clenched hands above his head and shrieked: 'Is there no God?'

Phil Mead was among the great English professionals who were sufficiently wary of Fender to attribute things to him for which he was not responsible. In Gover's presence at The Oval in 1931 Mead rocked backwards and forwards with his hands in front of his face in the professionals' changing-room when he was told that Stephen Fry had declared Hampshire's innings closed. 'He's done what?' Mead groaned, 'Oh no—it's that Fender—he's diddled us.' In a rain-ruined match, Hampshire closed their first innings at 127 without loss at lunch-time on the third day, thereby presenting Surrey with first innings points, although they had not taken a wicket. Surrey, who had made 245 in their first innings, went in again for seventy-five minutes before declaring and Hampshire in the end had to struggle to save the match. *Wisden* commented that 'what purpose could possibly have been served by Hampshire declaring will ever remain a puzzle.' Mead assumed Fry had been talked into his rashness by Fender but Fender remembered it was a straightforward attempt, by both captains, to obtain a definite result.

Neither Fender nor Mead ever forgot Kennedy's benefit match at Southampton in 1926 when Mead was dismissed in the last over before lunch by Bob Gregory. It was one of Gregory's earliest games for Surrey and Fender realized that Mead had never seen Gregory bowl. Nor had some of the Surrey team, for that matter, and there were smiles when he was put on. Fender had watched Gregory in the nets: 'Bob never turned a ball much in his life but he could roll them out of his hand steadily enough and I told him what I wanted him to do. I made a big fuss about putting three short legs behind square and Mead carefully smothered the first two balls safely down, looking all the time for what would have been off-spin to him. Third ball, Bob sent down a quicker one; Mead played too soon and got an outside edge; I caught a "dolly" at slip and in we went for lunch. We were lucky, of course, against a chap like Mead but we needed some luck when reduced to ploys like that.'

Herbert Sutcliffe was eighty-three when he recalled in the Yorkshire nursing home where he died in 1978, that Fender more than any other captain left him wondering what might happen next. Sutcliffe confirmed what he wrote about Fender in his book *For England and Yorkshire* (Edward Arnold, 1935): 'When you were batting against him or against the side he led, you had the feeling that there was some very powerful influence working against you—an influence that was ready to spot the slightest fault in your armour and widen it at the first opportunity. Fender was that influence. You knew that Fender was preparing a development in his attack that would test you to the full.'

Hammond was the English batsman who gave Fender as an opposing captain less hope than any other. 'Unless you got him out quickly there was not much you could do except to try and keep him quiet. I might bowl Gregory, Shepherd or someone else, who might not be thought to be a "regular", in order to make him "think". Sometimes we might "feed" his favourite cover drives in the hope he might lift one, but he scored a lot of runs against us.' Like others who watched Hammond in Australia in 1928–29, Fender thought he never batted so soundly, in some ways, again in his career. Fender omitted one story about Hammond from *The Turn of the Wheel*. Hammond made 251 in the second Test match, 200 and 32 (run out) in the third and 119 not out and 177 in the fourth, each time eliminating all risks and scoring most of his runs by hammering the ball through the covers on the back foot. Before the fifth Test Hammond was the guest of some Australians who ragged him that he never pulled or cut. If he did so he would be acknowledged as one of the great batsmen, but meanwhile they had reservations. Hammond deserted his proven method in the fifth Test and was caught at gully for 38 and 16 trying to square cut in each innings. 'Hammond was a fairly young man then and it wasn't the time to write the story, but I'm pretty sure he fell into the trap of trying to prove a point to his hosts. They are never slow to give advice in Australia. I'm sure he would have made a thousand runs in that series otherwise.'

This same tour brought Fender's most famous gaffe in print when he was critical in his book of what he felt were shortcomings in the youthful Bradman's technique. Irving Rosenwater, in his comprehensive biography of Bradman published by Batsford in 1978, dealt fully and sympathetically with the 'brilliant but unsound' verdict Fender passed. In his defence, Fender's own comments were: 'A lot of people in 1928–29 shared my reservations, initially, though they did not make them publicly known. Bradman had this marvellous pull stroke but fundamentally he did not play as straight regularly as some of us thought would be necessary to combat the variable bounce on English wickets. I genuinely thought this would be his undoing and I was not alone; some of the English players agreed with me. The fact that Bradman made so many runs in England, of course, showed what a fine player he was and my first thoughts were proved badly wrong.' The story of how Bradman, on his first appearance at The Oval, made 252 not out against Surrey, led by Fender, need not be repeated in detail here. Time and time again in later years Fender praised Bradman's skill, even if he sometimes argued that the opposing captain, or selectors, had made things easier for the Australian than should have been the case.

Part and parcel of Fender's qualified approval of Bradman, even in later years, came from his generation's belief that nobody could be a more complete batsman than Hobbs. This in turn stemmed from their conviction that the supreme test of anybody's ability was his batting on damaged turf, something they were not convinced Bradman could manage. Fender never saw Trumper, but like everyone else in his age group he had a Trumper story to tell. It arose from the wild hit that ended Bradman's second innings at Lord's in 1934 against Verity, who took 14 wickets that day. No stroke in Bradman's life incurred more criticism, and Fender put the poor shot down to Bradman's believing that his team's cause in the conditions was hopeless. After the game Fender found Warwick Armstrong, complete with cigar and with a drink in each hand, holding court in a Lord's bar. Fender asked Armstrong, as a man who had seen them both, how he would compare Trumper and Bradman. Armstrong removed the cigar from his mouth for the first time and said: 'Do you really want to know, Percy? Let me put it this way—if we won the toss on a doubtful wicket we always batted anyway. If Vic did not like the look of it, he would "shut up shop" and say "I think I better stay here till it gets better." Do you want me to say anything more?'

As a journalist, Fender gave his analytical approach to cricket free rein, but he was always readable and his articles were enjoyed by both players and public, as were his radio broadcasts. He also gave talks on Children's Hour and later still commentated for television. E. M. Wellings was unstinting in his praise for Fender, as a colleague on the *Evening News* for several seasons. Wellings described the play and Fender wrote the comment. 'Just imagine,' Wellings said, 'in those days an entire page of a broadsheet was devoted to a Test match each day. He had one half and I had the other and I suppose that together we churned out some 5,000 words, with the last copy being sent away at 5.15.' Fender kept his own scorebook in the press box, despite his heavy wordage commitments and devised his own system. It is common practice nowadays, but Fender's method was novel then and enabled him to tell how many balls a batsman had faced from a particular bowler. Being Fender, he rode his hobby-horses hard and once again he was frequently ahead of his time. In 1929, for instance, he was urging the provision of light meters for umpires, something that English cricket eventually adopted fifty years later.

Fender's criticisms of the cricket authorities were unexpectedly few and restrained in his newspaper work. He also refused pointblank to follow up the nocturnal activities of one Australian cricketer during a Test match in 1934. 'You employed me to write cricket,' the *Evening News* was told. Fender's writing contained only one instance where the grinding of a personal axe might be spotted. Fender's column in the *Star* of Saturday, 18 October 1930, told how he had been among the Union Castle Company's guests at Southampton as Chapman's 1930–31 MCC side sailed for South Africa. Fender, in his mention of Allom and Turnbull, referred to their literary efforts in New Zealand a year earlier, that had produced *The Book of the Two Maurices* (E. Allom, 1930). Fender went on: 'Their fame as authors has by no means decreased by the fact that they have, I understand, achieved the impossible in gaining from Lord Harris a favourable mention as cricketing scribes at their farewell dinner on Thursday night. Few things have gained more disapprobation from headquarters in recent years than the cricketer who writes for the public, yet, I understand, that they were even praised for their work.'

This particular farewell to a departing MCC side was always remembered by Fender because he and J. W. H. T. Douglas shared an otherwise empty compartment in the train back to Waterloo and something of a *rapprochement* took place between them. 'Nothing happened that you could put a finger on exactly but we talked about all sorts of things, including Australia in 1920–21. For the first time we seemed to get close. We were still talking when we got to London and he asked me to go and have a drink—and we had several together. In all the years we had known each other nothing like it happened before. We were both past being competitive by then and this may have helped, but when we parted we both felt, I think, that any past differences between us were finished. It can happen that way with people you have had a bit of a feud with.'

Two months later, almost to the day, Douglas was drowned off the Danish coast when the ship in which he was travelling collided with another. He died trying to save his elderly father, who also lost his life. Nobody could be sure precisely what happened. One version, that Fender gathered at the time, came from other survivors, was that Douglas believed mistakenly that his father was safe in a lifeboat and that Douglas drowned when he went below again to fetch his father's overcoat. The official inquiry did not go into such detail.

10. Farewell to Surrey and after

Few people, least of all Fender, had expected the 1935 season to be his last with Surrey. Like several other occasions in his cricket life, the ending when it came was tinged slightly with discord. A few newspapers took the chance for the last time to hint that not all the facts had emerged. They did not wield the cudgels too belligerently; Fender after all was in his forty-fourth year and he himself went on to take the final decision to finish his county career. There were sad undertones, though, to the way it happened and he stopped playing prematurely in the opinion of several Surrey colleagues, who felt he still had something to contribute.

Fender and Sandham were by 1935 the doyens of the Surrey side, but they continued to justify their places. Fender's matches were spaced out by journalistic and other business commitments and this was beneficial at his age. He played in half of Surrey's fixtures and in sixteen games that summer scored 440 runs and bowled 500 overs, taking 66 wickets, including 10 in the match against Warwickshire at The Oval. *Wisden* described Fender and Brown as the best slow bowlers in the side. For the last time, too, Fender captained Surrey, the opportunity arising when a leg injury in mid-June prevented Holmes from playing against Worcestershire at New Road. Fender put Worcestershire in to bat and Surrey won inside two days. Gover, with 12 wickets, was the man of the hour; the game was also a suitable requiem for Fender as a captain.

It was on a late April afternoon in 1936 that the axe fell on him. He was changing after net practice at Lord's, where he usually prepared for a new season because it was handier for his office than The Oval. Fender was joined in the dressing-room by Errol Holmes, who seemed ill at ease while some desultory small talk took place. Holmes suddenly blurted out: 'Have you thought which two or three matches you might want to play this season?' Fender was taken aback: 'Do you mean you only want me for a couple of games?' he asked. 'I think so,' Holmes replied. 'In that case I don't see any point in playing at all,' Fender said, and the matter dropped. Inevitably, as Surrey began their thirty-four-match programme and began to go through May without calling upon Fender, there was speculation by press and public about his absence. Fender did not remember at what stage later Surrey were more explicit about the matches they hoped he would play, but during May his cricket was limited to senior club matches and he also accepted invitations to lead MCC at Lord's in three-day games against Oxford University on 20 June and Cambridge University on 1 July.

Fender's position received its fullest public airing so far when the *Daily Telegraph* on Saturday, 16 May, carried a story in their news pages from Thomas Moult saying he had sought out Fender to get the mystery explained. Moult asked Fender whether the assumption that Surrey had not asked him to play for them was correct? Fender answered: 'No. I have been asked to play in a few matches. But as I had not heard from Surrey until the season was well started I assumed that I was not required.' (Moult explained at this point that counties usually checked on the availability of their amateur players at the start of the year.) Fender continued: 'Therefore I accepted certain other invitations.' The story went on to list five county games Fender had been asked to play and the reasons why he was only free to play two of them and possibly a third. Moult asked Fender what he felt about the position and Fender answered: 'I do not wish to say anything more.'

Fender's mood was, in his own words, 'black' at having been told he was not wanted as a player. During the days that followed Moult's story he decided it would be best if he finished completely. He let Holmes know and on 26 May wrote to the Surrey committee. Fender all his life never shirked the task of abiding by his own precepts but, as he stressed: 'I was dreadfully upset because I had never expected to finish so soon. In my calmer moments, though, I could see little point in turning out occasionally at the expense of some youngster. I had enough of that to contend with from other amateurs when I was captain.' The Surrey committee discussed Fender's letter on 4 June and nine days later both it and Surrey's reply were published in the newspapers. This seemed to have been at Fender's request and Leveson-Gower agreed, possibly remembering the rumours attached to Fender's deposal as captain in 1931. The Surrey committee approved their president's action at their next meeting on 18 June. By then the newspapers had printed their tributes to Fender and all conjecture had ended.

Fender's letter to the Surrey committee read:

'Gentlemen—As you may know from my letter to Mr Holmes, I have thought it best in the circumstances to advise the captain of the county eleven that I do not wish myself to be considered as being available this season.

'It is with the greatest possible regret that I have come to this decision but I could not see that it was for the benefit of the side or the individual players that I should join the side for an odd match on two or three occasions during the season.

'I should like to take this opportunity of expressing through you to the players, members and supporters of the Surrey eleven my most sincere thanks for the many, most delightful years which I have spent in their company, and in the service of the county eleven and also to thank them whole-heartedly for the magnificent support they have always given me.

'I can only say that the memory of those great days will be bright in my mind in my retirement and that my very best wishes will always go to the Surrey side with which I have been so proud to be associated for so long a period.'

In their reply the Surrey committee sent Fender a copy of a resolution, proposed by Leveson-Gower, which had been unanimously passed:

'That this committee have received Mr Fender's letter and wish to thank him very much for what he has written and at the same time to convey to him their sincere appreciation of the great services he has rendered to the Surrey County Cricket Club as a member of the Surrey county eleven and as captain.'

Fender never found out if there was anything further behind the events which led to his departure. Some of his contemporaries believed at the time that Holmes had been only the spokesman for a Surrey cabal who felt it was time Fender went. Fender still had opponents in the Surrey hierarchy after he finished as captain. He himself was elected to the Surrey committee in 1932 after losing the captaincy, but rather unusually his name was not put forward for re-election in 1936 when he retired by rotation. Fender was willing to stand, but he did not remember the background and the Surrey minutes remain mute about it. Fender, of course, was not temperamentally suited to committee work. Like many independent minds he held strong views and found compromise difficult. The minutes show his attendance record was moderate at general committees, but that he seldom missed any of the various subcommittees on which he served.

Fender had the assistance, among others, of two promising young professionals in Compton (D.) and Edrich (W. J.) as MCC beat Oxford by an innings in two days, but rain during the game with Cambridge spoiled what was to prove his last first-class match. The final day, Friday, 3 July 1936, however, was not without interest, with Fender hitting vigorously for his side's top score of 52 as MCC reached 155 in answer to Cambridge's 282. He pulled Wooller, Cambridge's most successful bowler, for one six and *The Times* said he played an innings 'which made it regrettable that he is not on permanent view at The Oval'. H. T. Bartlett led some aggressive Cambridge batting and MCC were set to make 283 to win in three hours. After a disastrous start when 5 wickets crashed with only 47 scored, T. N. Pearce (18 not out) and Fender (7 not out) checked the rout and the match was drawn.

Near the end *The Times* noted that 'a further wicket might have fallen had not a sparrow chosen to commit suicide in an altruistic attempt to save T. N. Pearce's wicket from a ball from M. Jehangir Khan. This gesture on the part of the sparrow might well have prevented the extra half-hour and an exciting finish.' As thousands of visitors to the MCC museum at Lord's know, the sparrow was stuffed and is preserved to this day. The incident was widely reported, earning the match far more space in the newspapers than might have been the case. Right to the end, Fender, directly or indirectly, was involved in the news.

Fender's life-span was not yet half-way completed, but his first-class cricket career has been the main subject of these pages. What followed can only be briefly touched upon though it was far from negligible in several spheres. For many years he remained in demand for club matches and charity games, and as a speaker at dinners. He could not positively remember his last cricket match: like many old men Fender's memory was clearer on the happenings of seventy years ago than on those of twenty years ago. Mr Brian O'Gorman, master-in-charge of cricket at St George's College, Weybridge, where Fender went before St Paul's, remembered Fender making an effortless 32 for the Forty Club against the school in June 1960 and Fender would then have been

sixty-seven. (Mr O'Gorman's father, Joe O'Gorman, played several first-team matches for Surrey under Fender in 1927. He was
one of the O'Gorman Brothers, a famous music hall comedy act,
which reached Royal Variety Performance level. Appearing in a
Surrey trial one year, Joe O'Gorman still fitted in a matinée at
the old Alhambra during the match.)

Perhaps the most notable occasion with which Fender was
associated later was the Surrey centenary match at The Oval on
23 May 1946, when the county met an Old England XI led by
Fender. It was a memorable and happy event, attended by King
George VI, and signified to the 15,000 present that the fearful
holocaust of world war had again receded. In sporting terms the
atmosphere was heavy with nostalgia, not least for regular Oval
spectators, with Hobbs and Strudwick walking out to umpire and
'Percy Fender' again in charge. Sandham, Jardine, Knight,
Allom, Holmes and Brooks were all in action, and Sutcliffe,
Woolley, Hendren and Tate, among others, were taking part.
For the players it was a wonderful reunion. Fender, as he had so
often done, played host, with an outing to a Jack Hulbert revue.
In a letter to *The Times* Fender thanked everyone for their
enthusiasm and support and, to this day, nobody present has forgotten the occasion. The idea for the match came from Holmes
and it was Fender who settled on 'Old England' as the name for his
side.

Fender rejoined the Royal Air Force in the Second World War
and, in the Services' phrase, became a 'movements officer' in
various parts of Southern England. In effect, he was responsible
for transporting men and supplies and was mentioned in dispatches
for his work in connection with the invasion of Europe and in
France. It was understandably less glamorous than the earlier
Flying Corps days, but it produced its share of anecdotes for him,
some more plausible than others. He remembered one package
which had to be given top priority and it turned out to be a corpse,
a practice run, he believed, for the 'Man Who Never Was' episode.
Then there was the hopeless task of trying to persuade the Prime
Minister to try on an oxygen mask before he left Lyneham for a
circuitous journey to Moscow. Fender had met Winston Churchill
in the past, hence the mistaken belief that Wing Commander
Fender might succeed where his current advisers had failed. The
oxygen mask had a hole specially cut for cigar smokers, but the
obvious contradictions in efficiency this would have brought,

made Churchill's refusal to have anything to do with it understandable.

Fender predictably found plenty of red tape to circumvent in his job, but the nearest he came to being court-martialled arose from the fact that he had corresponded with prisoner-of-war camps in Germany without his commanding officer's permission. Fender had written several times to cricketing friends in the camps, F. R. Brown, Bill Bowes and the South African Bob Catterall among them, trying to keep them up to date and making liberal use of cricket phrases to get news past the German censors. An obvious example was to refer to Garland-Wells's being elected captain at the Cairo Club. All the cricket world knew Garland-Wells as 'Monty' and Montgomery's appointment with the Eighth Army was not hard for the prisoners to deduce, but was, apparently, too subtle for the Germans.

Authority was still discussing Fender's transgressions when he was posted to movements work in South Africa and later to similar duties in New Zealand, Australia, the Philippines and New Guinea. One of his last wartime jobs was a sea voyage back to England as senior officer in a ship containing British wives and other civilian women from Japanese internment camps. On VE Day Fender managed successfully not only to over-rule the ship's captain on the subject of the ship's adhering to its teetotal regulations, but he had also ensured that suitable stocks were on board in readiness.

In common with everyone else, Fender had numerous domestic problems with which to contend during the war. He was a widower with children at boarding school; he had elderly parents living alone in London; his own belongings in store and his house were all bombed; and a private wine firm was not the easiest of businesses to run from a distance, in a time of rationing and restricted imports. In 1948 the firm moved to Balfour Mews, off Park Lane, and for the second time it was built up into a prosperous concern from almost nothing. Lionel Tennyson had pulled out, but Fender had the assistance of his son Peter this time, though eventually history repeated itself and son left father and launched out on his own. Peter Fender, a Free Vintner, had his own business at Topsham, near Exeter for several years but now works in insurance. Fender's daughter, known professionally as Pat Keevney, worked on the stage and in television in London and New York before her marriage.

8. Tom Webster drew this election poster for his friend when Fender successfully sought a seat on the LCC in 1952

From 1952 until 1958, Fender served two terms as a Conservative Member of the London County Council for the Norwood division of Lambeth and later he was appointed a Deputy Lieutenant of the County of London, and later Greater London, until resigning in 1976. It was during this period that he was sounded out as to whether he would consider accepting a knighthood, and in particular whether he would want the citation to read for public services or for cricket, but the Government changed and he heard no more. (It would have been several decades late but might have been considered an imaginative gesture for officialdom to recognize Fender in some way.) In 1962 he married again, but six years later his second wife died and he was a widower once more. Early in the 1970s Fender felt that the days of the private wine merchant were ending. With all the vision and forcefulness of his younger days, he launched the London Wine Exchange which, as he put it, 'operates for wines and cigars in much the same way as does the Stock Exchange for stocks and shares'. The essence of the scheme was that the purchaser placed his order with the Exchange, who passed it direct to the shipper or main dealer, who, in turn, delivered direct to the customer. This eliminated several middle men for the buyer and reduced transport costs to a single journey.

Like several famous cricketers, Fender was afflicted with blindness later in his life. It encroached slowly but remorselessly. He gave up driving on his eightieth birthday and as his sight worsened he moved to Horsham to live with his daughter and son-in-law. Fender was by far the oldest in the party when he flew with other former England Test cricketers to Melbourne in March 1977, for the Centenary Test match. Fender's enjoyment and staying power amazed everyone. He took with him as his guide his thirteen-year-old grandson, Nicholas Bensted-Smith, and the pair attracted a great deal of publicity. At Horsham in his own surroundings Fender moved around confidently unaided, and seldom complained about losing his sight. 'Even at my age blindness brings its compensations of a sort,' he said. 'My hearing has remained good and in some ways I find I have more perception about people and their characters, now that I cannot see them, than I did before.' Fender has secretarial assistance, but he continues to run his wine exchange by telephone. He retains all his interest in everyday affairs and seldom misses the television news. As a frustrated would-be barrister, he particularly enjoyed reports of court cases and must have been one of the last survivors among those who attended the Crippen trial in 1910.

It was indicative of Fender's spirit that he started to plan a dinner party in London to mark the sixtieth anniversary of his record fastest hundred. The actual date, 26 August 1980, however, coincided with other celebrations for the Centenary Test match at Lord's and Fender decided there was no point in organizing a private cricket function that week. Apart from several long-standing friends from late in Fender's own playing days, he hoped that the only two other survivors from the 1920 match would have been able to attend. These were Ben Bellamy, the Northamptonshire wicket-keeper, who was eighty-nine, and Sandham, who was ninety. (That 1920 Surrey team at Northampton provided a good example of cricket and longevity: eight of them reached their eightieth year or more and so, too, did Harrison, the twelfth man.) Meanwhile Fender was an honoured guest at the Lord's match, accompanied as at Melbourne three years earlier, by his grandson. For the first two days of the match Fender sat at the back of Q stand, greeting old friends, signing autographs and he was also interviewed on television. The occasion, though, rather taxed his strength and he returned to Horsham before the Test finished.

Fender has outlived all his most famous contemporaries in cricket and, by his own admission, he feels he has mellowed in old age. 'You don't live as long as I have without wishing you had dealt with certain situations in a different way.' One of the opportunities Fender remembered he missed came in a conversation he and Rockley Wilson shared on the ship returning from Australia in 1921. 'We were talking on deck late one night and he told me that he would never tour Australia again, but that I might. He said that if I wanted to do so I would have to watch my step. At the time I did not really understand what he was getting at—I knew he disapproved of the way I might not always get up too early in the morning and that I had a reputation for being outspoken, sometimes very undiplomatically so. I realize now that, if I had asked him, he might have groomed me out of some of my faults. My whole cricket life might have taken a different course. That was only one of the chances I missed.'

In Fender's moods of self-appraisal he stressed that his memories were happy ones, predominantly, but the realist in him would go on to add that, like everyone else, he had some of the other sort as well. His disappointments obviously included that he was never captain of England and that Surrey failed to win the champion-ship under him, but he was also aware that there had been times when he had been his own worst enemy. The manner in which Fender's MCC membership lapsed provided a classic example as late as 1972. By an oversight, Fender failed to amend his banker's order when subscriptions were raised. It was one of those irritating things that could happen to anyone. In due course the club, adhering to their rules, returned his cheque for the inadequate amount paid with a Roneoed letter, giving him the chance to apply for reinstatement. Fender, slightly irked, spurned the opportunity and wrote to Lord's: 'It is a sad finale to my fifty years or more of membership, but rules are rules and although, perhaps, I did not always respect them as I should have done in my younger days, at my now more mature age I must do so.'

On the back of this letter Fender typed part of a lyric from the musical *The Lilac Domino* (B. Feldman & Co. Ltd, 138/140 Charing Cross Road, London). As a text, it served to comfort him in many situations in his life. It is not inappropriate to end with it:

What is done you never never can undo,
　　Try as you may.
What is gone you cannot beckon back to you,
　　It's far away.
What is said, in time to come you may forgive,
　　But not forget;
In the memory all things live,
　　And all you can do is—regret.

Statistical appendix
Compiled by Michael Fordham

Batting and Fielding

	Matches	Inns	NO	Runs	Highest score	Avge	100s	50s	Catches
1910	2	4	0	19	12	4.75	—	—	1
1911	2	4	0	42	26	10.50	—	—	1
1912	21	30	5	606	133*	24.24	1	2	9
1913	29	51	2	1,163	104*	23.73	1	7	22
1914	25	37	1	820	140	22.77	1	3	29
1919				DID NOT PLAY					
1920	30	44	3	841	113*	20.51	1	4	43
1920–21 (MCC to Aust.)	9	13	1	325	60	27.08	—	3	7
1921	34	56	2	1,152	101	21.33	1	5	52
1922	30	38	4	1,169	185	34.38	2	5	42
1922–23 (MCC to S. Africa)	14	21	1	459	96	22.95	—	3	21
1923	36	54	5	1,427	124*	29.12	2	9	47
1924	31	40	2	1,004	107	26.42	1	5	39
1925	30	42	5	1,042	81*	28.16	—	8	29
1926	32	37	3	1,043	104	30.67	1	7	23
1926–27 (Tennyson's XI to Jamaica)	3	5	0	146	68	29.20	—	2	2
1927	27	32	5	863	100*	31.96	1	4	37
1928	31	40	3	1,376	177	37.18	3	6	43
1929	34	50	1	1,625	116	33.16	2	12	26
1930	24	25	2	700	96	30.43	—	5	25
1931	33	44	8	916	139*	25.44	2	3	28
1932	21	33	1	624	60	19.50	—	2	25
1933	22	31	4	741	106	27.44	2	5	19
1934	19	26	5	419	54*	19.95	—	1	15
1935	16	23	5	440	84	24.44	—	1	13
1936	2	3	1	72	52	36.00	—	1	—
Totals	557	783	69	19,034	185	26.65	21	103	598

Bowling

	O	M	R	W	Avge	Best bowling	5w in inns	10w in match
1910	3	1	14	1	14.00	1–14	—	—
1911	7	0	47	0	—	—	—	—
1912	122	29	408	16	25.50	5–42	1	—
1913	316.3	59	1,193	34	35.08	6–98	2	—
1914	597.2	140	1,917	83	23.09	6–83	2	—
1919			DID NOT PLAY					
1920	794.3	138	2,653	124	21.39	8–66	3	1
1920–21 (MCC to Aust.)	233	17	983	32	30.71	7–75	4	1
1921	1,057.2	188	3,563	134	26.58	6–63	7	1
1922	1,116	208	3,329	157	21.20	7–37	14	3
1922–23 (MCC to S. Africa)	380.1	81	1,136	58	19.58	7–55	3	1
1923	1,324.2	307	3,558	178	19.98	7–34	8	1
1924	723.4	175	2,065	81	25.49	6–91	2	—
1925	1,142.2	304	2,889	137	21.08	6–31	11	1
1926	1,044.2	237	2,749	112	24.54	7–76	5	1
1926–27 (Tennyson's XI to Jamaica)	118	17	379	10	37.90	4–146	—	—
1927	931.1	241	2,292	89	25.75	7–10	4	1
1928	1,226.3	334	3,099	110	28.17	8–24	5	1
1929	911.1	185	2,801	88	31.82	8–74	3	1
1930	636.2	117	1,827	65	28.10	5–47	2	—
1931	665	116	2,028	84	24.14	7–58	5	—
1932	665	152	1,760	63	27.93	5–58	2	—
1933	759.4	150	2,331	88	26.48	8–29	7	—
1934	595.5	69	2,291	79	29.00	8–79	7	3
1935	500.2	60	1,983	66	30.04	7–89	3	1
1936	36.4	5	162	5	32.40	2–45	—	—
Totals	15,907.1	3,330	47,457	1,894	25.05	8–24	100	16

Centuries (21)

133* Sussex v. Oxford University (Horsham) 1912
104* Sussex v. Cambridge University (Hove) 1913
140   Surrey v. Warwickshire (The Oval) 1914
113* Surrey v. Northamptonshire (Northampton) 1920
101   Gentlemen v. Players (Lord's) 1921
185   Surrey v. Hampshire (The Oval) 1922
137   Surrey v. Kent (The Oval) 1922
124* Surrey v. Gloucestershire (Bristol) 1923
103   Surrey v. Nottinghamshire (The Oval) 1923
107   Surrey v. South Africans (The Oval) 1924
104   Surrey v. Essex (Leyton) 1926
100* Surrey v. Yorkshire (The Oval) 1927
110   Surrey v. MCC (Lord's) 1928
177   Surrey v. Yorkshire (Bradford) 1928
101   Surrey v. Kent (Blackheath) 1928
116   Surrey v. Essex (The Oval) 1929
100   The Rest v. England (Lord's) 1929
100* Surrey v. Derbyshire (The Oval) 1931
139* Surrey v. Somerset (The Oval) 1931
106   Surrey v. Nottinghamshire (Nottingham) 1933
100* Surrey v. Nottinghamshire (The Oval) 1933

The nearest Fender came to scoring two centuries in a match was for Surrey v. the South Africans at The Oval in 1929 when he made 79 and 98.

Seven or more wickets in an innings (19 times)

8–66   Surrey v. Nottinghamshire (Nottingham) 1920
7–64   Surrey v. Lancashire (The Oval) 1920
7–75   MCC v. South Australia (Adelaide) 1920–21
7–59   Surrey v. Lancashire (The Oval) 1922
7–37   Surrey v. Leicestershire (The Oval) 1922
7–55   MCC v. Orange Free State (Bloemfontein) 1922–23
7–34   Surrey v. Warwickshire (Birmingham) 1923
7–72   Surrey v. Middlesex (Lord's) 1923
7–76   Surrey v. Essex (Leyton) 1926
7–86   Surrey v. Sussex (The Oval) 1926
7–10   Surrey v. Middlesex (Lord's) 1927

8–24   Surrey v. Warwickshire (The Oval) 1928
8–74   Surrey v. Northamptonshire (The Oval) 1929
7–58   Surrey v. Somerset (Taunton) 1931
7–96   Surrey v. Hampshire (Southampton) 1933
8–29   Surrey v. Essex (The Oval) 1933
7–73   Surrey v. Middlesex (Lord's) 1933
8–79   Surrey v. Glamorgan (Cardiff) 1934
7–89   Surrey v. Worcestershire (The Oval) 1935

Fender took 6 wickets in an innings twenty-five times and 5 wickets fifty-six times.

Ten or more wickets in a match (16 times)

10–124   Surrey v. Lancashire (The Oval) 1920
12–184   MCC v. South Australia (Adelaide) 1920–21
10–150   Surrey v. Essex (Leyton) 1921
10–128   Surrey v. Gloucestershire (Bristol) 1922
10–152   Surrey v. Warwickshire (Birmingham) 1922
10–186   Surrey v. Middlesex (Lord's) 1922
10–102   MCC v. Orange Free State (Bloemfontein) 1922–23
10–178   Surrey v. Lancashire (The Oval) 1923
10–112   Surrey v. Sussex (The Oval) 1925
10–124   Surrey v. Essex (Leyton) 1926
11–81   Surrey v. Middlesex (Lord's) 1927
11–106   Surrey v. Northamptonshire (The Oval) 1929
10–175   Surrey v. Nottinghamshire (Nottingham) 1934
10–178   Surrey v. Middlesex (The Oval) 1934
11–142   Surrey v. Glamorgan (Cardiff) 1934
10–103   Surrey v. Warwickshire (The Oval) 1935

Fender took 9 wickets in a match twenty times.

Hat-tricks (2)

Surrey v. Somerset (The Oval) 1914
Surrey v. Gloucestershire (The Oval) 1924

Three wickets in four balls (2)

MCC v. Griqualand West (Kimberley) 1922–23
Surrey v. Lancashire (The Oval) 1925

Four wickets in five balls

Surrey v. Middlesex (Lord's) 1927

Fender in this spell took 5 wickets in seven balls and 6 in eleven balls.

The double — 1,000 runs and 100 wickets (6 times)

	Runs	Wkts
1921	1,152	134
1922	1,169	157
1923	1,427	178
1925	1,042	137
1926	1,043	112
1928	1,376	110

Fender also held 52 catches in 1921, the first time anyone had reached 50 or more catches in the same season in which he did the double.

Match double

104 and 10–124 (3–48 and 7–76), Surrey v. Essex (Leyton) 1926

All-round play

9 and 104*, 6–98, Sussex v. Cambridge University (Hove) 1913
53 and 42, 6–109 and 3–47, Surrey v. Hampshire (Bournemouth) 1921
24 and 91*, 6–119 and 0–56, Surrey v. Leicestershire (Leicester) 1922
62, 3–41 and 6–71, Surrey v. Middlesex (The Oval) 1922
69 and 8, 6–60 and 4–118, Surrey v. Lancashire (The Oval) 1923
61, 5–55 and 5–57, Surrey v. Sussex (The Oval) 1925
104, 3–48 and 7–76, Surrey v. Essex (Leyton) 1926
94, 1–78 and 5–50, Surrey v. Hampshire (Southampton) 1928
177, 6–116, Surrey v. Yorkshire (Bradford) 1928
94 and 53, 0–42 and 5–38, Surrey v. Warwickshire (The Oval) 1929

64, 7–96 and 2–53, Surrey v. Hampshire (Southampton) 1933
54*, 4–50 and 5–91, Surrey v. Gloucestershire (The Oval) 1934

In thirteen other matches Fender scored 50 and took 5 or more wickets in an innings.

Fielding

Fender held 6 catches in Surrey's match with Leicestershire at Leicester in 1928. He held 4 catches in an innings four times.

Test matches

Batting and fielding

Matches	Inns	No	Runs	Highest Score	Avge	100s	50s	Catches
13	21	1	380	60	19.00	—	2	14

Bowling

O	M	R	W	Avge	Best Bowling	5w in Inns	10w in Match
363	67	1,185	29	40.86	5–90	2	—

Bibliography

The books most widely consulted, in addition to those mentioned in the Acknowledgements were:

H. S. Altham, *A History of Cricket*, Volume I, Allen & Unwin, 1962.

L. E. G. Ames, *Close of Play*, Stanley Paul, 1953.

John Arlott, *Alletson's Innings*, Epworth Press, 1957.

R. L. Arrowsmith, *A History of County Cricket: Kent*, Arthur Barker, 1971.

Denzil Batchelor, *The Book of Cricket*, Collins, 1952.

Rowland Bowen, *Cricket: A History of its Growth and Development throughout the World*, Eyre & Spottiswoode, 1970.

W. E. Bowes, *Express Deliveries*, Stanley Paul, 1949.

Gerald Brodribb, *Next Man In*, Putnam, 1952.

Frank Browne, *Some of it was Cricket*, John Murray, Sydney, 1965.

S. Canynge Caple, *The Cricketer's Who's Who*, Lincoln Williams, 1934.

Dudley Carew, *To the Wicket*, Chapman & Hall, 1946; *England Over*, Secker & Warburg, 1927.

A. W. Carr, *Cricket with the Lid Off*, Hutchinson, 1935.

J. D. Coldham, *Northamptonshire Cricket: A History*, Heinemann, 1959.

The Cricket Quarterly, 1963–70.

Edward Docker, *Bradman and the Bodyline Series*, Angus & Robertson, 1978.

Leslie Duckworth, *S. F. Barnes: Master Bowler*, Cricketer, Hutchinson, 1967.

P. G. H. Fender, *Defending the Ashes*, Chapman & Hall, 1921; *The Turn of the Wheel*, Faber & Faber, 1929; *The Tests of 1930*, Faber & Faber, 1930; *Kissing the Rod*, Chapman & Hall, 1934; *An ABC of Cricket*, Arthur Barker, 1937.

W. H. Ferguson, *Mr Cricket*, Nicholas Kaye, 1957.

J. H. Fingleton, *Cricket Crisis*, Cassell, 1946.

David Frith, *The Fast Men*, Van Nostrand Reinhold, Wokingham, 1975.

Edward Grayson, *Corinthians and Cricketers*, Naldrett Press, 1955.

W. R. Hammond, *Cricket My Destiny*, Stanley Paul, 1946; *Cricket My World*, Stanley Paul, 1948; *Cricketers' School*, Stanley Paul, 1950; *Cricket's Secret History*, Stanley Paul, 1952.

J. B. Hobbs, *My Life Story*, the *Star* Publications, 1935.

E. R. T. Holmes, *Flannelled Foolishness*, Hollis & Carter, 1957.

H. Larwood, with Kevin Perkins, *The Larwood Story*, W. H. Allen, 1965.

H. W. Lee, *40 Years of English Cricket*, Clerke & Cockeran, 1948.

Sir H. D. G. Leveson-Gower, *Cricket Personalities*, Williams & Norgate, 1925; *Off and On the Field*, Stanley Paul, 1953.

W. J. Lewis, *The Language of Cricket*, Oxford University Press, 1934.

M. W. Luckin, *South African Cricket 1919–1927*, published by the author, 1928.

Ronald Mason, *Jack Hobbs*, Hollis & Carter, 1960; *Walter Hammond*, Hollis & Carter, 1962; *Plum Warner's Last Season*, Epworth Press, 1970.

Laurence Meynell, *Famous Cricket Grounds*, Phoenix House, 1951.

Playfair Cricket Monthly, 1960–73.

E. W. Padwick, *A Bibliography of Cricket*, The Library Association, 1977.

Jack Pollard, *Bumpers, Boseys and Brickbats*, John Murray, Sydney, 1971.

E. L. Roberts, *Cricket in England, 1894–1939*, Edward Arnold, 1946; *Yorkshire's 22 Championships 1893–1946*, Edward Arnold, 1949.

Gordon Ross, *A History of County Cricket: Surrey*, Arthur Barker, 1971.

E. H. D. Sewell, *A County Cricketer's Searchlight on English Cricket*, Holden, 1926; *Cricket Up-to-date*, John Murray, 1931.

E. E. Snow, *A History of Leicestershire Cricket*, Edgar Backus, Leicester, 1949.

Herbert Strudwick, *Twenty-five Years behind the Stumps*, Hutchinson, 1926.

Surrey CCC Handbooks and Yearbooks 1914–1937.

E. W. Swanton, *The World of Cricket*, Michael Joseph, 1966.

Roy Webber, *The Playfair Book of Test Cricket*, Volumes I and II, Playfair Books, 1952–53; *The County Cricket Championship*, Phoenix House, 1957; *The Phoenix History of Cricket*, Phoenix House, 1960; *The Book of Cricket Records* (revised edition), Phoenix House, 1961.

Index

With the obvious exception of P. G. H. Fender himself, this index lists the names of all the individuals mentioned in the book.

THE PAVILION LIBRARY

All books from the Pavilion Cricket Library are available from your local bookshop, price £12.95 hardback, £5.95 paperback, or they can be ordered direct from Pavilion Books Limited.

In Celebration of Cricket
Kenneth Gregory

Batter's Castle
Ian Peebles

The Best Loved Game
Geoffrey Moorhouse

The Ashes Crown the Year
Jack Fingleton

Bowler's Turn
Ian Peebles

Life Worth Living
C. B. Fry

Lord's 1787–1945
Sir Pelham Warner

Cricket Crisis
Jack Fingleton

Lord's 1946–1970
Diana Rait Kerr and Ian Peebles

Brightly Fades The Don
Jack Fingleton

P. G. H. Fender
Richard Streeton

Cricket Country
Edmund Blunden

Through The Caribbean
Alan Ross

Odd Men In
A. A. Thomson

Hirst and Rhodes
A. A. Thomson

Crusoe on Cricket
R. C. Robertson-Glasgow

Two Summers at the Tests
John Arlott

**Benny Green's
Cricket Archive**

Please enclose cheque or postal order for the cover price, plus postage:

UK: 65p for first book; 30p for each additional book to a maximum of £2.00

Overseas: £1.20 for first book; 45p for each additional book to a maximum of £3.00

Pavilion Books reserve the right to show new retail prices on covers which may differ from those previously advertised in the text or elsewhere and to increase postal rates in accordance with the Post Office's charges.